Enjoying the Ride

Two Generations of Tragedy & Triumph

MITCH STURGEON

Casco Bay Publishing, LLC

ISBN: 978-1-7323137-0-5
Library of Congress Control Number: 2018906449

published by
Casco Bay Publishing, LLC
South Portland, Maine
www.cascobaypublishing.com

produced by
Great Life Press LLC
Rye, New Hampshire
www.greatlifepress.com

To wheelchair people,
and to those who stand behind us.

Contents

Foreword

I first met Mitch Sturgeon, or at least the virtual version of him, about ten years ago at an online multiple sclerosis patient forum devoted to people with Primary Progressive MS. We'd both been diagnosed with the insidious disease within a year of each other, and it seemed we were following similar paths.

In 2009 I launched my blog, Wheelchair Kamikaze, and Mitch contacted me via email, thus starting a more active correspondence between the two of us. In one of my early blog posts, I wrote about my love for the Boston Red Sox, born of my college days spent in Beantown during the 1980s. I promptly received an email from Mitch, which to my surprise included an invitation to meet him at Fenway Park the following weekend to take in a Red Sox-Yankees game, for which he had two coveted tickets. I was taken aback by his generosity. Although we had previously exchanged several online notes, Mitch hardly knew me from Adam. I couldn't make it to Boston due to the MS beast's insistence on making impromptu long-distance travel difficult if not impossible for me, but his surprising offer left an indelible impression and had me thinking this Mitch person must be one hell of a guy.

As our friendship blossomed through the years, that first impression of Mitch the man versus Mitch the online avatar proved to be spot on. We routinely Skyped one another to discuss topics ranging from the latest MS treatments to sports, politics, religion, and astrophysics (we agree on the multiverse theory but disagree as to whether some version of Mitch and Marc exists in an infinite number of universes).

Eventually we met in person. My wife, Karen, and I gave Mitch and his wife, Kim, their first tour of Central Park. A few years later, they introduced us to their lovely oceanside neighborhood in South Portland, Maine. Mitch and Kim are salt of the earth people. The two share honesty, integrity, and a no bullshit attitude that is a rare and refreshing commodity in this self-aggrandizing, social media driven world of ours.

These true-blue personality traits are on full display in Mitch Sturgeon's writing, both on his own blog and in this memoir. Mitch simply tells it like it is. His analytic mind parses details and distills the most relevant—and entertaining—observations into the story of his personal journey through life, whether it be his first experience deer hunting in the back woods of Maine or the initial, ominous signs of the disease that would forever alter his life.

The fact that Mitch's condition would place him in a situation eerily similar to that of his beloved mother, makes *Enjoying the Ride* a compelling narrative on multiple levels, at once a roadmap of a life diverted by disease and also an intensely personal story of familial ties, echoes of the past, and a transcendent mother-son relationship. Throw in a long-held family secret, and you have the makings of a thoroughly enjoyable, thought-provoking, and intensely personal telling that res-onates long after the final word is read.

The world could use more people like Mitch Sturgeon, and more writing like *Enjoying the Ride*.

Marc Stecker
Founder, WheelchairKamikaze.com
New York, New York
2018

— PART ONE —

☙

CHAPTER 1

A Conspiracy is Born

I n the end, we succumb to death. Given all she had endured, however, my mother's passing was more an achievement, a victory, a
finish line crossed with arms raised high.

Three days after she died, I sat in the front row at Clay's Funeral
Home surrounded by my extended family, except my daughter, Amy.
She stood tall and straight at the podium and read the eulogy I had
written. My closing words were these:

> I haven't asked my father, but I wonder if once or
> twice these past few days he's heard my wheelchair coming
> down the hallway at his house and confused it with the
> sound my mother's chair made in that same hallway for the
> past forty years.
>
> I'll consider myself a success in life if, once or twice,
> anyone confuses anything I do for something my mother
> might have done. She set the standard for how to live with
> humility, grace, strength, and most of all, love.

After the ceremony, someone asked, "Mitch, you were so young. Can
you remember your mother walking?"

"Yes," I responded without much thought. Then I paused for a
moment before continuing. "Well, sort of. I still have a few memories
from those early years, but I don't remember her walking any more
than I remember her breathing. Her love and comfort come to mind,
but nothing about her legs, one way or the other."

* * *

When Vernice Sturgeon arrived at the hospital that October day in
1963, the nurse on duty correctly diagnosed her condition. She eased

my mother into a standard issue wheelchair. As they pushed Mom down the hall toward the delivery room, she hoped and prayed for a little girl. That was the plan—the reason they had decided to have one more child. Instead, my birth added another sports-crazed, hunting and fishing obsessed, outdoor urinator to a household already thick with them.

If my father was disappointed to have a third boy, he didn't show it. Dad teased the men in town who weren't lucky enough to have produced a son, by offering his assistance, guaranteed boy, first try. When Mom heard him deliver that line, she rolled her eyes. On this subject, Dad was all talk.

Because I grew up in the sixties, and because I was a curious boy, I learned about war at an early age. As a five-year-old, I began eavesdropping on my parents when they watched the nightly news. The program led off with clips from Vietnam. A few minutes later the anchorman ran through a series of routine announcements including the stock market closing and the number of American war casualties that day. For all I knew, soldiers fighting and dying was as ordinary as the sun rising and setting.

One day in that summer of 1969, I stumbled upon a hatchet in the garage, and I knew what to do with it. I snuck across the field behind our house, in search of enemy soldiers. I let my guard down for a moment, and a platoon of hostile white birches ambushed me. I pounced on one of the smaller trees, chopping it down before the other birches could come to its defense. Hopelessly outnumbered, I scurried back to home base, dropped the hatchet on the lawn, and rushed into the house full of the spunk a boy feels when he has engaged the enemy and scored a kill.

My mother, waiting for me in the kitchen, scooched down and placed a hand on each of my shoulders. She didn't scold me for running with a sharp object, failing to wear a hard hat and safety glasses, or harvesting timber without a permit. No. She was only concerned about one thing. "Mitchy, I watched you from the window. You can't chop down those trees. That's not our land." These were different times.

The spunk hissed out of my body like air from a punctured tire. I hated to disappoint my mother. She continued, "Your father wouldn't be happy knowing you had damaged another man's property." She paused, looked out the window and down the hall, then lowered her voice and continued, "I won't mention this to him, and neither should you."

In my mother, I had a protector.

There were a million ways to anger Dad. I spent my childhood, and significant portions of my adult life, tiptoeing around this man. He never laid a hand on me and rarely yelled. He didn't need to, because his booming voice and the words he chose were intimidating enough.

Although I rarely stood up to Dad, man to man, I sometimes engaged him in battles of will. Once, he became so fed up with my fussy eating that he wagged his finger at me and threatened, "You will sit there until you finish your green beans if it takes all night."

Nothing in this world could have made me eat even one of those slimy green snots. Hours later, when he went to bed, Mom slid the offending vegetables in the trash and whispered, "We'll just tell Dad you ate the beans, but you still don't like them."

To this day I won't touch green beans. Dad is long gone, but I refuse to capitulate.

Mom also found ways to resist Dad's will. On those summer days when he took out the electric clippers to give my two older brothers and me crew cuts, Mom grabbed my hand and led me upstairs to the spare bedroom, where she read to me while running her fingers through my curly hair, saving it, at least temporarily, from the blade.

Mom also tiptoed around Dad—the Edith to his Archie Bunker. When he worked the midnight shift at the paper mill, which was every fourth week, he dragged himself home at 6:30 in the morning as the rest of us were starting our day. He was partially deaf from exposure to heavy artillery in the Army and heavy equipment at the mill. Yet, he could hear the slightest noise when he tried to sleep during the day. On those occasions, my mother did what she could to exercise some control over her three rambunctious boys and an ever-changing collection of dogs.

Her goal was to prevent Dad from staggering out of his bedroom, naked except for boxer shorts, lips drawn into his mouth because his dentures were on the nightstand, scolding everyone, including guests.

A knock at the door from friends, relatives, or the occasional traveling salesman meant disaster. The dogs would bark, the intruder would try to speak over them, and my father would wake up. Eventually, when he worked the midnight shift, Mom taped a piece of paper on the door reading, "Don't Knock, Ted Is Sleeping." That only worked, however, on the folks who bothered to read it.

* * *

Although I didn't satisfy her wish for a girl, because I was the youngest and the last, Mom treated me as her special child. In addition to protecting me from Dad, she tried to address my every want and need in life. If my older brothers and their friends wouldn't allow me to join in a game, she intervened. When I fell, she picked me up. If I asked for whoopie pies, she baked them. My mother and I forged a silent promise, an unspoken agreement. I would stay by her side, and she would coddle and protect me. The kids in my neighborhood, and even a few adults, called me a mama's boy. I objected, but not so much that I pulled away from my mother. We were conspirators, after all. Us against Dad. Us against the world.

CHAPTER 2
A Broken Promise

Our family didn't own a summer place on one of the local ponds, but we knew many people who did, and we escaped the in-town heat to visit them. On these outings, I watched the stress melt away from the grown-ups as they laughed, played cards, and told stories while sipping on their drinks, sometimes all day and well into the night.

On Saturday, September 13, 1969, we swam and barbecued at a friend's camp on Little Narrows Pond. After a few hours Mom and Dad deposited my two older brothers and me at home with a babysitter, and they returned to the camp for some adult time.

When I awoke the next morning, the same babysitter greeted me in the kitchen.

"Hello, Mitchy."

I ignored her and peeked around the corner into the living room. Empty. I glanced out the window to the driveway. No car. "Your parents aren't here now. Your dad will be home later to explain things."

That didn't make sense. Mom explained things. Dad hunted and fished, worked at the mill, and growled at my brothers and me for acting like knuckleheads.

In the afternoon I heard a car pull into the driveway. The kitchen door opened and slammed shut. Dad yelled, "Andy, Tommy, Mitchell, I need to talk to you." He dismissed the babysitter. I, the five-year-old, followed my brothers, twelve and eight, into the kitchen. "Sit down," Dad ordered, motioning toward the table. Mom wasn't with him. Again, it didn't make sense.

He was a mess. Dad's comb-over hairstyle was supposed to cover up his bald spot. Instead, long stringy hair hung off the right side of his head. I had only seen this look when he came out of the water after swimming. A commotion arose in my gut. All I knew was that everything would be better once Mom got home.

Dad sat down with us at the table, took the last drag of his cigarette, and ground it into the ashtray. "I have to tell you boys something. Your mother . . . " Dad's voice cracked. Six big, unblinking eyes stared back at him. He shifted his gaze down to the ashtray.

"Your mother had an accident."

Silence followed until Andy, the oldest, gathered the courage to ask, "What happened?"

Dad sat up straight in his chair, cleared his throat, and took a deep breath. "We returned to the lake after dropping you off. Your mother was walking down the stairs to the wharf and slipped on a wet step. She fell backward and broke her neck. She's paralyzed and will be in the hospital for . . . I don't know . . . a long time."

Having said what he needed to say, Dad stood and walked over to the kitchen window, his back to us. Maybe he saw his reflection because he flipped his unruly hair back over the bald spot.

Although the gravity of the moment was not lost on me, I had no basis for comparison, no frame of reference. I looked at my brothers for guidance or comfort or anything. They stared blankly at the refrigerator, so I stared too.

It was bad.

Dad's cigarette lighter snapped open, the ignition wheel spun, and the cover clanged shut—a sequence my father executed several times per hour, every single day.

"I need to get some sleep, so go play outside and try to be quiet. Your grandmother is on her way. She'll be staying in the spare bedroom until I figure something out." And with that, he left his three boys alone in the kitchen.

In recent years I have asked myself if my father lied to us, and to everyone else in town, back in 1969. But I prefer not to think of it in such terms. After all, he was the sort of man who would do or say whatever was necessary to protect those closest to him.

* * *

Although surrounded by family, I felt an unbearable loneliness creep in. My father and brothers were important to me, but they weren't my voice, my defender, my everything. Mom was. And what of our silent promise—that she would protect me, and I would stay by her side? If she was going to the hospital for a long time, why didn't she bring me? I felt our promise drown behind my eyes in tears I would not shed. At five years old, I already understood that Sturgeon men didn't cry.

As we shuffled outside I mustered the courage to ask Andy what *paralyzed* meant.

"Mom won't be able to walk anymore. She'll be in a wheelchair."

I sat alone on the back steps and considered my plight. I sure had a lot of questions, and they weren't complicated ones like why do bad things happen to good people? No, I worried about who would take care of me. How would I know what to wear, what to eat, when to go to bed? Would I still get my bath on Sunday night? Only Mom knew these things. I wasn't sure what else she was secretly in charge of. Would the television still turn on, the phone ring? Would the sun rise? Would soldiers still die?

From my perch on the steps, I could see the stand of birch trees across the field. Their trunks shone as white as the paper Dad brought home from the mill. But the leaves had already begun their seasonal fade from green to yellow. As the breeze wafted among the trees, they shifted back and forth, dancing together in the wind. An isolated birch, however—the tree I had chopped down earlier that summer—still lay broken in the field.

CHAPTER 3

Smells like Money

My family lived deep in the woods of Maine. Tourists flocked to our state's picturesque coastline, but most didn't travel inland, and we preferred it that way. Those out-of-staters offended our sensibilities, and we didn't need their money. Our town did quite well, thank you, by converting trees into paper, as if spinning straw into gold.

Men like my maternal grandfather cut and limbed trees at nearby forest operations. Pulp trucks loaded the timber and headed for the paper mill in the center of town. When the logs disappeared into the mill, men like my father and my paternal grandfather chipped, steamed, digested, washed, and bleached the fiber to a pulp. They took the pulp and refined, colored, filtered, dried, cut, and wound it into giant paper and tissue rolls, before packaging and labeling it. The finished products emerged from the other end of the mill and were loaded into trucks heading south. Always south. To the north there were just more trees, potato fields, and the Canadian border.

Union workers could only guess how the mill would run for them each time they punched their time cards. Best case, their shift proved mind-numbingly dull, leaving ample time for crossword puzzles, the dinner they brought from home, and browsing through girlie magazines (only on the night shift). Worst case, they faced eight hours, or sixteen if their relief called in sick, of exhausting manual labor with exposure to heat, noise, chemicals, and other hazards. But no matter how much the mill took from them during the week, on Friday each worker stopped at the guard shack, extended his hand, and the mill gave back.

These manufacturing processes were so complex that only a few employees understood them. To everyone else, it may as well have been magic. But the magic came at a cost. The towering smokestacks emitted water vapor, soot, and airborne toxins in clouds that varied from white to black, depending on how the boilers were running. On clear days, this discharge blasted high and true, like a steam locomotive. On humid or drizzly days, however, it oozed out the top of the stacks, never rising far enough to be swept away by the prevailing winds. This viscous haze enveloped the town and permeated our homes.

Workers who picked up cigarettes and beer at Sampson's grocery store or grabbed a bite at the Rose Bowl Restaurant wore the stench as a badge of honor rather than a source of shame. It meant each of them had a secure, high-paying job, presumably for life, unlike the store clerks and restaurant staff who waited on them.

At least a dozen towns in Maine smelled as bad or worse than we did. Rumford and Millinocket reeked, and Westbrook polluted Maine's largest city, Portland. But no other mill town had a name with such an unfortunate rhyme. "Stinkin' Lincoln!"

My father didn't put up with the insult. When outsiders disparaged his town and his employer, he growled, "Smells like money," and that would be the last word on the matter.

On his days off, when my father hunted ducks on the Penobscot River, he used a machete to cut through the wall of rotting fiber that had accumulated in the weeds close to shore, so he could set the decoys and retrieve the ducks. We never fished in this otherwise magnificent river. Anything we caught would have been too toxic to eat. It wasn't only our mill. The two Great Northern Paper facilities were situated just upstream. And downstream of us, mills in Old Town and Bucksport further harassed the Penobscot on its way to the Atlantic Ocean. After all, before the Clean Water Act of 1972, dilution was the solution to pollution.

Despite these issues, most of us felt Lincoln was the best place on earth to live. The mill engendered enough prosperity that our little town of five thousand served as the hub for the even smaller towns surrounding us. The downtown area was defined by its bookend statues—the Civil War monument on the north end of Main Street, across from the Lincoln Theater, and the World War I monument at the south end, across from Albert's Barbershop. That quarter-mile stretch teemed with businesses like Candyland, Warren Bate's Sport Shop, and Lakeside Lanes. The Memorial Day and Homecoming parades drew huge crowds on Main Street.

In the 1960s and '70s, young people "rode the monuments" in Lincoln on Friday and Saturday nights, continuously making the loop around the two war memorials. They smoked cigarettes, sipped drinks, and made themselves visible to all the other young people in town looking for something to do.

We had everything anyone needed right in Lincoln. Although many of the ladies liked to go to Bangor for the shopping opportunities, men like my father had no use for the big city.

Lincoln suffered no calamities like hurricanes, tornadoes, wildfires, or droughts. While Nor'easters paralyzed Boston and New York, we celebrated the snow. Dad took us ice-fishing, snowmobiling, and once we were old enough—rabbit hunting. Mom taught my two older brothers how to ski. I had to learn from her friend, Hazel.

The wilderness surrounding us harbored no poisonous insects or snakes, no alligators or man-eating tigers. Crime was rare, traffic jams unheard of. Nobody protested about civil rights; we all had the same skin color and prayed to the same God. As a child, I never met a Jewish or African-American person. The State had sequestered most of the Native Americans in squalid reservations at Indian Island and Princeton. French-speaking Canadians, who had immigrated from Québec over the years, comprised our most prominent ethnic minority. I lightheartedly called them "frogs," like everyone did.

Not far outside of town, the pollution from the mill diminished. From these pristine waterways, we ate trout, salmon, perch, pickerel, and whitefish, but not smallmouth bass. My father considered them an invasive species. When we landed one, he pulled the boat close to shore and threw the offending fish into the woods as far as he could, sending a message to all the other smallmouth in the lake.

The forests teemed with wildlife. Sporting camps catered to wealthy out-of-staters who paid top dollar to hunt for a trophy buck or bruin. Boys as young as ten showed up late for school with blood on their pants and were heralded as conquering heroes. Families filled their freezers with game each fall, such as woodcock, partridge, ducks, deer, bear, and occasionally a goose. Later, when they became legal to hunt, we added turkeys and moose. I grew up on a diet heavy in venison. Sometimes the steaks were so tough that I would chew on them for a few minutes, give up, and spit out the remains before taking another bite. My father made things worse by insisting our deer meat be cooked well done.

Although nobody would ever accuse my father of being a romantic, he did have a soft side. Each year he picked mayflowers, lilacs, cattails, and pussy willows for Mom. These wildflower bouquets situated on the kitchen table not only pleased the eye, but they offered us respite from that pervasive odor, that seductive smell of money.

CHAPTER 4

Reason to Fight

My brothers and I chased Dad through the maze of hallways at Eastern Maine Medical Center in Bangor, an hour's drive from our house. A few weeks had passed since Mom's accident, and we were visiting her for the first time. Dad coached us as we walked.

"Don't cry or look scared. It will upset your mother."

I kept falling behind the three longer-legged Sturgeons.

"She's going to look different, but don't stare."

I slipped farther back until Dad took pity, stopped my brothers, and waited for me.

"Does everyone understand what I've just said?" Dad looked from boy to boy.

I peeked at my brothers. Yes. The answer was yes. Three heads bobbed up and down.

Dad ushered us into the room, one at a time. I went last. Inside, it smelled a lot like heavy-duty cleaners and a little like pee. Everything shone bright white or shiny steel, nothing soft or soothing anywhere. Although the collection of high-tech equipment reminded me of the bridge on Star Trek, I didn't like it one bit. A person lay in the middle of the room, hands folded on belly.

Something wasn't right. Dad had said we would be visiting Mom, but I didn't see her anywhere. She had beautiful black hair. The top of this person's head had been shaved, and two steel rods were bolted to the skull. Besides, Mom would be in a wheelchair. Andy had said so.

I found myself drawn to the person with the shaved head. As if sneaking up on a frog in my backyard, I inched closer.

The eyes, nose, mouth. These are familiar. It's a woman.

She wore bright red lipstick—a flowering rosebush in a

snowstorm. Unable to look directly at me because the rods kept her head aimed at the ceiling, she broke into a most familiar smile.

"Come here, Mitchy. I won't bite. How do you like kindergarten?" Mom spoke in her usual, cheerful way. Her eyes soothed; her voice comforted. I smiled right back.

This may have been the most important five minutes of each of our lives. If Mom hadn't been up to the task of comforting and reassuring her sons, I don't know what would have become of us. Or her.

A few days later Mom's friend, Audrey, visited her. To prevent pressure sores, Mom's bed could spin like a rotisserie, and Audrey found my mother momentarily upside down, staring at the floor. Audrey positioned herself on the floor, looking up at Mom. Audrey worried whether the time my mother had spent with my brothers and me had broken her heart or strengthened her resolve. Before she could even ask, my mother settled the issue.

"I have to get out of here," Mom said. "I need to get home to take care of my three boys."

* * *

Things didn't go well for my mother those first few weeks at Eastern Maine Medical Center. She couldn't feel anything below her neck, yet she suffered constant pain in those regions. Her fractured spinal cord remained unstable, and her survival uncertain. Friends dreaded answering their phones for fear it would be *the call.*

Even if she lived, the prospects of her ever getting out of a hospital bed were dim. When it became apparent that Bangor didn't have the resources to treat such a severe injury, she transferred to Massachusetts General Hospital in Boston. There, a team of experts evaluated her at a special clinic for patients with spinal cord injuries.

In Boston, my mother went through a series of roommates, including an 18-year-old girl who had broken her neck in a diving accident. She couldn't move any part of her body except her eyelids. The nurses set up a string of letters over her bed. They instructed the girl to shut both eyes tightly when they touched the letter she wanted.

Thrilled at the prospect of giving this girl a voice, my mother and the nurses watched with anticipation when they tried out the system for the first time.

"P-L-E-A-S-E-K-I-L-L-M-E," the girl spelled.

At first my mother's injury baffled even the brilliant Boston neurosurgeons. But a resident on weekend call took a personal interest in her case. He researched options and developed a surgical plan to stabilize her spine. The goal moved beyond saving her life to creating a life for her outside the hospital, albeit as a quadriplegic. Multiple surgeries later, and a couple of months after her accident, my mother was out of immediate danger and no longer in pain. The grueling rehabilitation process could begin.

* * *

When I was a young adult, my father told me the story of how the Boston doctors allowed my mother to come home for a few days at Christmas in 1969, three months after her accident. He described the drive from Boston to home, accompanied by Roger, the owner of the camp where Mom got hurt.

"I couldn't afford to pay for an ambulance to bring her home, and she wasn't able to sit up in a car seat for that long of a drive. So, Roger and I threw a mattress in the back of the station wagon, picked her up in Boston, and set out for home.

"In fact, she was leaving Boston for good, and after Christmas we would take her to the hospital in Bangor. Anyway, we were about halfway home when she said, 'I think I'm leaking back here. You better pull over and see what's going on.' I did. And she was."

"You mean . . . "

"Yup."

"Had they given you any training on how to handle *that stuff?*" I asked, scrunching up my face.

"Absolutely not. Your grandmother promised to take care of *that stuff* when we got home. We figured out that her urine bag had filled up, but I didn't know how to unhook it and empty it on the side of the road. I could see a little valve on the bottom of the bag, so I grabbed the mattress and pulled your mother halfway out of the back of the station wagon."

"On the side of the road?"

"The interstate, actually. I opened that valve and let it fly. Your mother didn't complain because we had no choice. It was about then I realized our lives would be full of moments like that, and I stopped giving a damn what anyone else thought."

* * *

While Mom was away at the hospital for so long, everyone pitched in to help take care of us boys. I could be a bit of a challenge, as I only liked a few foods, and I only spoke a few words. One of our regular babysitters, Sue, related this story to me from before my mother's accident.

Mom asked me what I would like for dinner. (We called the noontime meal dinner and the five o'clock one supper.) I stopped and looked up at her, but didn't say a word.

Mom cupped my face in her hands, stared into my eyes, and enunciated each word as if English were not my first language. "Mitchell, what—do—you—want—for—dinner?"

My eyes met hers, but I remained mute.

"He wants a peanut butter sandwich, no crust," Andy said.

"He wants a hot dog with the skin peeled off," Tom said.

"Let him speak," my mother implored, never taking her eyes off mine.

Not a word escaped my lips.

My various caregivers treated me well while my mother was away, though they didn't do everything the way they were supposed to. I ate a lot of hot dogs, skin and all, and a lot of peanut butter sandwiches, crust and all. Cruel world.

* * *

Even though my father had full employee benefits at the paper mill, the hospital bills mounted. On top of that, he had hired a carpenter, his friend Junior Bowers, to build a wheelchair-accessible house for my mother. Dad worked his regular shifts at the mill and as many extra shifts as he could manage. His union brothers agreed to bend the rules so he got more opportunities for overtime. He also took a second job printing the weekly newspaper on Wednesday nights. These moves enabled him to pay Junior Bowers and Haskell Lumber every week, on time. They completed the house in just a couple of months. People close to my father suggested he declare bankruptcy to get a fresh financial start, but he managed to remain solvent and pay all his bills. No handouts.

In the spring, Mom transferred from Eastern Maine Medical Center to the nearby Ross Home, where therapists trained her in the essential skills of wheelchair living. Although classified as a quadriplegic, my mother had some use of her arms and hands. I can imagine the first time she tried to hold a coffee cup and bring it to her mouth.

"Mrs. Sturgeon, try to stick your fingers through the handle this way."

"Oh please, it's Vernice. Call me Vernice."

The cup was probably empty and made of lightweight plastic, and at first she only pretended to drink from it. Maybe after a week of bringing the cup to her lips and tipping it, they added a little water. After another week, cup half full. One month in—a full cup and no spillage.

I'm sure Mom concentrated on domestic skills like food preparation. I can imagine how pleased everyone must have been when she learned to fry a piece of meat, bake a potato, warm up a can of peas. Each day at the Ross Home she practiced maneuvering her manual wheelchair, feeding herself, and assisting in her own daily care. She learned about the proper use of her urinary catheter system and how to direct caregivers to evacuate her bowels on every third morning.

In the early summer of that year, about nine months after her accident, Mom graduated from her rehab program and prepared to return home.

CHAPTER 5

Homecoming

Before my mother came home from the hospital, Dad spoke to his 13-year-old son, Andy, to temper his expectations. He explained that people in Mom's situation lived an average of only ten years. Tom and I remained ignorant of this prediction, which was probably a good thing.

A few days before moving into our new house, Dad marched my brothers and me down to the Lincoln Maine Federal Credit Union on Taylor Street, bank books in hand. He instructed us to empty our savings accounts. I had ninety dollars in mine. I can't remember where the money had come from. Perhaps it was intended to be a college fund, but we had more urgent needs. We pooled our money and bought three twin beds for the new house.

Move-in day brought with it a fresh start. Once more, we were a complete family under one roof. Not only did I have my mother back, but I loved the new house, situated in a neighborhood ripe for exploration and adventure.

The house was surrounded by a huge yard, but Dad refused to waste money on loam or grass seed. Instead, we spent long hours those first summers walking around the yard and picking rocks and sticks out of the soil. Eventually, a nice-looking lawn did take hold.

Dad built a unique centerpiece for the backyard—a raised dog pen to house our beagles. These dogs, Polly and her offspring, Smokey, were not so much pets as they were rabbit hunting dogs. Part of the pen consisted of an elevated, insulated doghouse with sawdust on the floor. The doghouse opened into a raised box, framed on all sides with wire fencing. This way, the beagles could see outside their pen and enjoy the open air while their droppings slipped through the fencing to the ground below—a self-cleaning dog pen.

With such delectable morsels piling up below their pen, pigeons couldn't help themselves, and they feasted. We didn't like pigeons, so Dad allowed us to shoot them from our back deck using a BB gun. Thus, dead birds were added to the pile. Occasionally, our aim would be so poor we would hear the BB ricochet off the solid door to the pen. Once, after I shot at a pigeon, I heard Smokey yelp. My bad.

We may have been simple people in a backward town, but the home that Dad and Junior Bowers had designed represented the latest in wheelchair accessibility. The kitchen was laid out so my mother could operate items like the faucet and the stovetop. She could reach some drawers and cupboards. All the work areas in the house had cutouts so Mom could pull her wheelchair underneath the counter or sink. The master bedroom featured an attached bathroom with a roll-in shower. The rear deck afforded her a space to enjoy the back-yard. The attached garage provided a staging area for Mom to get into and out of her vehicles. She couldn't have asked for a better setting to come home to.

The house provided the infrastructure, but the procedures my mother developed made it a functional home. Her home. Mom's complicated morning ritual required a lifelong parade of paid female helpers. Some of these women became like family. The unfriendly or lazy ones, and the one we suspected of stealing, didn't last long.

My father usually accomplished the more straightforward task of putting Mom to bed in the evenings. Paid helpers, volunteers, or friends stepped in if he worked the 3-11 shift. Because the process involved some degree of immodesty, Dad was the only man in the world allowed to put Mom to bed.

By the time I was eight or nine years old, and my brothers were involved in afterschool sports programs, I was given more responsibility for helping my mother. I felt a surge of pride whenever I pushed her through Sampson's grocery store or helped her get from the car to the sideline at one of Andy's high school football games. I learned to appreciate the importance of a disabled person getting out in the world, and I took my caregiver responsibilities seriously. None of my other friends' parents had entrusted them with such tasks. Plus, Mom had become a minor celebrity in our town, and some of that notoriety rubbed off on me.

Most weeks she made a grocery list and sent someone else shopping. She used an electric typewriter to print items in the precise order they would be encountered as we walked down the aisles, starting with the deli on the right side of the store and finishing up with the frozen goods on the far left. Every so often she went shopping in person to learn where things had been moved, and she updated her list accordingly.

Sometimes, having a quadriplegic mother proved educational. Our family physician, Old Doc Gulesian, had a son who was one of two dentists in town. As a child, I ate a lot of sweets and suffered a mouth full of cavities. Young Doc Gulesian would put some numbing compound on a Q-tip and place it in my mouth for a few minutes. When removing the Q-tip, he would instruct me to "Close your eyes and cross your legs." I would feel a pinch in my mouth, but I never peeked. I was a good boy.

Once, when my mother needed dental work, Young Doc Gulesian made a house call and treated her in our kitchen. I watched. He didn't tell her to close her eyes and cross her legs when he removed the Q-tip and gave her a shot with a long syringe, *inside her mouth*. I was flabbergasted. Afterward, I asked her about it, and she said, "How do you think he numbs your mouth when he gives you a filling?"

"The stuff on the Q-tip."

"No, that's only to numb your mouth, so the shot doesn't hurt."

If not for my mother being in a wheelchair, I wonder how long I would have gone without knowing dentists numbed their patients' mouths with a syringe.

Despite her disability, I felt my mother did more for us than most non-disabled mothers did for their kids. She cooked our meals and baked tasty desserts, only needing help during physically challenging steps in the cooking process. Mom ran a tight ship, fiscally.

Although her handwriting was barely legible, she maintained notebooks of budget versus actual spending. She kept all of us on a weekly allowance, including Dad.

Mom remained a giving person, perhaps to a fault, as if overcompensating for some perceived debt that she owed us. If my father wanted green beans, she made me peas or carrots. If she overcooked part of a meal, she ate the burnt food. When we got to the end of a loaf of bread, she took the heel. My mother and her hired helpers did most of the cleaning and all the laundry. She loved running a household, and she exuded positivity. We didn't suffer a disadvantage for having a disabled mother. In fact, we are better people today having been raised by such a caring and inspirational person.

When Mom first came home from the hospital, she started out with a manual wheelchair. After three or four years, it became apparent that this sapped her strength, and her doctor authorized the purchase of a second wheelchair—a power model. She still used the manual chair at least a couple of days a week to keep muscle tone in her arms. We kids weren't allowed to touch her power wheelchair, but when her manual chair sat idle, my friends and I had great fun with it. We pushed each other up and down the hallway until we annoyed my father enough to provoke him. "That's not a goddamned toy!" he would bellow.

Sometimes I would sit in her manual wheelchair and quietly push myself around the house. In those instances, I wasn't playing with her chair. I was pretending to be paralyzed, just like Mom.

CHAPTER 6

Holding Court

Some folks in my parents' circle of friends worried about how Ted would react to Vernice's injury. Would he be up to the task of taking care of her and their three boys? They didn't think poorly of him, but he was such an active person, they weren't sure he could adapt. By any objective measure, however, he performed spectacularly that first year. Vernice came home to a house specifically designed for her needs, a house superior to our previous one in almost every way. Ted accomplished this without going into debt. His hard work had been instrumental in Vernice's ability to reestablish herself in the family and the community.

Still, he was no joy to live with.

My father didn't tolerate frivolous people. He rarely spent time with casual acquaintances. His close friends, like Jack, Doug, and Nick, seemed larger-than-life to me. They were honest, industrious, intelligent, and devoted to my father and, by extension, to everyone in the family. They had made an effort to cut through his rough exterior and know the man within, finding a friend for life. Few people took on this challenge, though, and I can't blame those who chose not to.

My father disliked going out. He used my mother's disability as an excuse. She enjoyed socializing, but she never argued with him if he said, "It looks like it's going to rain, and you know we can't get your wheelchair wet."

That wasn't true. They could get the wheelchair wet.

He loved to hold court at his kitchen table, however, over a half gallon of Jack Daniels and sometimes a deck of cards. He taught me at a young age how to count my cribbage hands.

"Fifteens first, pairs next, and runs last. Like this: fifteen two, fifteen four, a pair is six, and three is nine."

And he taught me how to mix bourbon and whiskey drinks for him and his guests:

"Pour the alcohol first, one third the way up the glass. Then fill the glass with ice. Top it off with mixer if they want any. This is the most important part. If they take their bourbon on the rocks or with water, then serve them Jack Daniels. But if they mix it with goddamn ginger ale or anything else, make sure you only give them Jim Beam. That's all they deserve."

We had no wine in the house, and beer only in the summer.

Despite my father's shortcomings, Mom remained devoted to him, even more so after the accident. He was the man who fell in love with her and married her those many years ago. He stayed with her in hard times and didn't run. He paid her medical bills and built her house.

One time my brother Andy found out just where things stood in this relationship.

"Make me a cup of coffee," Dad said to Mom at the breakfast table. He gave this command plainly, the tone neither friendly nor unkind. He had a need, and he conveyed this need to his wife.

"Yep, just a minute," Mom replied while she fixed him a piece of toast, a complicated task for her.

Andy had seen this a hundred times before, but he had reached his limit. "Why don't you get off your ass and fix your own cup of coffee?"

Andy felt proud of himself for standing up on his mother's behalf. It had been long overdue. He braced for a sharp response from Dad, but Mom spoke instead.

"Don't ever talk to your father like that. I'm perfectly capable of making him a cup of coffee. That's my job."

Dad looked at Andy with a knowing grin, and Andy realized the cause was hopeless. Mom had sealed her fate. If Dad's requests ever became too burdensome, our chivalry would be unwelcome.

* * *

My father didn't take us on traditional vacations. We didn't go to Disney World. We didn't visit the Grand Canyon or Aunt Vivian and my cousins in California. Although we listened to the Boston Red Sox baseball games on our radios every day, or watched them when they were occasionally on television, my father never took me to Fenway Park, a five-hour drive away.

This isolation was not unusual in our corner of the world. I didn't feel deprived. Instead of extravagant vacations, we went on hunting or fishing trips, and we made the two-hour drive to Southwest Harbor once every summer, even after my mother's accident. There, we visited my namesake, Gardner Mitchell. My father had met Gardner in the Army, during the Korean War, and he became part of Dad's small inner circle.

Southwest Harbor is one of four towns on Mount Desert Island, the second largest island on the eastern seaboard. Only Long Island, New York surpasses it. As we approached Southwest Harbor, we drove through a gauntlet of tourist traps: a low-budget zoo, a go-kart track, mini golf, and a store shaped like a round block of cheese. I never dared ask Dad to stop and let us explore these treasures. Neither did my brothers, at least in front of me. I knew what the answer would be.

When I have kids, I thought, *I'll stop in all these places.* And I did.

As we crossed the bridge, the acrid smell of the ocean almost took my breath away, especially at low tide. The sulfurous odors emitted by the paper mill in our hometown, which caused first-time visitors to gag, didn't bother me, but I found the natural ocean smell to be most disagreeable. It was worth it, however. As the youngest of three boys, I rarely occupied the high ground. But when we traveled to Southwest Harbor, it was all about Mitchells of one kind or another, and I felt my stature in the family grow, even if my brothers didn't notice.

These trips became the highlight of my summers. Although we didn't get to ride the go-karts, on Mount Desert Island we enjoyed fishing, hiking, and sightseeing.

Due to her spinal cord injury, my mother had lost the ability to perspire, and thus control her body temperature in the heat. This issue came to the forefront one year on a sweltering drive to Southwest Harbor. By the time we arrived at the Mitchells', she had no energy and felt ill. Inside the house, we placed her in front of a fan and assumed all would be well. The men and boys went fishing.

When we returned to Gardner's house a few hours later, Mom had not cooled down. In fact, her condition had deteriorated.

My father called the local hospital. Before bringing her in, they suggested we try to cool her down ourselves, using whatever means necessary. My father and Janet, Gardner's wife, placed Mom in their shower and turned on the cold water. This did the trick, and within an hour she had recovered. Once the danger passed, Dad suggested we return home. Mom didn't like that idea. She had traveled so far and been through so much that day; she wanted to enjoy the rest of our visit. The adults feasted on lobster and clams, the kids on hamburgers and hotdogs, then we headed back home in the cooler evening air.

* * *

One early June day in 1975, my father called our schools and summoned us home. When I arrived at the house, I watched the ambulance crew wheel my mother out of her bedroom on a stretcher. Dad told us to give her a kiss. She was going to the hospital for a few days. Mom smiled and issued us a cheery goodbye as if she were going on holiday.

As the ambulance backed out of our driveway, lights flashing but sirens quiet, my father told me to go outside and play, and off I went. My mother's calm and sunny demeanor worked on me. I wasn't nearly as concerned as I should have been.

Meanwhile, Old Doc Gulesian, our family physician, sat down with my two older brothers and my father at the kitchen table.

Dr. Gulesian explained that one of my mother's kidneys had failed—a complication of her paralysis. Furthermore, he expected the other kidney to fail within a couple of years. They would try dialysis for a while, but it would be only a short-term solution.

There was never any discussion of a kidney transplant for a quadriplegic.

My mother had adjusted so well to her situation that I didn't consider our family to be different from anyone else's. Dad worked. Mom stayed home. I had two siblings and a couple of dogs. I didn't worry about my mother's health. She looked just fine to me. Then, one day shortly after my mother had returned from her kidney operation, a fifth-grade classmate named Kristin pulled me aside on the playground and said, "Guess what I heard? When your mother dies, you're going to come live with me."

"What are you talking about? She's not dying," I replied.

"Yes, she is. My mother said so."

The invocation—somebody's mother said so—amounted to irrefutable evidence in fifth grade. I had never considered the possibility that Mom would die, from breaking her neck or otherwise. I didn't know the seriousness of her kidney problem, or that more than half of her expected 10-year lifespan had already passed, but other people in town did.

If my mother died I would be sent to live in a home I had never even visited before, with people I barely knew? I spent the rest of the school day in a daze. As soon as I got home, I found Mom and asked her, "If you died, where would I go live?"

"Well, you would stay with your father, of course."

"I wouldn't go live with Kristin and her mother?"

"Where is this coming from?"

"Kristin told me that her mother said you're going to die, and I'll move into their house."

Mom laughed a comforting laugh. "Kristin doesn't know what she's saying. I have no plans to die, Mitchy, but if I did, you would not go to live at their house. Believe me." And I believed her, because, to a fifth grader, the only authority higher than someone else's mother was your own.

* * *

It wasn't only people in the community who imagined worst-case scenarios. After my mother's accident, and for the rest of my father's life, he assumed every uncertain situation would have a disastrous outcome.

When Tom was in ninth grade, and I in sixth, he played quarterback for the junior varsity football team. At a game in the town of Dover-Foxcroft, he dropped back on a passing play, and a defender tackled him from the blind side, helmet first, squarely in the back. Tom crumpled to the ground and passed out from the pain. Dad rushed on to the field.

Tom woke up to Dad screaming, "Can you feel your toes? Can you feel your toes?" Tom mumbled that he could feel his toes, a minor consolation for Dad. Bad stuff could still happen, and in his mind, it probably would.

Ray Roy, the father of a teammate, had driven to Dover-Foxcroft in a station wagon. Oblivious to the fact that they shouldn't handle a potential spinal cord injury victim themselves, they stuffed Tom into the back of the station wagon and drove him to the small local hospital. The emergency room doctor gave Tom a shot for pain and lifted him up into a sitting position. Tom screamed in agony, Dad screamed in anger, and he and Ray Roy dragged Tom back to the station wagon. They drove 30 minutes to Eastern Maine Medical Center in Bangor—the same hospital where my mother had spent so much time after her accident. They diagnosed Tom with a cracked vertebra but indicated he had no spinal cord damage, and that he should enjoy a full recovery. He did, and he played football at a high level from his sophomore year through his senior year.

My poor father. Spinal cord issues kept coming back to haunt him.

It made no sense to me how Tom could break his back and recover while Mom broke her neck and became paralyzed. When I asked Mom, she explained that the spinal cord is part of the central nervous system and is encased in the vertebrae. An injury to the vertebrae can heal. An injury to the spinal cord—not so much. This physiology lesson would come in handy later in my life.

CHAPTER 7
Blood on My Hands

When I turned 13 my father decided it was time I became a deer hunter. He didn't ask if I wanted this any more than he asked if I wanted to go to college. Dad made certain decisions for us.

On my training hunts, he didn't allow me to carry a firearm, and he ordered me to follow about 20 feet behind him. When he stopped, I stopped. When he moved, I moved. But if he saw something interesting, a teachable moment, he motioned for me to join him. Dad educated me on how to identify deer tracks and signs of mating activity, like buck scrapes on the ground and antler rubs on saplings.

Certain terrain allowed for almost silent walking—mossy or otherwise damp ground for example. However, walking on a forest floor covered with dry, frozen leaves and sticks was about as quiet as roller skating on sheets of bubble wrap. Still, Dad scowled at me every time I made a noise. When he snapped a twig or let fly one of his smoker's coughs, well, that couldn't be helped.

On November 13, 1976—Tom's sixteenth birthday—Dad and Andy went hunting without me, and I didn't mind. I had grown tired of the dirty looks, and I disliked hunting without a gun. Tom didn't go that day because he had basketball practice. Dad surprised me by returning home at mid-morning and saying, "Put on your hunting clothes. You're going to tag a deer for your brother."

The State of Maine allowed each licensed hunter to harvest one deer per season. Andy had shot a small deer that morning, and Dad decided I would register it so Andy could hunt for a bigger one. Once again, he didn't ask if I wanted to perpetrate this fraud. It wasn't optional nor unusual back in those days.

Dad and Andy had taken the canoe up Passadumkeag Stream that morning, and Andy continued to hunt while Dad retrieved me from the house and coached me on the ruse we were about to execute. When we arrived at the boat launch, he pulled out Tom's .30-30 lever action rifle and taught me how to load and fire it. "Just in case the game warden doesn't believe you shot the deer and wants proof you know how to handle a rifle."

I had fired a shotgun before. In fact, I killed a partridge with Dad's 20-gauge just a few weeks earlier, on my third try. After I missed the first bird I shot at, he teased me incessantly. After I missed the second one, he got downright mad at me. I was glad I didn't miss the third partridge.

Firing a rifle was a bigger deal, though. Dad instructed me, "Hold this the same way you do a shotgun, and when you're ready to shoot, pull back on the hammer to cock the gun. It helps to steady yourself if you exhale all the way and hold your breath just before you pull the trigger. Now, see if you can hit that pine tree over there."

I lifted the gun, cocked it, and watched the front and rear sights dance around and around. I tried to time it so that the post at the end of the barrel passed through the notch at the front of the barrel at the exact moment everything lined up on the tree. I exhaled and held my breath. It helped, but not enough.

This is going to be ugly.

But Dad was waiting, and I risked passing out from lack of oxygen. I pulled the trigger and felt the recoil on my shoulder. The rifle kicked harder than a shotgun, but not as severely as I had feared.

"Look at that! You hit it in the center. Nice shot. Now let's get going up the stream. I'll show you where the deer is, in case the game warden still doesn't believe you and wants to see the gut pile."

I attempted to pass the gun back to Dad, but he raised both hands and said, "I'm not lugging that gun. You are."

Finally.

We shoved off in our 20-foot Grumman canoe and motored against the current for about 15 minutes. Dad pulled ashore, and we tied up the canoe. He and I made our way through the woods toward the downed deer. For the first time, Dad allowed me to walk beside him instead of behind. I didn't notice when he picked up his rifle and aimed, so the blast startled me.

"I just shot a doe," he said.

We approached the carcass. I had seen many dead deer over the years, although never a fresh kill. I wondered how Dad could be sure it was deceased and wouldn't bite or kick us. But he wasted no time pulling out his hunting knife and cutting her open. He proceeded deliberately and taught me how to field dress a deer.

"We don't eat the heart and liver," he said while holding them up for me to see. "We'll give them to old Luther Martin." Luther was a friend of my grandfather. Both Luther and Grampy Sturgeon were old and serious, and they made me uncomfortable. But their eyes lit up, and they almost smiled when we showed them the game we had shot or the fish we had caught.

I had cleaned the guts out of many fish and partridge. I thought that cleaning a deer would be similar, and it was as far as what I could see and feel. But when I knelt down close—oh, the smell. I had never in my life experienced anything so foul. Dad was teaching me men's work, however, so I carried on as if a bouquet of roses had come out of that deer's gut.

"You stay here by this doe, and I'll go back to the canoe to get more rope to drag her with," Dad said.

As the crunch of his steps faded, I became bored. After setting my brother's .30-30 against a tree, I wandered around and kicked at the dirt. I began daydreaming, undoubtedly about girls. A twig snapped, but the sound came from the opposite direction from where my father had gone.

Must be Andy.

It wasn't. I peered into the woods, and a real, live white-tailed buck peered back at me, not 20 paces away. This being the height of the rut, he had been following the doe with keen interest.

I remained frozen by indecision. The young buck did, too. My choices were to do nothing or try to shoot him. His choices were to stay close to the doe or flee. Like me, his brain was addled each day, at least this time of the year, by a vague yet overpowering desire to be with the opposite sex. My urges led to frustration, awkwardness, and occasional humiliation. His could lead to death.

My mind raced. We already had two deer down. Would Dad be angry if I made it three? Would he be angry if I didn't? It might not matter because I stood a good distance from my brother's loaded rifle. After walking over and picking it up, I looked for the buck, but of course, he had disappeared, making my decision for me.

I won't even tell Dad I saw a deer. He'll yell at me or tease me endlessly for setting my gun down.

Then I heard another noise. The buck had only moved a few feet to his left. In Dad's absence, I made an executive decision. I lifted my brother's rifle, watched the front and rear sights dance all around the deer's front quarter, cocked the gun, and squeezed the trigger. The report from the .30-30 reverberated throughout the woods, and the buck vanished in a flurry of hooves and fur and antlers. I heard him crash through some underbrush and then—silence.

Dad feared I had either fired my gun to amuse myself, which he expressly forbid, or I had fired the gun by mistake, which would be a frightening prospect. He yelled, "What the hell are you doing down there?"

"I just shot at a buck!" I answered.

Dad arrived at the scene huffing and puffing. He wasn't angry, not even close. He asked me to show him the details—where I stood, where the deer stood, which way he ran, and so forth. Andy showed up too, having heard the gunshot. At 19, he had already earned a reputation as an expert tracker. He found a tuft of deer hair at the spot where I said the buck had been standing, a positive sign.

The tedious tracking process began. When Dad or Andy found a drop of blood on a leaf, or a footprint in the mud, or any other sign of the wounded deer, they stood me at that location while they walked in ever larger, concentric circles around me. When they found the next sign, they moved me to that spot, and so on. This continued for about an hour, and I accepted that I had screwed up and not hit the deer in a vital part. Then Andy called from just beyond my field of vision, "Come here, Mitchell."

I wondered which variety of tracking evidence he had found this time, and asked, "What is it?"

"You'll see."

I gawked at the healthy-looking—although very much dead—animal with its perfectly formed six-point rack. Dad and Andy shook my hand, patted me on the back, and congratulated me repeatedly. I had never seen Dad so animated without Jack Daniels involved, and I had never in my life received so much praise.

Andy took charge of field dressing the deer while Dad explained, "This is the last time we're going to help you do this. You'll gut your own deer from now on." (I did.)

Andy had me elbow-deep in the deer's chest cavity. I ended up with blood all over my hands, but I didn't mind—a rite of passage. We dragged all three deer out of the woods, packed them into the canoe, and shoved off. In case I didn't appreciate how exceptional this day was, Dad summarized it for me. While speaking over the steady drone of the six horsepower Johnson outboard, which strained to push the overloaded canoe down the stream, he observed, "Three men and three deer, and you getting your first deer, this is a day we'll never forget."

As I contemplated his words and basked in the glory, I realized he was right. If I took all my birthdays and all the Christmases I had experienced up to that point, threw in the day Mom came home from the hospital, and topped it off with that one time I had kissed a girl, it still wouldn't have equaled the satisfaction I felt at that moment.

At school on Monday, my neighbor Ronnie said, "I saw your father come home in the middle of the morning and take you off in your hunting clothes. He shot too many deer and had you tag that buck. You can't fool me." No matter what I said, I could never convince Ronnie of the truth.

* * *

Growing up, our Christmases were right out of Currier & Ives: cold and snowy weather, traditional holiday treats, opening gifts, mistletoe. I miss those Decembers.

Each Christmas Eve, my parents hosted an open house—a party that started in the afternoon and lasted until late at night. Everyone in town admired my mother. She had been through so much, yet endured with uncommon grace and good spirit. I think the reason we had such a robust turnout each year was that people just wanted to be around Vernice, especially at Christmastime.

The guests entered our house amid great fanfare—handshakes and hugs and wishes of Merry Christmas and a Happy New Year. Dad always hung a sprig of mistletoe in the living room. He knew which female visitors would play along and allow a friendly kiss on their lips—he wasn't satisfied with a cheek or a forehead.

Most of the guests brought something delicious and homemade, but Dad's favorite visitors were those who placed a fifth or half-gallon of Jack under the tree. My father was a social, happy drinker. I never considered that he had a problem with alcohol, and looking back I still don't. In fact, I enjoyed being around Dad when he got into the Jack and water. He was so much more pleasant.

On Christmas Eve the adults shuffled me off to bed at my regular time. But I would lay awake for hours listening to the raucous, alcohol-fueled conversations drifting down the hallway from the kitchen and living room. I loved to eavesdrop on stories I was not supposed to hear. December 24th became the most educational night of the year for me.

During the open house a couple of months after I shot my first deer, Dad shouted, "Mitchell, come here!" He was half in the bag already. "I'm going to give you your Christmas present right now. It's under the sink in our bathroom. Go get it."

I hurried into my parents' bathroom. Under the cabinet, I pulled out a beautiful set of deer antlers, professionally mounted on a plaque—my antlers. I carried the trophy out into the kitchen, and everyone oohed and aahed. Dad told the story for the millionth time and ended it the way he always did: "I said to the man at the deer registration station, 'I don't care if you believe me or not, but the smallest hunter shot the biggest deer!'"

Uncle Fuzzy, Dad's genial and outgoing brother-in-law, came every Christmas Eve with my Aunt Brenda. He asked me, "Where are you going to hang those antlers?"

"Over my bed," I responded.

Everybody laughed.

"I don't think you want to hang those sharp antlers over your head. We'll find a place," said my mother, coming to my rescue like she always did.

A couple of years later, my mother surprised me by announcing, "There will be no Christmas Eve open houses for the next seven years."

What an oddly specific thing to say.

"Dad will be working the three-to-eleven shift on December twenty-fourth each of those years." My father worked a rotating shift called the southern swing. He could foresee his schedule as far out as he cared to look.

It was worse than Mom had predicted, however. The open houses, my favorite part of Christmas, never resumed.

CHAPTER 8

The Unfortunate Popcorn Incident

Although I had matured from the shy little boy who wouldn't speak to anyone, I still suffered from a common flaw of adolescent boys. I was both obsessed with, and terrified of, pretty girls.

The custom in middle school required that I express my interest in a girl only through a shadowy conduit of passed notes or whispers in the hallway between my people and hers. If the girl shared my interest and responded in the affirmative, we would become boyfriend and girlfriend. I would then feel so shy and intimidated that I would ignore her until she became frustrated with my behavior and, through our surrogates, would terminate the arrangement.

In seventh grade, on the heels of my successful deer hunt, I pulled off a major coup when Lynn agreed to be my girlfriend. She was a grade ahead of me and gorgeous, with beautiful blond hair, an outgoing personality, and the mystique of being French-Canadian. Although I remained terrified to speak with her in person, we developed a profound relationship over the phone, where I must have exhibited some degree of adolescent charisma. We talked for hours at a time, and this relationship continued for almost a year.

Occasionally, Lynn and I ventured out on something resembling a date. We went to the movies one September night when Lynn was a freshman at the local high school, and I still languished in eighth grade at the middle school. Lincoln had an antiquated movie theater with a single screen. The seats were vinyl, the floors sticky. Every once in a while the proprietor strolled up and down the aisles with a flashlight and scolded any kids who talked, or put their feet up on the seatbacks in front of them, or buried their hands too deeply in one another's clothing. Lucky for us, he spent extended periods of time in his office, and we did pretty much what we wanted.

Early in the movie, Lynn whispered that she was going to buy popcorn and would return shortly. She never came back. Before the show finished, I snuck out of the theater and positioned myself across the street so I could spy on everyone as they exited. Sure enough, Lynn walked out hand-in-hand with a smug-looking senior. He carried himself with all the confidence in the world. This guy was in another league from me and didn't know that I existed. As I glared at him, hatred and jealousy boiled up. He might as well have reached all the way across the street, stuck his hand down my throat, pulled out my heart, and stomped on it. But when I saw the smile on Lynn's face, and how comfortable she looked with him, I realized he wasn't the person responsible for my pain. The one stomping on my heart was Lynn, which hurt all the more.

The senior who Lynn walked out of the movies with that night was no ordinary man. After high school, and after he and Lynn had gone their separate ways, Master Sergeant Gary Gordon became a member of Delta Force special operations. He was killed during the Battle of Mogadishu, an ambush reenacted in the movie *Black Hawk Down*. He was posthumously awarded the Medal of Honor. A true American hero.

By my freshman year in high school, I had matured to where I could sometimes speak with pretty girls in person. I remember one short-lived relationship with an attractive and popular eighth-grader named Gayle. I had toiled at odd jobs so I could afford to buy my class ring. As we sat together in the movie theater (there wasn't much else to do in Lincoln), I showed this gaudy piece of jewelry to Gayle for the first time.

She perked up. "Oh, look at that. Can I hold it for a second?" She tried the ring on each of her fingers, and we laughed about how large it appeared on her delicate hand. She pulled her feet up into her seat, turned, batted the lashes on those big brown eyes, and asked, "Can I keep it?"

What a dilemma. She was so cute that I wanted to make her

happy, but I needed more information.

"You mean go steady?" I asked.

"Sure, I guess."

I noted her lack of enthusiasm.

Wearing a high school boy's ring on a string around her neck would solidify her social standing in the eighth grade. I, on the other hand, had put a lot of work into purchasing the ring, and it symbolized my new status as a member of the class of 1982. I had only worn it for a couple of days, and I wasn't ready to part with it for anything less than true love.

"How about this?" I proposed. "Let's go steady, but I'll still wear my ring. I just got it on Wednesday."

She pushed the ring into my hands, turned away and ignored me for the rest of the movie. The next day, Dave approached me and said, "Gayle told me to inform you that it's over. She is breaking up with you."

I looked at my ring, shrugged, and said, "I'm okay with that."

CHAPTER 9
Rules of Romance

During my sophomore year on the high school track team, my future wife stood out among the other freshman runners because of her blazing speed, playful personality, and nice ass. When I showed interest in her, Kim responded flirtatiously, and we began to seek each other out during track practices and on the bus rides to and from meets. At that time, I socialized with the popular kids, and she didn't. I like to think I rescued her from a life of obscurity. She likes to think I caught her on the upswing.

If a boy wanted to get anywhere with a girl, he had to follow a certain process, or so I was told. It started at handholding, followed by putting your arm around her at the movies, then kissing (and more) if you were so fortunate. Like a video game, the boy had to win at one level before he could advance to the next. Sometimes I didn't know what each stage entailed, in which case I asked Dave. He knew everything about girls. As was my nature, I assumed the steps should be performed more or less clinically, without eye contact, affection, or passion.

On our first date I held Kim's hand as we walked into the movie theater. Step one, check. We saw *The Electric Horseman*, which garnered an Oscar nomination for Best Sound. I don't remember anything about the sound. Early in the movie I raised my right arm and put it around Kim. Step two, check. I felt nervous as hell, but at least I had the manual, the Standard Operating Procedure, to guide me.

I can do this.

I never considered that girls could have a different instruction manual than boys, or no manual at all. I expected to be in complete control until she said "no" or "stop." Instead, Kim improvised by leaning in and laying her head on my chest. Questionable behavior, borderline affectionate. I let it slide. Then, she gently stroked my forearm. This was a most unexpected development.

What kind of freak am I dating?

Despite these misgivings, I found myself intoxicated by the rise and fall of her breath on my neck and chest, the tickling of a stray hair on my cheek, the smell of her shampoo. I experienced a heightened sense of awareness, not unlike when I saw that buck standing in the woods a couple of years earlier, although not the same either. This was better. When she stopped stroking my forearm for a moment, I wanted to tell her to continue, but I couldn't find the words. I consulted the manual. It was mute on the subject.

I wondered if there might be more to this process than the mechanics. Could I appreciate some gestures for what they were, and not for where they might lead? Kim had nudged me into uncharted territory. This turn of events fascinated me. This girl intrigued me. If she had asked for my ring, I would have given it to her. If she had gone to get popcorn, I would have followed her.

When Kim returned home from the movies, she pulled the ticket stub out of her pocket and placed it in her scrapbook, where it still sits today. Even though I found my evening with Kim to be groundbreaking, I didn't see the big picture. She knew from the beginning.

Kim remembers the first time I took her to meet my mother. As we walked up the hill toward my house on Edwards Street, I said, "Did you know my mother's in a wheelchair?"

"I didn't. Do you mind if I ask why?"

"She was out at a camp and slipped on some wet steps going down to a dock. Broke her neck."

"She just slipped?"

"Yup. Just slipped."

I didn't appreciate how unlikely it was that I would still have a mother to introduce anyone to. Nobody had told me about her expected 10-year lifespan, which she had now exceeded. Nobody told me that her remaining kidney was in danger of failing (it never did). Out of ignorance, I assumed her survival to this point had been unremarkable.

Kim was the first girl I ever brought home for dinner with my family. Mom wanted desperately to make Kim comfortable, and the first question to pop into her head on this June day was: "So, Kim, do you get many trick-or-treaters at your house?"

Before Kim could answer, Tom spoke up. "Really, Mom? How many trick-or-treaters does she get?" We all had a good laugh at Mom's expense, including Mom.

My parents fell in love with my new girlfriend. Kim immediately bonded with my mother, but it took a while longer with my father. We started going steady that summer, and the ring changed hands.

* * *

In eighth grade, I had begun to experiment with alcohol. My best friend Dave and I skimmed a little off the top of his parents' liquor bottles, replaced it with water, and thought we were clever. Recently, my adult daughter told me she did the same thing to our liquor bottles.

By our freshman year, my friends and I started drinking almost every weekend. We participated in late-night and sometimes all-night parties at gravel pits, campsites, lake cottages, or homes where the adults were away for the night. We told our parents we were staying at one another's houses, and we stayed somewhere else altogether. My mother and father remained oblivious until the Molly Hatchet incident during my senior year.

Kim had little interest in such activities. I faced a conundrum. After a year of trying to balance my social life with my girlfriend time, I felt trapped. My buddies were going to parties and organizing fishing and hunting expeditions while Kim wanted me always by her side, away from them—a story written a million times. One evening in her parents' living room, curled up in an embrace on the couch, I gathered my courage and blurted out, "I don't think this is working anymore. I want to break up."

Kim didn't recoil, but instead burrowed deeper into my arms and said, "No."

"No?" I asked.

"Right. We're not breaking up."

I didn't know somebody could refuse a breakup. I hadn't prepared for that. A few minutes passed, and I said nothing. As with our first date, Kim had blown up my scripted performance. Finally I asked, "Why aren't we breaking up?"

"You don't want to."

I made my case about the parts of our relationship that I disliked. She understood and promised to do better. When I remained unconvinced, Kim began to sob gently. I had no sisters and few female friends, so this was a strange and unwelcome development. The crying needed to stop, immediately.

"Okay. Let's not break up. I didn't mean it."

That's the closest we ever came to splitting—a feeble attempt by me and superior defensive maneuvering by Kim. Again, she saw things I didn't, and she trusted her instincts. This was one of those extraordinary moments in life where a single decision, made on the spot, determined which of two diverse paths I would take. If I had followed through with the breakup, I have no doubt it would have been the biggest mistake I ever made.

CHAPTER 10
Superdog

Most people have that one special dog in their life. Mine was a black lab named Tarr. Andy used his paper route money to purchase Tarr as a puppy shortly after we moved into the Edwards Street house. But, as Andy and then Tom went off to college, it sure felt like Tarr became my dog. Although I had only a twin bed, he slept with me every night. His intelligence, loyalty, and love made him the perfect companion, except that he was acutely aware of his confinement.

For the twelve years Tarr lived with us, we couldn't leave a door open or he would burst through it, run down the street, and work his way from house to house. If he happened upon a cat, he chased it. If he encountered a dog, he fought it. My cuddly pal turned into a monster, terrorizing the neighborhood until we caught him and dragged him home. More than once, we had to pry his mouth open to get him off another animal. My father seemed to admire this side of Tarr's personality. I hated it, but I always forgave him.

Tarr had a part-time job in the family. He retrieved the ducks we shot. He would jump into any situation, no matter the water temperature or weather conditions, and he always got his bird. He possessed superior athletic skills and became an invaluable member of our team. Tarr was Superdog.

By the summer after my junior year in high school, Tarr's old age showed in the gray hairs on his snout and in the way he struggled to walk around the house. One afternoon, too weak and lame to get up and go outside, he lay on the hardwood floor in the living room with a sheepish look on his face and emptied his bladder in front of my parents and me. My father stood and announced, "Well, we need to have him put down. Mitchell, clean up that mess, and after supper we'll go out to the woodlot and dig a grave."

When my father walked out of the room, I pleaded with Mom. "Why do we have to put Tarr down? Shouldn't we give him another chance? He just made that one mistake."

Always defending my father's decisions, Mom said, "He's an old dog. If he can't control his bladder anymore, it's time. Your father is right."

My father and I drove outside of town to a piece of property he owned. We did some hunting on this land, but its primary purpose was to supply us with firewood for heating the house all winter. Once there, we dug a nice, deep grave for Tarr or, rather, I dug, and my father supervised. As I finished up the hole, he broke the news to me. "I'm working the day shift the rest of the week, so you need to take Tarr to the vet and have him put down. Bring him out here afterward, lay him in the grave, and cover him with dirt."

This wasn't a request, but an order. Even though I disagreed with the course of action, I didn't protest. I wanted my father to know that I had matured enough for this assignment, and I felt proud that he trusted me with it.

The next day I drove Tarr to the animal clinic. I held on to his head and rubbed his ears as the vet gave him the lethal injection. He took his last breath in my arms. I wrapped him up in a blanket and placed his body in the back of the pickup truck. As soon as I started driving to the woodlot, a couple of tears formed in my eyes, and then I began bawling. I had never cried so hard before, nor have I cried that hard since, even after the deaths of people closest to me. The tears made it difficult to see the road, so I drove as carefully as I would have in a torrential rainstorm.

When I arrived at the woodlot, I parked near the grave, picked up Tarr's body and laid him in the ground. I covered him with the dirt and the stones we had prepared, said a quick goodbye, and left. On the drive home, I began to wonder why my father had me do this by myself. We could have waited until he got out of work in the afternoon and done it together. He made it sound like there was no other way, but there was. Maybe he didn't want me to see him cry. Maybe he didn't have the nerve to go through with it. Whatever the reason, he passed this off to his 17-year-old son. For the first time, I felt I had behaved in a more manly fashion than my father.

But disappointment, as it turned out, would be a two-way street.

CHAPTER 11

The Molly Hatchet Incident

In the fall of my senior year, four of my buddies and I bought tickets to a Molly Hatchet concert at the Bangor Auditorium. This southern rock band recorded only one hit song—"Flirtin' with Disaster," an apt description for our adventure that night.

On the drive to the concert, we encountered a state policeman who confiscated all our booze and pot. Because the driver of our car knew the cop, we got off with only a speeding ticket, or so we thought. In fact, while we were at the concert, he called a meeting with our parents and told them what he had found, and that he had decided to let them dole out the punishment instead of running us through the legal system. It wasn't only the legal system he saved us from, because four of the five of us were starters on the football team and would have been kicked off.

When I got home after the concert, I tried to quietly walk past my parents' bedroom on the way toward mine. But their light was on, and my father beckoned me in. A chair had been placed between their beds, and I was instructed to sit down in it. My father did all the talking.

"Where did you buy the pot?"

"What pot?" Given that I had been ambushed, I fell back on this reflexive, if desperate, defense.

"Don't play dumb. The police told me everything."

"It wasn't my pot." This happened to be true.

"Bullshit. Tell me who you bought it from."

I paused long enough to think about the broader consequences of my answer. "Even if it was mine, I couldn't tell you where I got it."

"Why not?"

"Because that's something you just don't do."

"Well, you've put yourself in a difficult position, haven't you? Needing to protect some slimy drug dealer. How long have you been smoking pot?"

"This was the first time," I lied.

"Bullshit."

A long silence ensued. Then, he continued. "This is far from over. We'll talk about it more later."

But we didn't. My father and I never had another conversation on the subject.

My parents, and many people their age, didn't know the difference between occasional, recreational pot smoking and heroin addiction. I came to understand this the morning after the concert when my mother, in a supportive tone, said, "I want to ask you something. Do you need to go away for a little while to a hospital, for . . . you know?"

"No, Mom, I'm not a drug addict."

Until that moment I had been in a defensive, combative mode. Mom's naïve question shifted my perspective and broke my heart.

This dual identity I had so carefully nurtured—scholar and athlete by day and party animal by night—finally caught up with me. Although I now recognize that my fall from grace had been inevitable, back then I'd never considered the possibility. While my relationship with my parents had been damaged, school and sports and my bond with Kim remained unaffected. I focused on those interests, and I merely went through the motions at home. I did what I had to do there, and either spent time in my room or left the house altogether.

The next weekend I had a football game at Dexter High School, about an hour's drive from Lincoln. During warm-ups before the game, I canvassed the crowd and saw that my father had made the trip, as he always did if his work schedule allowed. I became hopeful that perhaps his heart had softened. I started the game at running back, and I pulled off my longest touchdown run of the year. We won handily. When I saw my father at home afterward, he said, "I only went to that game to watch Timmy, not you." (Timmy was the son of a family friend.) This was the first time my father had spoken to me since that night after the concert, and his words could not have been more hurtful. I scoffed at myself for not expecting it. I should have known from watching him gut a deer that my father was an expert at cutting to the bone.

After my senior year of football concluded, my head football coach and English teacher, Mr. Crawford, asked to speak with me one day after school. I dreaded the conversation. I had the utmost respect for Mr. Crawford, and I hoped he hadn't found out about what happened the night of the concert.

"Have a seat. There's something important I need to talk to you about."

Oh crap.

"Mitch, I nominated you for the Tom McCann Scholar-Athlete of the Year Award, and I'm happy to tell you that you are the winner for Class C schools. Congratulations."

Are you kidding me? Good news?

I thanked Mr. Crawford, shook his hand, and went on with my day. It had been a rough few weeks at home, so this gave me a much-needed morale boost. I became hopeful that I could start to climb out of the hole I had dug.

Even if my parents wouldn't congratulate me and share in my joy, I looked forward to telling them, because this would be more evidence for my side of the argument—that I was a good person, and I was not throwing away my life. At dinner that night I explained the award to them. Mom smiled and asked questions and carried on the same way she would have if not for the recent tensions.

My father grunted, "That's nice."

Progress.

The town manager and the superintendent of schools sent me congratulatory letters. The *Bangor Daily News* and the *Lincoln News* each published prominent articles. The award's selection committee presented me with a plaque at halftime during one of our high school basketball games. My father, beginning to soften ever so slightly, attended the award ceremony and said to me afterward, "See what you almost gave up?"

I believe my father had good intentions. He didn't understand my behavior, and he feared I would waste my opportunities, my gifts. A more modern, enlightened parent might have counseled their high school senior to avoid these temptations and added, "If you must partake, at least make sure you don't drive, and you don't get in a car with anyone who has been smoking marijuana or drinking. In fact, if you find yourself without a safe ride, call me, and I'll come get you." But parenting hadn't evolved to that point in 1982, at least not in rural Maine.

Why did I risk so much by smoking pot and drinking alcohol in high school? I hated the thought of being known only as a smart kid, because smart kids were nerds, misfits. I didn't tell my friends that my favorite TV character was *The Professor* on Gilligan's Island. I didn't want them to know that I loved the smell, the feel, the possibilities that came with a shiny, new book. The progress reports with all As on them? I was too proud of that accomplishment to keep it a secret. I liked being known as a mischievous and unpredictable teenager as much I liked being known as a successful one. Neither of the labels appealed to me without the balance provided by the other. I wanted to be good at everything.

To be clear, I didn't hate the activities that earned me a reputation as a bad boy among my friends. I thoroughly enjoyed the partying. Today, I marvel at how many chances I took and how many people I let drive me around when they were drunk. I am amazed that I came out of it relatively unscathed. Like so many youths, I chose to walk through a minefield just to pick up some candy along the way.

* * *

Throughout the spring of my senior year in high school, the good news kept coming. I was named valedictorian of our class. And then, shortly before graduation, the University of Maine, the only college I applied to, awarded me a half-tuition scholarship that increased to full-tuition for my final three years. As the honors accumulated and time passed, my mother celebrated my achievements. My father grudgingly acknowledged each one, baffled by how I could break his rules and still meet with success.

At my graduation ceremony, I won the coveted Larson Scholarship, sponsored by Lincoln Pulp and Paper, my father's place of employment. This was the largest and most prestigious scholarship awarded at our graduation each year. The university had taken care of my tuition, and this would pay my room and board costs for four years.

As valedictorian, I wrote and delivered a speech during graduation—a harrowing experience for an introvert, but I survived.

After the ceremony I helped my mother get into her wheelchair van for the ride home. I sat in the passenger seat, and Dad drove. She and I chatted about the ceremony. So many folks had congratulated them on raising such a fine young man. Dad said nothing during the ride. So much had happened in just a few hours, but I wondered if anything had changed.

As Dad pulled into the driveway, we all grew silent. He hit the remote control button for the garage door, waited for it to inch open, and pulled the van inside. Still in my graduation gown, I got out and prepared to help my mother disembark. Dad came around the back of the van, walked up to me, and, for the first time since I was a little boy, he pulled me to him and gave me a big hug. He then backed away, his hands on my shoulders. Looking me straight in the eye, he started to say something, but couldn't form the words. After a moment, he nodded his head, patted me on my left shoulder, and walked into the house.

I held the button to lower my mother to ground level, and as she rolled off the lift, she looked up at me, smiled, and said, "Your father is proud of you. We both are. Winning the university scholarship, the Larson Scholarship, valedictorian, giving such a beautiful speech. That was quite something."

Dad never again mentioned the Molly Hatchet incident, and he never told me how proud he was of me. But I knew.

I didn't hate my father. I loved him. I didn't fear my father. I felt safe around him. Yet I couldn't wait to move out of that house. It wasn't only the fallout from the pot-smoking incident or having to put my dog down by myself. It was simply difficult living with him. As far back as I could remember, he had been like this. His rigid ways may have helped mold me into the person I became, but it was time for the molding to end.

On the other hand, nothing about my mother made me want to leave her. I assume she didn't want me to go either. I was the last in the line of children who gave her life so much purpose. She had fulfilled the pledge she made to her friend Audrey from her hospital bed: "I need to get home to take care of my three boys."

All of us were successful. Andy had started his own surveying company. In the fall, Tom would be a senior in the civil engineering program at the University of Maine. Now, Mom was about to send her youngest son off to college with a boatload of scholarships and awards. She must have been so pleased with our accomplishments.

At this stage in our lives, however, we played a zero-sum game. For as much as my world and my brothers' worlds were opening up, hers would be closing down. I was about to leave her alone with Dad. Yet I didn't think about the effect it would have on her. I had become too absorbed in my own life. On this occasion, it was I who broke our silent promise to remain together forever.

One summer evening before leaving for college, I made a new agreement, but this time with Kim, and this time it wasn't unspoken.

"I promise you this," I began. "I'm getting the hell out of this backward little town, and away from this stinking paper mill. I'm going to see the world and do big things. Are you with me?"

"I'm with you, no matter what."

Tom, Andy, Vernice, Mitch 1964.

Mitch circa 1969.

Vernice, Ted 1951.

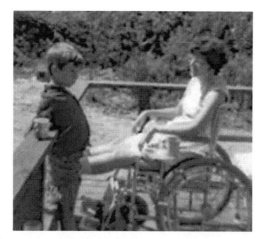

Mitch, Vernice 1970 first picture of us after her accident.

Mitch, Andy, Tom 1971 near Southwest Harbor, Maine.

Mitch, Tarr 1976.

Mitch 1976, first deer.

Kim, Mitch 1980, first formal date.

— PART TWO —

ᗚ

CHAPTER 12
Delightful Romp

In the summer of 1999, Kim and I agreed to coach our daughter Amy's softball team for nine- and ten-year-olds. Kim served as head coach, and I her assistant, because my work responsibilities took precedence. Chemical Engineers at Lincoln Pulp and Paper didn't keep bankers' hours, after all.

At one practice session, after an hour of dropping fly balls, throwing in the wrong direction, and swinging and missing, I felt we needed a change of pace. I ended the day by timing each girl as she ran around the bases. After the last one had finished, the team begged Kim and me to take a turn. We ignored the girls' pleas and tried to release them to their waiting parents, but they persisted. Kim, a high school track champion, ran the bases faster than anyone and solidified her status as the coolest mom in town.

I planned to ratchet up the fun. Maybe I would run the last leg backward or cruise around the bases twice. I raced to first base and then second like the next coming of Willie Mays. Somewhere between second and third base, however, the effort required to pick my legs up and put them down became overwhelming—not an unfamiliar sensation. I had felt like this before, but only after much longer sprints. When I realized I wouldn't be able to finish at full speed, and that I might be slower than Kim, or even some of the faster girls, I pretended to trip over third base. Hamming it up for the crowd, I landed flat on my back in the grass and howled with laughter.

While I lay there, gazing up at the puffy clouds on that warm summer afternoon, Kim and the girls ran to my rescue and laughed with me. They helped me up, dusted me off, and we walked away from practice in high spirits.

* * *

Nobody was more surprised than Kim and me that we ended up back in Lincoln in our mid-twenties.

After my freshman year at the University of Maine, Kim joined me there. We both enjoyed academic success, made lasting relationships, and had lots of fun. I became president of my fraternity, where I lived for three and a half years. Kim lived there for about two and a half years if you count the number of nights she stayed over as my guest.

Upon graduating, I took a job in Cleveland, Ohio, at a high-tech firm. My primary goal was to get away from Maine and away from the paper industry. After two months on my new job, I flew back to Lincoln, and Kim and I married in my parents' backyard. Kim's mother and my mother sat at the kitchen table and cried the next day when we left for Ohio.

Kim finished her college credits at Cleveland State University, earning a degree in Early Childhood Development. Over a two-year period in Ohio, we made lifelong friends and went on mad adventures. But we felt the itch to return to New England, and, in 1988, I took a project engineering job at a paper mill near Burlington, Vermont. I realized that to live where I wanted to live and make the money I wanted to make, I had few employment options outside of the paper industry.

Just when I thought I was out . . . they pulled me back in.

My parents never visited us in Ohio or Vermont—Dad didn't like to travel—but we made two or three trips home each year. Kim's parents drove to both locations, multiple times if I remember correctly.

After living in Vermont for less than a year, Lincoln Pulp and Paper invited me to move home and become the first Larson Scholarship winner to work there full-time. My college classmates and I had considered the Lincoln mill to be the last place any self-respecting chemical engineer would ply his trade. It was a dump. But I learned they had formed a new management team and were hiring talented people, including my good friend Marco. We had graduated together from the University of Maine, and he was such a brilliant engineer he could have worked at any mill in the country.

Kim was eight months pregnant with Amy at the time, and the idea of raising our children near their grandparents appealed to us. We made the move in June of 1989 when Amy was 11 days old. Within a couple of months, we purchased our first home, and domestic bliss ensued.

Kim took a job as a teacher in the Lee school District, one town over from Lincoln. As a first-year teacher in northern Maine, she made less than half of what I did. I couldn't reconcile this, given that she had gone to college as long as I had and did more meaningful work than mine.

Three years later, in 1992, Kim gave birth to Zachary, and I took the necessary step to ensure our family didn't get any larger. I was uncomfortable for the entire weekend. Kim was unsympathetic.

We remained content in our starter home until 1994 when we looked at and fell in love with Old Doc Gulesian's house. To this day I remember house number two as my favorite.

For the decade of the '90s, we had it good. When I wasn't working, I golfed, snowmobiled, hunted, camped, lounged by our swimming pool, and partied almost every weekend. Kim did all those things with me, except the hunting.

Our three households—Kim's parents, my parents, and us— formed a comfortable, loving, mutually beneficial arrangement. Kim and I enjoyed active social lives, so we often left the kids with one or the other sets of parents. Holiday meals were shared, often with both sets of parents visiting our house. When anyone needed help, someone was always there. My mother and Kim's mother became best of friends.

The dire predictions about my mother's life expectancy turned out to be false. Due to medical advances, quadriplegics began to routinely live for decades. An operation that rerouted my mother's urinary tract saved her other kidney. Mom's health remained stable for many years.

* * *

A couple of weeks after my failed attempt to run the bases, our softball team found ourselves in the postseason tournament against the

first-place, undefeated team. They had the best athletes and a no-nonsense coach (Kim and I believed a certain amount of nonsense was
necessary for morale). To everyone's surprise, we went to the top of the
last inning trailing by only one run. We loaded the bases with nobody
out. All our girls on the bench stood and screamed in support. Their
parents, after a season spent cringing at their daughters' mistakes and
consoling them after their losses, rose from their cold, hard bleacher
seats and dared to hope something special would happen.

Something special did happen.

Our batter struck the ball sharply at the third base person, who
caught it in the air for the first out. Instead of staying at their bases,
all three runners reacted to the loud ting of the aluminum bat and ran.
Kim and I yelled and pointed and swung our arms wildly, imploring
the girls to turn around. But it was too late. The third base person
threw to second for a double play, and the second base person threw
on to first for an inning-ending, game-ending, season-ending, Little-
League-softball-coaching-career-ending, triple play. Special indeed.

I soon forgot any disappointment from this freakish loss. Instead,
I reflected on my coaching experience with only profound satisfaction.
We instilled in the children an appreciation for good sportsmanship,
and we inspired them to work hard and have fun with sports, and
that was enough.

As for my inability to run the bases, I couldn't have imagined I
would remember that day for anything other than the delightful romp
it appeared to be, if I remembered it at all. I didn't blame it on old age.
I was only 35, arguably in the prime of my life. I chalked it up to too
much beer on weekends and too many donuts at the office.

Even if I had done the math and realized that my mother was
35 at the time of her accident, I wouldn't have entertained any sort
of mysterious connection. As a man of reason, when I looked for
explanations I used a logical, scientific approach. Only weaker minds,
I believed, would have ascribed causation where there was only
correlation.

CHAPTER 13
A Charmed Life

In February of 2000, the winter after the softball triple play, I began an exercise program. Several times a week, I made my way down to our cavernous finished basement, which had been the medical office for Old Doc Gulesian before he retired and sold the house to us, the very same medical office I visited many times during my childhood.

One morning, as I jogged on the treadmill, my left foot began to make an audible *slap slap* sound when it landed. I concentrated and forced the foot to go quietly from heel to toe, heel to toe, like my right foot did. It worked, but only for a few minutes. Then my left foot resumed its *slap slap* cadence. Again I made a concerted effort. Again my left foot came into compliance, and I finished the workout. This routine went on for weeks, although it concerned me little.

In April, I moved my exercise program outdoors, foot slap and all. A few days later, my uneven jogging gait caused shin splints, a common runner's ailment. Because this problem had impacted my ability to exercise, I decided to have it looked at. I hadn't been in for a routine checkup in a long while anyway. Maybe I had a pinched nerve or muscle strain. I might need a few sessions of physical therapy.

While I waited for the appointment date, my co-worker and good friend, Tim, told me that a young salesman who called on us at the paper mill had been diagnosed with multiple sclerosis. "He has only a slight hitch in his walking gait now, but it will get worse," Tim said. "They gave him a desk job to make things easier."

I made a mental note—*ask doctor if I have multiple sclerosis.*

The news about the young salesman troubled me, but not because I found MS to be scary. He was such a brash, hardworking guy with unlimited energy, who visited every corner of our plant to help us diagnose and solve problems (and to make a sale). I knew he would be miserable with his new assignment. A desk job—what a horrible fate.

After describing my lone symptom to Dr. Anderson, I asked, "Is multiple sclerosis a possibility?"

"This will be a process of elimination, and I expect we can eliminate MS first if you are worried about it," he said.

"Not worried. Just wondering."

"Let's get you scheduled for a brain MRI. That will tell us if MS is in the picture."

"MRI?"

"It's like a CAT scan, but it gives us better diagnostic imaging for neurologic disorders."

Lincoln had no MRI machine. Dr. Anderson explained that the mobile MRI people would call me to set up an appointment. "It might take a while to get you in."

"No hurry," I said.

I wasn't concerned; things always had a way of working out for me—a charmed life and all.

CHAPTER 14
Stations in Life

Around the time of the mysterious foot slapping phenomenon, and after having lived in Lincoln for most of our lives, Kim and I discussed the possibility of relocating to the more populous coastal region of southern Maine. My career had progressed too slowly at the paper mill. Although I demonstrated ability and ambition, several older, entrenched managers blocked my upward mobility. I had fallen behind my peers—my college classmates and other thirty-something engineers I knew. They were rising to senior management positions all around the country.

If we made this move, I wouldn't only leave Lincoln. I would also leave the paper industry—a field I should never have entered in the first place. The life of a production manager in a paper mill, even at its best, is demanding. I made myself available 24 hours a day, 365 days a year. I missed vacations, weddings, anniversaries, and house closings. The mill's operating schedule determined what time we opened our Christmas presents. Even when I was not at the mill, my phone rang, or my beeper beeped, day and night. The mill compensated us handsomely for our troubles, and we accepted these positions of our own free will, but eventually I recognized this as a career for a different sort of person. Many of my friends have flourished in this environment. Me? I wanted a different career, a different life.

Throughout this process, we remained oblivious to one of the most important reasons for me to consider a career change. Managers in paper mills walk miles every day, climb countless flights of stairs, and need the stamina to work absurdly long hours. We didn't know a thief had taken up residence in my central nervous system and would soon steal all these abilities from me.

Kim and I had issues outside the mill, too. Although we enjoyed an occasional card game with Dean and Amy, or sitting by the fire with Preston and Nancy or Marco and Jean, we had grown bored with our routines. We needed to shake things up.

After a particularly frustrating day at the mill, I asked Kim if she was ready to put our relocation plan into action. Always the adventurer, she responded with enthusiasm.

The 1999-2000 school year had been Kim's first as a school counselor (what we used to call a guidance counselor) instead of a teacher, and she loved her new profession. Within a few weeks, she lined up seven interviews for school counselor positions in southern Maine, her first one being with the Cape Elizabeth School District. We knew Cape Elizabeth only as one of the suburbs of Portland, Maine's largest city. Nothing special. The interview went well, and soon after Kim made the three-hour drive home, the principal at Cape Elizabeth Middle School called with a job offer and a generous fifty percent increase in salary.

"They need an answer by Tuesday," Kim said after hanging up. Exuberant, we celebrated over a few cold beers. The next day we told my brother Tom and sister-in-law Diane our secret. Diane taught in southern Maine and could give us some insights.

"Cape is not just another suburb," she explained. "It's the most affluent community in Maine. When you get a job offer from the Cape school system, you take it."

Kim had hit the career jackpot, first try. She wanted to accept the offer, but we had to consider my situation, too. Our three previous moves, from Maine to Cleveland, from Cleveland to Vermont, and from Vermont back to Maine, revolved around my jobs. Chemical engineering positions were hard to find, whereas education jobs were plentiful. My earning potential remained higher than Kim's, although less so when we considered the money she would make at Cape Elizabeth.

It came down to how much confidence I had that I could find suitable employment in southern Maine. "Let's go," I said. "You take the job in Cape Elizabeth. I'll find something. Portland is a big city with tons of good companies."

She clapped her hands together, broke into a smile, and screamed, "I can't believe we're doing this!"

"We're doing it. No turning back now," I assured her.

The next day Kim accepted the school counselor position in Cape Elizabeth for the fall of 2000. By mid-May she notified her school district that she would not return in the fall. In early June, afraid the mill would hear about Kim's resignation, I told the mill manager I had begun looking for employment in southern Maine. I asked him to keep me on while I conducted my job search. He agreed. It took me a while to find a job in southern Maine, so I helped them hire my replacement, and I stuck around for a while to train him.

Kim and I dreaded telling our parents. We were about to take a wrecking ball to the little utopia we had cultivated with them in Lincoln.

When we told Kim's recently retired parents of our decision, they appeared to take it well, but we suspected they were distraught on the inside. They weren't. Carole and Clair seemed unruffled because they had no intention of staying behind. As soon as we gave them the news, they began devising their own relocation plan which unfolded over the ensuing months.

My parents were different. They would never leave Lincoln. Kim and I sat down in the living room with them, in the usual arrangement. My father commanded the chamber from his corner recliner, a TV tray to his right piled high with paperback books, and the lamp stand to his left, on which rested the ceramic ashtray, a lamp resembling an oak tree, and the television clicker. I positioned myself on the sofa at the other side of the lampstand. My mother parked her wheelchair to the right of my father's TV tray, and Kim sat to my left on the couch.

"Well, we've made a big decision," I began. I worried that my voice would tremble, but it didn't.

"Is that so?" My father placed his cigarette in the ashtray and turned to give me his full attention.

"As you know, I've held the same job title at the mill for a couple of years now."

"Yeah."

"And I don't see any opportunities for advancement in the next few years."

"I agree. None of those other peckerheads are going anywhere."

Having worked most of his adult life at the mill, Dad knew all the personalities and the politics.

"So my career is going to suffer if I stay," I continued.

It had pleased my father when we moved back to Lincoln eleven years earlier, but he had a practical mind. In fact, he had warned me the paper mill might not satisfy my long-term ambitions.

"As you know, there aren't many engineering jobs in this part of the state, so, reluctantly, we've been looking in the Portland area. In fact, Kim has already found a job for next fall in Cape Elizabeth."

Dad picked up his cigarette, took a draw, and spoke while exhaling.

"When I got fed up with the bullshit at the mill, I had no alternatives. I didn't have a degree. But your education gives you options, so I understand if you need to move on."

Dad wanted all his children to exceed his station in life. I think he knew it would come with consequences.

My mother cared little about stations in life. Her family was her profession, her reason for living. But she could conceal her emotions with the best of them, and she was on her game that day. I suspect she was dying on the inside while Dad went along with our plans to rip her youngest son, her beloved daughter-in-law, and two of her grandchildren away.

"So, you're moving to Cape Elizabeth?" she asked.

"Yes, somewhere in that area. I told the mill manager today, and he agreed to keep me on while I look for a job."

"We're certainly going to miss you. Have you told the kids?" Mom asked.

"Soon. Wish us luck."

Mom forced a smile and drilled us with questions. "When

will you leave? Will you sell your house? What about your pets? Your furniture? Will you take your lawnmower or buy a new one?" Surprisingly, she didn't ask if we expected many trick-or-treaters in Cape Elizabeth.

When I had gone off to college 20 years earlier, I left my mother, breaking our silent promise. I was doing the same thing again. In Sturgeon households, however, discussions like this brought no tears, no pleading, no outpouring of emotion. Those frailties were for weaker families, or so we thought.

If the conversations with our parents required the most compassionate approach, the impending conversation with our nine- and twelve-year-old children would require the most strategic. When I was their age, monsters, earthquakes, and bullies didn't scare me nearly as much as the fear that one day my parents would tell me we were moving, and I would be the new kid at some other school. For this reason, I felt especially guilty for what we were about to do to Amy and Zach. But Kim and I had a plan.

Before telling the kids about the move, we scheduled a three-day vacation for the family in the Portland area. We took them to an amusement park, a skateboard park, the ocean, and the largest shopping mall in the state. We refrained from scolding them, making them brush their teeth, or in any way tainting their memory of this glorious vacation.

"I wish we lived down here," Amy said at one point. Sweet music!

Our kids had a typical sibling relationship. Zach drove Amy crazy with his immaturity and lack of understanding of how the world worked. Amy used her superior intellect and strength to always remind Zach of his place in the family pecking order.

Because of Amy's somewhat volatile personality, we didn't dare tell her about the relocation while we were at home. She might run off to any of several hiding places before we finished. So, a few days after we returned from Portland, the four of us piled into the car to get an ice cream cone. Instead, I drove down a dirt road near our house. The kids, enmeshed in their video games, didn't notice the bumpy ride at first.

"Dad, why are we going down this road?" Amy asked after a few minutes.

"We have something to tell you," I said, parking the car.

Kim and I turned to face the kids. I began, "Didn't we have a great time in southern Maine? Remember, Amy, how you said you wished we lived down there? Well—good news. We're moving to the Portland area."

Amy's eyes darted from mine to her mother's, for confirmation. I sometimes said things that weren't true, just to get a reaction out of people. Amy saw no backpedaling in Kim, and as she switched her gaze back to me, her eyes began watering.

"No, you can't do this. It's not fair."

"You said you loved our time in southern Maine, Amy."

"Just for a visit," she screamed, and the tears flowed.

I don't know what came over me. We didn't negotiate with our kids on matters like this, but I blurted out, "What will it take to make you agree to this move?"

She didn't hesitate—her lifelong dream. "TV in my room."

"Done."

Well played, Amy Sturgeon. Well played.

CHAPTER 15

A Good 20 Years

A few days after my MRI scan, I called Dr. Anderson's office. "The radiologist's report indicates that you have a lesion or lesions on your brain consistent with multiple sclerosis," Dr. Anderson said. "You need to see a neurologist to obtain a firm diagnosis, and we can set up that appointment for you." He spoke as dispassionately as if he were placing a telephone order for replacement vacuum cleaner bags. I'm not finding fault. I don't know what the appropriate tone is for delivering such news.

This was another seminal moment in my life, like the day I couldn't race around the softball field. However, this moment didn't require the passage of time to give it perspective. This was a slap upside the head from the class bully as he stood over me and asked, "What are you gonna do now?"

Even though I had considered the possibility of an MS diagnosis, the doctor's words stunned me. My body engaged its fight or flight mode, but I couldn't see an enemy to defend against, and I had nowhere to run.

An awkward silence ensued. My entire body of knowledge about the disease still consisted of the brief conversation I had with my co-worker about the young salesman with MS. After a while my brain re-engaged, and I settled on what seemed like the best question. "If I do have MS, what would that mean for me?"

"Well, I can't say. You'll need to talk to a neurologist about that."

He was hedging, and I knew it. Just like an X-ray technician won't tell you if you have a broken bone, a family doctor won't discuss your neurologic disease, even though each of them understands more than they let on.

I rephrased the question in a way he might feel comfortable

answering. "I meant to ask what the typical prognosis is for a person newly diagnosed with MS?"

I heard him rustle some papers and clear his throat. After a few seconds he responded, "Let's see. How old are you?"

"Thirty-eight."

"You probably have a good twenty years left."

What the fuck?

I only had twenty years left to live? I would never make it to retirement age, grow old with my wife, or watch my future grandchildren get married? What about restricting me to a desk job, like they did with the young salesman I knew?

The room started to tilt. I became lightheaded and nauseous. I had been given a death sentence, albeit a deferred one.

Dr. Anderson told me I would hear from a neurologist in Bangor soon to schedule an appointment. I'm not sure I said goodbye when I hung up the phone.

I had placed this call from Kim's grandmother's house in Lyman, Maine, where Kim had established her home away from home since the beginning of the school year. During the week, she slept at Grammy Ida's house and commuted 45 minutes each way to her new job in Cape Elizabeth. On the weekends, she drove back to Lincoln to be with the kids and me. The three of us had stayed behind until I could find employment in southern Maine. I happened to be visiting Kim at Ida's house because I had a job interview in South Portland later that afternoon.

After I hung up the phone, I jumped into my truck and drove to Cape Elizabeth Middle School. When I walked into her office, Kim was on the telephone. She looked up at me, saw my pained expression, and ended her call.

"What is it? What's wrong?" She motioned for me to sit down and then closed the door.

"Dr. Anderson got my MRI results, and I probably have MS," I managed to say despite losing control of my voice at the end of the sentence.

"MS? What does that . . . I don't even . . . " Kim stammered, having no context for what these two otherwise innocuous letters, these initials of mine, might portend for our future. We didn't know anyone with multiple sclerosis.

"It means I only have twenty years to live."

I broke down and cried for the first time since burying my dog, Tarr, 20 years earlier. Kim put her arms around me, and we hugged in silence. After a moment she gently pulled away and took control of the situation. "I need to tell my principal that I'll be unavailable. Are you okay for a minute or two?"

I nodded. When she returned, Kim suggested we go to Fort Williams, a mile away. In the short time she had lived in southern Maine, this park had become our favorite spot by the ocean. Always thinking clearly, even under pressure, Kim printed out several pages of general information about MS from the Internet.

When we arrived at the park, we sat on one of the granite benches and skimmed over the materials Kim had brought along. We soon recognized the absurdity of Dr. Anderson's statement regarding a 20-year life expectancy. MS didn't kill you, except in rare instances, and researchers had developed a growing number of treatment options. Many patients led long, fulfilling lives after diagnosis. This news reassured us, but I became angry with the doctor for having put me through the worst two hours of my life.

As our mood improved at Fort Williams, we gazed out over the seascape from our cliff-top perch. It was a perfect September day on the southern Maine coast. I watched one ocean wave after another march dutifully toward the shore and impale itself on the jagged rocks below me. The collisions heaved sheets of water in the air where they crystallized into droplets and rained down on anyone who dared wander too close. I shut my eyes, turned my face upward to the noontime sun, and let the soothing ocean breezes embrace me. I took several slow, deep breaths—in through my nose and out through my mouth. Bad news earlier in the day had initiated a fight or flight response from the primitive part of my brain. Now the beauty of nature and calming effect of my meditations brought comfort to that same element. The initial storm had passed, and we had weathered its fury.

It wasn't until fourteen years later, when I sat down to write this book, that I considered the possibility I had misunderstood Dr. Anderson. I thought I heard, "You probably have a *good twenty years* left." Today, I'm almost certain he said, "You probably have *twenty good years* left." This would imply twenty years of decent health and mobility before MS would kick my ass, a conclusion I could imagine him drawing from certain long-range MS studies. Although that's not a statement he should have made to a potential MS patient—those statistics are dubious at best—I dragged it out of him against his will, so I accept responsibility.

* * *

Later that September I visited a neurologist in Bangor, fully expecting him to confirm the MS diagnosis. Instead, after reading the MRI film, he became incredulous. "Who said you might have MS? They shouldn't have done that. I doubt these minor symptoms indicate something as serious as MS. And I must say, you could find a tiny brain lesion like this on nearly anyone's MRI."

He ordered a battery of tests, some quite uncomfortable, all inconclusive. We decided to wait and see if anything further developed. I didn't know what to think. Only days earlier at Fort Williams, I had battled these MS fears, these demons, and survived the encounter. Now I was being told the demons never existed, although they seemed real to me. I had mixed feelings, but each day after that, I thought less and less about MS.

In late October we decided to complete our relocation to southern Maine, job or no job for me. Life in this transitional state had worn on us all, especially the children. We decided to join Kim at Grammy Ida's house. Zach and Amy would attend school in Cape Elizabeth with their mother. I would commute to Lincoln a couple of days a week to pick up some consulting work at the mill while I continued to look for employment in southern Maine.

Below is an excerpt from my Friday, October 20 email, written after I dropped the kids off for their last day of school in Lincoln. On Saturday, they would move to southern Maine. Since Kim had started her new job, I sent her regular updates during the week. I knew she struggled to be away from us, and I hoped these little notes might lessen the separation anxiety.

> Friday, October 20, 2000 8:15:10 AM
> Kim,
>
> Here are the morning news updates:

ZACH STURGEON TO SPEND HIS LAST NIGHT AT FRIEND'S HOUSE

In an unexpected move, the mother of one of Zach's best friends, John, contacted Zach's dad about spending his last night in Lincoln at John's house. Zach is thrilled. When asked about the impending move, Zach repeated an oft-used phrase during this campaign, "I just can't wait to meet all those new friends."

IN RELATED NEWS, AMY STURGEON TO HAVE SOME GIRL NAMED MELISSA SPEND THE NIGHT TONIGHT

As a counter move to the above story, young Amy Sturgeon coerced her helpless dad into letting her have a friend over tonight. After all, it was only fair, she said.

And then this . . .

PIXIE TO GO SOUTH—CHILDREN REJOICE

Sources close to the Sturgeons indicate that Mr. Sturgeon told his children this morning that the much-loved family feline "Pixie" will indeed be making the trip south this weekend. The news was greeted by the children with much hubbub.

And finally . . .

STURGEON HAVING DIFFICULTY GETTING HIS
WORK DONE

Is the world renowned former Assistant
Superintendent finally washed up? Some people think so.
"He can't even get 40 hours per week in!" said some guy
that looks in Sturgeon's windows all day and writes down
everything he does.

"If Sturgeon tries to charge the company for
40 hours, I'll tell them the truth, and he will finally suffer
the public humiliation that he deserves."

When interviewed, Sturgeon replied, "If that guy
continues to watch me next week he'll see a whole different
person. Hell, I may work 41 hours!"

Love ya,
Mitch

A few days after Thanksgiving, I landed a job at an engineering and
consulting firm just outside of Portland. Finally, we could get on with
our new lives. Soon afterward, Kim's recently retired parents, Carole
and Clair, proceeded with their escape and moved into the same house
with us, Carole's childhood home. They planned to stay with Ida and
take care of her in her waning years (which they did).

On Christmas Eve of that year, we packed up the car and drove
to my parents' house in Lincoln. As we exchanged gifts the next
morning, Kim helped my mother open the present she had bought
her. Mom seemed delighted when she saw the sweater, but you never
knew with my mother. She could fake it with the best of them. My
father couldn't.

From across the room he growled, "She doesn't like pink. She
won't want that."

Taken aback, Kim said, "Well, okay . . . I can return it."

Mom whispered, "Don't worry, dear. It's not your fault."

After we had opened all the gifts, Mom asked Kim to help her
with something in the bedroom. When out of earshot from my father,
Mom said, "I just wanted you to know that Ted is the one who doesn't

like me in pink. I wore that color the night I got hurt."

"I'm so sorry," said Kim.

"You couldn't have known. Would you mind exchanging it for another color?"

None of us ever had a more personal conversation with my mother about the night she got hurt.

After Christmas dinner, we drove back to the chaotic living situation in southern Maine. During this six-week period in December and January of 2000-2001, seven people, three cats, and two dogs lived in this three-bedroom, one-bath house. Perhaps that is why we rushed and bought house number three, which was unsuitable for someone who might have MS. Then again, the only neurologist I had visited scoffed at the idea that the lesion on my brain was in any way concerning, let alone life-changing.

Our new place had a multi-level, contemporary layout with short staircases everywhere we turned. The little hitch in my step hadn't affected my stair climbing. The house was located in Scarborough, a slightly less affluent suburb than Cape Elizabeth. The kids had adapted so well to attending school in Cape that we decided they could continue there indefinitely and ride each day with Kim. They loved the idea, and we all loved the house. *Finally, a home we'll never leave.*

Shortly after I had put in my notice the previous summer, Lincoln Pulp and Paper filed for Chapter 11 bankruptcy. This meant that they could keep operating, but were under the supervision of a bankruptcy judge. A few years later they filed for Chapter 7 bankruptcy and shut down for the first time since before my mother's accident.

In 2004 a buyer came along and restarted the mill. They operated it, mostly in the red I think, until November of 2013 when a major explosion occurred in the recovery boiler, the part of the mill where my father had spent most of his career and that I had managed for my last few years at Lincoln Pulp and Paper. Thankfully, nobody was hurt. After the explosion, with half of the mill down, they held on for a couple more years until they could hold on no longer. In the fall of 2015, the mill went back into Chapter 7 bankruptcy. Again, a buyer came along, but not a paper company. This time, the mill was bought by a salvage company.

Lincoln's paper mill had employed thousands of people, including my grandfather, my father, and me. A bustling little town had sprung up around it. Today, the mill sits there, gathering rust, a reminder of what used to be. I hope the salvage company does its job thoroughly and takes everything away so that the town can one day emerge from the shadow of the mill.

CHAPTER 16

The Jordan Pond Incident

One must negotiate a gauntlet of institutional nonsense before being granted an audience with a medical specialist, face-to-face, in his or her inner sanctum:

1. Meet with primary care physician to exhaust their expertise and obtain a referral.

2. Receive a call from the specialist's office to schedule an appointment six to eight months out.

3. On the appointment day, if still alive, drive to the doctor's office, exit vehicle, present credentials to the check-in desk.

4. Fill out reams of paperwork, which the doctor never reads, then find the perfect seat in the waiting room which maximizes average distance to all other patients in the waiting room.

5. Pick up a magazine and surreptitiously scan the waiting room to assess the population you now belong to, without making eye contact and certainly without speaking. Try to guess each patient's ailment.

6. When the door to the inner sanctum opens and a medical assistant calls out your name, drop what you are doing (these are very busy people), hustle to the door, apologize for being slow, and follow the assistant to the treatment room they indicate.

7. In the treatment room, there will be fewer and more out-of-date magazines. Pick one up nonetheless and browse through it while analyzing the posters on the wall and the implements of torture lying around the room. Try to guess which one hurts the most. Remember, you are almost certainly being watched and evaluated through secret cameras.

When steps 1 through 7 have been dutifully completed, and sufficient time has expired, and then excessive time has expired, the object of your desire, the medical specialist, will knock on the door and enter the treatment room. It always works this way, without exception, except when it doesn't.

Shortly after moving into our Scarborough home, I had the good fortune to meet Dr. Sara Freedman, who to this day remains my compassionate and able family physician. After I explained my situation to her, she said, "I doubt this is something as serious as MS." In her defense, almost every other doctor I met felt the same way. She referred me to a back specialist, who found nothing to explain my left foot problem, and then to the office of Dr. Paul Muscat, neurologist.

On a spring day in 2001, I sat in the waiting room (step 5) at this large neurological practice. Magazine in hand, empty chair on either side of me in the waiting room, I watched as patient after patient had their names called by medical assistants, and disappeared behind the door (step 6). A gentleman about my age, slender and bald, opened the door and called out my name. As I approached, he said, "I'm Dr. Muscat. It's a pleasure to meet you."

A physician showing himself in the waiting room? How odd.

Dr. Muscat directed me down a long hallway toward the last examining room on the left. He confessed later that he liked to retrieve patients himself, mostly to study their walking. In this way, the exam started before patients even realized it.

"Mr. Sturgeon, what brings you to a neurologist today?"

I started with the left foot slap story, skipped the embarrassing part about the 20-year life expectancy fiasco, and continued all the way up to the recent back specialist.

Dr. Muscat asked to see the MRI films I had brought and, after studying them for a few minutes, said, "I tend to agree with the other neurologist. It seems unlikely that you are experiencing something as serious as MS. I know he ran you through a gauntlet of tests, but I need to get my own data. I hope you don't mind."

Oh, I minded. However, I respected his desire for reliable information.

"No problem," I said.

Dr. Muscat asked me questions, not only about my health issues but all aspects of my life. I suppose, when you're dealing with diseases of the nervous system, it's best to start with the view from 30,000 feet and work your way down. As an engineer, I spent much of my time methodically troubleshooting technical problems. Dr. Muscat dealt with medical problems in much the same way. Most importantly, he treated me like an equal. It has remained this way for all the years I've worked with him. By mutual agreement, I am the manager of my healthcare; he is my expert consultant.

After a battery of tests, Dr. Muscat found nothing conclusive. Like the northern Maine neurologist, he prescribed more wait-and-see. My symptoms continued to progress slowly throughout the summer of 2001. The foot slap became more constant and pronounced—almost a visible limp. I also began to experience general muscle fatigue in both legs, which I noticed during activities such as mowing the lawn. Still, the changes were subtle and not frightening. Based on the collective wisdom of everybody, except for Dr. Anderson in Lincoln, this was nothing serious.

* * *

Acadia National Park holds a special place in Kim and my hearts. As a youngster, I traveled there with my parents when we visited my name-sake, Gardner Mitchell, in Southwest Harbor each summer. In high school, I accompanied Kim and her parents on camping trips near the park. Much of our early romance played out on those weathered rocks and sandy beaches. One weekend in particular, which should be remembered with only tenderness and affection, is steeped in contro-versy to this day.

We both agree that on this camping trip Kim became the first one to say, "I love you." We disagree about what happened next.

I remember replying with my own, "I love you, too," but Kim

insists that I responded with the much less romantic, "Me too." I wish there were an afterlife, where we could rewind the videotape-in-the-sky to that moment. I would gloat when proven correct, if gloating is allowed in the afterlife.

Over the Fourth of July holiday in 2001, a few months after my initial visit with Dr. Muscat, we went on a camping trip near Acadia with Kim's parents, her two brothers and their wives, and our combined six children. One morning someone came up with the idea to take the whole gang for a hike in the park. Since our group would have some youngsters in it, we chose an easy, three-mile loop around Jordan Pond.

We arrived in three separate vehicles, found the parking lot, and piled out on to the trailhead. Away from the coast, residents struggled with the hottest weather of the year, but Acadia's temperatures remained comfortable because of its proximity to the chilly Atlantic Ocean. As I stood at the edge of Jordan Pond, I could see the reflection of the North and South Bubble Mountains at the far end of the water. The sky resembled one big blue dome, interrupted only by the mid-summer sun. Ridges of evergreen and exposed rock stood guard to the left and the right. We had slipped inside a snow globe—isolated from the rest of the world.

At first I found the trail flat and hard, then the footing became uneven. When it did, that damn left leg, the one that went *slap slap* on the treadmill, refused to step over even modest obstacles. By the time we hit the halfway mark, I could no longer hide my walking difficulties. I didn't want to draw attention to myself, so I feigned a sprained ankle. I stole a moment of privacy to explain the situation to Kim, and she helped me fashion a rudimentary walking stick. As I limped around Jordan Pond, my wife and I exchanged knowing glances. Both of us recognized the significance of this new development. The game had changed. The snow globe had been shaken, if not turned completely upside down.

At my next appointment with Dr. Muscat, we discussed the Jordan Pond incident, and he got an idea. The most common form of

MS, called relapsing remitting multiple sclerosis (RRMS), produces lesions primarily in the brain. However, about 10% of patients suffer from a form of the disease called primary progressive multiple sclerosis (PPMS), where the trouble often starts in the spinal cord. And in those cases, MS leaves patients more severely disabled.

This time Dr. Muscat ordered an MRI of my spinal cord in addition to my brain. A few days later we met.

"I have your MRI films," he said. "I haven't looked at them yet. Shall we?"

"The moment of truth," I responded.

"I don't expect we'll find anything, but we have to follow a process of elimination."

We walked from the examining room into a common area of the practice. He lifted the oversized translucent prints from the manila envelope, one at a time, and placed them on the backlit viewing panel. "Nothing interesting here," Dr. Muscat muttered under his breath while examining the first few films. "Nope, nothing here."

Then his demeanor shifted. He pulled his glasses to the end of his nose, leaned in and squinted. I peeked over his shoulder, oblivious to what I was looking at. Discerning the stuff that is supposed to be on an MRI from the stuff that isn't is a skill akin to reading a blurry ultrasound of an unborn child to determine the baby's gender.

Without a word, he snatched the offending film from the light board and hustled it across the corridor to one of his associates. I exhaled and held my breath to keep things in focus—a skill my father taught me when shooting a rifle for the first time. The two neurologists studied the film, each of them pointing to the same area of the MRI. They looked at one another and nodded, reaching agreement on my fate.

Remember to breathe.

Dr. Muscat returned and put the MRI back up on the light board. He laid his finger beside what appeared as an innocent blurry spot on my spinal cord, in the middle of my neck. "This looks like MS."

Breathe.

CHAPTER 17
Answers

After discovering lesions on my cervical spine, Dr. Muscat invited me into his office to continue the conversation. I maintained my composure, unlike a year earlier when Dr. Anderson first mentioned MS. If nothing else, I wanted to show strength in the presence of Dr. Muscat, whom I'd already grown to admire. We were objective troubleshooting partners after all, and there's no crying in troubleshooting.

The walls in his office were adorned with oversized, framed certificates, covered in Latin phrases, from places like Columbia University, Mount Sinai Medical Center, Beth Israel Deaconess Medical Center, and more. *He's well-qualified. Good to know.*

This office was more than a shrine to his accomplishments, however. It was a functional space full of files, reference books, and papers. His desk sat up against the wall so that it never came between him and his patients. After I had made myself comfortable in the guest seat, he settled into his office chair and swiveled to face me. I had his full attention, although he didn't exactly have mine. My brain was going in a hundred different directions.

"If we are talking MS, and I'm almost certain we are," he began, "this is not the end of the world. Many of my MS patients get up every day, go to work, and lead fulfilling lives."

I didn't want the MS 101 talk right then. I knew the basics from my previous flirtation with the disease. Later, I would pick his brain on everything related to MS, but at that moment, I felt a strong desire to get the hell out of there.

"In the last ten years, researchers have made a lot of progress with MS," he continued. "I'm not saying we are close to a cure, but—"

"I'm familiar with MS," I interrupted. "If that's what this is, I can deal with it. What's our next step?"

"Okay. We need to confirm your diagnosis with a lumbar puncture, also known as a spinal tap. After that, we'll discuss treatment options. Let's talk to my scheduler and see when she can get you in."

On my drive home, I called Kim. I knew she was watching Zach play a flag football game. "I guess Dr. Anderson had it right after all. Dr. Muscat is pretty sure I have MS. He found more lesions on this MRI."

"Damn."

"He has to run another test to confirm it. We'll talk more when you get home," I said in a steady voice.

As I drove, I thought, *It's in the neck, just like my mother's injury.* I recalled the time when I first noticed her surgical scars. I was six years old.

"Why do you have marks on the back of your neck, Mom?"

"When I slipped and broke my neck, they had to operate. They couldn't fix it all the way, but they did enough so I can use my wheelchair and do some other things with my hands."

"I'm glad they fixed your neck."

"Me too, Mitchy. Me too."

I pulled into the driveway. As I walked from my truck into our kitchen, I reached around to the back of my neck. I didn't feel any scars on the outside, like my mother had, but the lesions were there, on the inside. My mother broke her neck, and now, in a sense, so had I.

I sat at the dining room table, waiting for Kim to get home. Zach led the way, barreling through the door to tell me all about his football game. I listened as patiently as I could and then asked him to go clean up.

"It's in my neck," I said to Kim as soon as Zach was out of earshot. "The MS lesions are in my cervical spine—the same place as my mother's injury."

"Strange."

We sat in silence for a moment, uncertain where to even begin. Finally, I took a stab at it. "Now that I understand what's happening to my body, I can start the fight."

"I feel the same way. I'm not happy you have MS. Since you do have it, though, it's good to know." She embraced my hands in hers and squeezed. "It's good to know." She broke eye contact and seemed to be somewhere else.

"What are you thinking about?"

"Keeping things in perspective. I've dealt with something today that's worse than MS. You know Amy's friend, Joni? Her dad committed suicide last night. I found out as soon as I got into school."

"Oh, oh my God. That's terrible."

"It sure is. I helped out where I could all day—consoling crying girls in my office, informing Joni's teachers of what happened. I even spoke to Joni's mother. It's been hell. So, when you called with your news, it didn't seem horrible in comparison. You're still sitting here in front of me, and I expect you will be for a long time, right?"

"That's my plan. Things could be much worse. And frankly, I don't think MS has a chance against me—you and me."

"I wouldn't bet against us," Kim said with a smile. I smiled right back.

We were so naïve.

* * *

At the spinal tap appointment a few days later, Dr. Muscat said, "I've consulted with every neurologist in the practice, and they all agree that the MRI indicates MS. This spinal tap is a mere diagnostic formality. Let's make an appointment for about a week out. We'll go over the results and discuss a path forward."

"What if the tests come back negative?" I asked.

"It doesn't matter. We *will* be talking about MS at the next appointment. Now let's get started. I used to be an anesthesiologist, so I'm gentle. You'll hardly feel a thing."

He had me raise my shirt and lean over his examination table. He felt along my lower spine until he identified the perfect location. He marked that spot with a pen. Next, he applied a soapy solution and an antiseptic to sterilize the region. Then he injected a numbing agent just under the skin. It burned a little.

"Now I'll insert the needle. You will feel—"

"Wait!" I realized he might be about to make a huge mistake. "How are you able to stick a needle into my spinal cord without damaging the nerves?"

"I'm surprised more patients don't ask that. Your spinal cord stops before the bottom of your spine. I go into a region where there is nothing but spinal fluid—no nerves."

"Okay. That makes sense."

"May I proceed?"

"Yes, of course."

The jab hurt less than when he marked my skin with the pen. He told me that spinal fluid was flowing nicely, and it wouldn't be much longer. Dr. Muscat's laid-back bedside manner had put me at ease. Other than the fact that I had a needle sticking out of my back, I felt fine.

He pulled out the needle, applied a small Band-Aid, and told me we were done. He informed me of a possible, though unlikely, side effect—a post-lumbar puncture headache, potentially starting that evening or the next day. "It's something that happens if the perforation in the spinal cord doesn't seal completely, and spinal fluid leaks out. If this occurs, it's more comfortable to lie down rather than sit up. If the headache lasts more than a couple days, call me."

I woke up the next morning with a dull headache. I stayed in bed. If I tried to sit up for a few minutes, my head felt like the bass drum in a marching band. This went on for three miserable days before clearing up. The post-lumbar puncture headache experience had been so unpleasant, I swore I would never submit to another spinal tap.

At my next appointment, Dr. Muscat informed me that my spinal fluid tested positive for MS indicators. On October 22, 2001, with Kim at my side, he gave me the official diagnosis. Not only did I have MS, but based on my presentation, clinical exams, MRIs, and test results, I had primary progressive multiple sclerosis.

The bad kind.

CHAPTER 18

Climate Change

Kim and I adopted a simple philosophy regarding MS disclosure: tell everybody who might care, everything they might want to know, and do it sooner rather than later.

For some folks, maintaining privacy in matters like this is paramount. Not so for us. Kim or I can be trusted with a confidence when it's necessary, but if we can unburden ourselves, then so much the better. And we did, beginning with my brother Andy and his wife, Karen.

The four of us went out to dinner at Street and Company in the Old Port section of downtown Portland—a high-end restaurant suitable for special occasions. The last time we made a big announcement to them at a restaurant, it was about Kim's first pregnancy. That went poorly (the announcement, not the pregnancy). When we ordered drinks and Kim requested a diet cola instead of a glass of wine, Andy asked her when the due date was.

"There's something we need to speak with you guys about," I began. "It started in the winter of 2000 when I was jogging on my treadmill."

I laid out the whole story for them—from visiting the doctor in Lincoln, to being told I had 20 years to live, to hiking Jordan Pond, to the official diagnosis just a couple of days earlier.

"What is your prognosis? What does this mean?" Andy wanted to know.

"It's impossible to say. Everyone has a different course of MS. I may have a mild form, or I may have a severe form. Only time will tell. But for the short term, not a lot will change in my life."

"What can we do to help?" This was Andy's standard

problem-solving approach. First, understand the challenges, and then find solutions.

My vague answers frustrated Andy. He leaned back in his chair, and Karen took over the questions.

"How are you and Kim holding up?"

"I think we're doing fine," Kim replied. And we were.

Andy told me later that we surprised them with our disclosure. They hadn't noticed the subtle physical changes I had experienced over the last year. They knew some people with MS but not anyone having a particularly difficult time with it, at least outwardly. My announcement felt like one of those nonspecific threats that wouldn't affect the family until years down the road: "College will be so expensive by the time our kids get there," or, "If we don't do something about climate change, one day our coastal cities will be underwater."

Kim and I agreed on a protocol for the remaining disclosures. Close friends and relatives shouldn't hear about this from more distant friends and relatives. Nobody important to us should find out from a mere acquaintance. As many people as possible should hear it from me so they would learn the truth, or the truth as I knew it, or at least the truth as I chose to portray it.

One of my primary goals this night with Andy and Karen, and at all subsequent disclosures, was to downplay the seriousness of my diagnosis. I hated being the subject of pity. I was not and still am not pitiable. Even if I were to descend into wretchedness, it would do me no good to see that condition reflected on someone else's face. I keep things positive; I like to leave people happier than I found them.

The next conversation would be with our children.

At the dinner table, I began by saying "We have something important to tell you," much like I had the previous night with their Uncle Andy and Aunt Karen. Zach was nine years old and Amy twelve. I placed extra emphasis on the possibility of a mild course of MS. I finished with, "Do either of you have any questions?"

"Can I go outside now?" asked Zachary.

"Well, Amy, do you have any questions?"

"Nope."

In situations like this, children take their cues from the adults, and we had portrayed the seriousness of MS as somewhere between that of a hangnail and a broken leg. What could have been a heart-wrenching disclosure, and arguably should have been, was a non-event in their lives. If our goal was to give them a realistic assessment of what our family might face in the coming years, we failed. I don't remember what our goal was.

I would have a few more conversations about MS in the coming days and weeks, but none more delicate than telling my parents. That weekend I drove north to break the news to them. On the way, I stopped at my brother Tom's house and brought him and Diane up to speed. Although I mentioned to them I had primary progressive MS, they didn't appreciate the difference between that and the relapsing remitting kind. They knew only one person with MS, and that individual showed few symptoms after 20 years. So their initial level of concern was mild. Like Andy and Karen, Tom and Diane thought this might be something I wouldn't have to deal with until years down the road. Over the ensuing weeks, however, Tom researched primary progressive MS and realized what I faced. He became distressed that our family had been dealt another severe health blow. Hadn't we suffered enough?

When I gave my parents the talk, beginning with, "There's something I need to tell you," I expected the worst, but the conversation went remarkably well. Again, I maintained an upbeat and positive attitude as I explained to my quadriplegic mother and my always-assume-the-worst-case father that I had a chronic, disabling, incurable disease, while using none of those adjectives. They asked a few basic questions and seemed unflustered. As I left their house, I felt satisfied with the experience. *What troopers they are*, I thought.

On the drive home, I phoned Andy to let him know how well things had gone with our parents.

"Not really," he said. "They called me as soon as you left, and they were inconsolable."

Their point of reference was a friend up the street who had secondary progressive MS, an advanced form of RRMS with symptoms similar to PPMS. She still walked, but had trouble with fatigue and vision, and felt miserable. At least my parents didn't seem to associate MS with wheelchair use, or it might have been even worse.

That's the Sturgeon way: Always remain stoic when receiving bad news (or good news, or any news at all). I would have to prove to them I was okay, which would take time. No prepared speech would suffice.

The diagnosis marked a turning point in my relationship with my father. It's not that we grew closer. He just started treating me better. He never again took a harsh tone with me or second-guessed my decisions in a condescending manner. I appreciated my father's newfound civility, no matter his motivation. Although he made accommodations for me, he treated everyone else the same as always. Take Kim, for example. From the moment he met her in the summer after her freshman year in high school, he saw her as someone he could playfully bait, and she would fight back. He preferred this type of relationship, so she became his favorite daughter-in-law.

When Kim and I lived in Lincoln as a married couple and visited my parents often, my father might say to Kim on any given summer afternoon, "Mix me a drink."

"Mix your own goddamn drink," she would reply.

"Either you mix me a drink, sweetheart, or Vernice will have to do it."

Kim knew Vernice would mix Ted a drink in a heartbeat, even though it was a complicated procedure for her. Kim might say, "You are such an ass," and then get him his Jack Daniels and water. Having thoroughly enjoyed the interaction, he would grin from ear to ear and jiggle his drink just to make the ice cubes sing.

* * *

MS patients are often advised, "Once you disclose your MS, you can't undo it. So be cautious." I get that. People with MS sometimes face discrimination in the workplace. If you don't have to tell your employer, maybe you shouldn't. But that's not how I operated. I continued with our strategy of liberal disclosure. I couldn't keep it from my employer because a big part of my job involved walking, and it had become apparent that my legs were failing me. The HR manager and my boss were supportive. They thanked me for filling them in and told me to let them know if they could do anything to help.

The process of informing my friends and loved ones about my diagnosis went smoothly, at least as far as I knew. No one asked me a question for which I wasn't prepared. At no point did I become nervous or emotional.

I'm ready, I thought. *Bring it on.*

CHAPTER 19

Treatment

W hen processing bad news, people typically experience sadness or grief. However, from the time Dr. Muscat laid his finger on the MRI and said, "This looks like MS," I felt invigorated.

Given that I had a diagnosis, a name for my tormentor, I could develop and implement a plan. I could fight back, maybe even win.

Another factor came into play. At thirty-eight years old, my life had become mundanely comfortable. As far back as I could remember, I had envisioned myself leading an exceptional life, and it wasn't happening. I feared my greatest achievements were behind me, and I expected only continued descent toward mediocrity. For these reasons, part of me welcomed the opportunity to take on a fresh challenge, despite its unpleasantness. Although I wasn't happy to have MS, I responded with energy and commitment, and when I'm energized and committed, it's a feeling akin to happiness.

Perhaps the most important factors in my resiliency, however, could be traced back to my mother. There seemed little doubt that I inherited her upbeat nature, or learned as much by observing her, or both. And maybe subconscious forces worked some of their magic. Consider this. My mother's disappearance left a gaping wound in my five-year-old psyche. Her return from the hospital nine months later may have stopped the bleeding, but the wound never completely healed. When I learned that I had developed a disease in the same part of my body that my mother had injured, perhaps my subconscious considered the diagnosis as some sort of shared legacy with my beloved mother—neither a curse nor a reward, but a part of her once again living within me, like before her injury. Like old times.

If this is true, because of my diagnosis maybe the silent promise each of us had broken over the years became reestablished in my mind, and this served as another source of strength for me. I'll never know; my subconscious isn't talking.

* * *

At my next appointment Dr. Muscat said, "I like to be upfront with you, and I think you appreciate that." He paused for confirmation.

"I would have it no other way."

"I expect you will experience a more severe course of MS than most people. No single issue accounts for this. It's a combination of several factors."

Bring it on. I'm ready, I said to myself.

"First, you are a man. Statistically, men have a worse time with MS."

I already read that somewhere. Next.

"Second, at thirty-eight you are older than average at diagnosis. This correlates with a poor prognosis."

Okay, but that doesn't scare me. Next.

"Third, you presented with leg weakness and walking difficulty as opposed to sensory problems. People who start out that way tend to accumulate disability more quickly."

Big deal. What else?

"And fourth, your lesions are primarily in your cervical spine instead of in your brain."

Yup, cervical spine is screwed up, just like my mother's.

He paused. My turn. "I understand the first three. However, I would think that lesions in the brain would be worse than lesions in the spine. The brain is a more complex organ."

"True, but consider the cross-sectional area of the brain. It's about this big." He positioned his hands as if holding a human head between them. "Now think about the cross-sectional area of the spine." He held up his thumb as an example. "Assuming the same lesion load, you can see how the spinal cord can be affected to a greater degree than the brain."

"I get it," I said. "Thanks for being upfront with me."

Although Dr. Muscat laid out the harsh truth, I didn't flinch. My shoulders didn't droop. My voice remained clear and strong. I didn't even let out a heavy sigh. The more bad news I heard, the stronger my resolve became.

I suspect my mother behaved similarly when the doctors told her she had a severed spine and would never walk again—might not even get out of bed again. I can imagine her response as something like, "Thanks for being upfront with me. What do we do now?"

"So, what do we do now?" I asked Dr. Muscat.

He explained that the Food and Drug Administration (FDA) had approved three drugs for the treatment of MS, but only for the most common form of the disease, RRMS. There were no approved treatments for PPMS. Anecdotal evidence existed, however, that these treatments worked for some folks with my form of the disease, so we considered them.

Avonex was a once-a-week, self-administered injection. Dr. Muscat judged it suitable only for milder courses of MS. Next, we discussed Betaseron, an every-other-day shot. This treatment had better results but came with flu-like side effects. Dr. Muscat considered the third drug, Copaxone, to be largely ineffective.

Then we reviewed the most aggressive option, a chemotherapy drug called Novantrone. The FDA had recently approved Novantrone for some types of worsening MS. Although primary progressive MS didn't make that list, the manufacturer was conducting a Novantrone trial for PPMS patients. At least the pharmaceutical company was willing to invest money in this possibility. We agreed that I would think things over for a week and come back with an answer.

I reached my decision in a day. I saw only one way forward.

At the next appointment I said, "Based on the prognosis you gave me, and everything we discussed about the treatment options, I don't want to mess around. Let's go straight to the chemo."

Dr. Muscat nodded. "Excellent. That's what I would've selected if I were in your situation."

This was crazy. Almost nobody jumped straight to Novantrone after diagnosis. Patients only tried it when everything else had failed. But why should I wait for everything else to fail? Why not get the good stuff immediately and preserve as much of my functionality as I could?

One reason to wait was that Novantrone treatments carried some risk. This drug could affect the heart's ability to pump blood, which might, in turn, have a deleterious effect on one's health. The protocol required a full cardiac checkup before starting on the course of treatment. Today, the cardiac checkup is required before each infusion. As a further precaution, Novantrone has always had a maximum allowable lifetime dosage.

Because Novantrone is a chemotherapy drug, I received my treatments at the cancer infusion center—an IV drip once every three months. I knew I had joined the big leagues when the person sitting to my left in the waiting room spoke with the person sitting to my right about where they stood in the complex process of getting their personal affairs in order. I wondered if the cancer patients could tell I was not one of them because of my healthy glow. They probably just thought I was a newbie.

I followed Cheryl, the oncology nurse, into the treatment area. She had a stout, sturdy build, and the top of her head didn't reach the bottom of my chin. When she spoke, she smiled, not only with her mouth but with her entire face, with her whole being. I couldn't guess her age—anywhere from 40 to 70. Her role was to provide comfort, both medical and emotional.

Cheryl directed me to one of the infusion stations, which consisted of a recliner, television, IV stand with a computerized pump, ample pillows, and one of those hospital tray tables on wheels. I hadn't had many IVs in my life, so I didn't know what to expect. Cheryl studied both of my arms from the elbow to the knuckles. She tied tourniquets here and there and gently slapped certain blood vessels to make them show up better. She spoke to my veins like they were shy, little puppies. "Come on now. Be a good vein and show yourself!" But my veins were naughty puppies.

Cheryl went after a vein on the back of my left hand. It hurt when she punctured the skin. I expected that. It hurt even more when she wiggled the catheter around, chasing the elusive vein. After I had contorted my face in pain enough times, she gave up on that hand and started on the other, running into the same problem. With each failure, she sighed and apologized.

"I'm going to find Florence. She is the vein whisperer," said Cheryl. "She'll get you."

"What do we have here?" asked Florence when she arrived a few minutes later. "Some sort of troublemaker?"

I liked her immediately. She was as short as Cheryl, rail thin and about my age. She displayed no comforting smile, really no smile at all, but her quick and precise movements, her dry humor, exuded competence. Florence started on my left, inner forearm. Again, the penetration hurt, and the poking around hurt more.

"Hmm," she said as she pulled out and taped a piece of gauze on the wound. No apology.

She felt around on my right arm until she found a vein she liked, on the thumb side of my wrist. "These wrist veins are leathery," she said. "I'll soften it for five minutes with a hot towel."

It worked. She successfully placed the IV, then said, "For the rest of your Novantrone infusions, we won't waste time. We'll go straight for the hot towel and the wrist vein."

When Cheryl attached the bag of Novantrone, I took note of its distinctive, almost soothing, dark blue color. At this first infusion, they administered the drug in an exceedingly slow manner to make sure I didn't have an adverse reaction.

Naturally, after they pumped fluids into me for a couple of hours, I had to pee. I dragged my IV stand with me into the bathroom, lifted the seat, and started emptying my bladder. Back then I was still a stand-up-and-pee kind of guy. After a few seconds, I looked down for a routine check, and I burst out in laughter. The cancer patients must have heard me. My typically yellow or clear urine had turned a lovely blue color. I had read weeks earlier about this harmless phenomenon, but it had slipped my mind.

I finished the treatment before noon, drove through McDonald's, wolfed down a burger, and continued on to the office. It was important that I report to work. In my pitched battle against MS, I didn't want the disease to see me blink.

Novantrone has a mixed side effect profile. Some patients tolerate it well, and others suffer from nausea and fatigue. I had no problems. In fact, the day after my second dose I went on a 225-mile snowmobile ride.

Throughout the treatments, everyone wanted to know if I felt any different.

Different than what?

Did they want to know if I felt different than before I had MS, different than just before I started treatment, different than I would have felt had I not gone on the treatment? Of course, it's the last comparison—different than I would have felt had I not been on the treatment—which really mattered. Unfortunately, that was the very question I could never hope to answer. This conundrum would repeat itself time and again over the coming years.

After five infusions of Novantrone over a period of twelve months, my leg weakness continued its steady progression. Reluctantly, Dr. Muscat and I decided to halt the program.

Afterward, Kim and I reflected upon this experience. "You must be disappointed with Novantrone," she said.

"It's not just that," I replied. "I thought the worst-case outcome would be that I used this wonder drug, this silver bullet, too early in the disease progression instead of waiting until a time when I might need it more. But what actually occurred is disheartening. I tried the most potent treatment available on the market, and it failed to have an impact, even in the early years of the disease. That's scary."

"I'm sure they'll come up with something else soon," she said.

We sincerely believed this.

A friend of mine had seen the world-renowned neurologist and

MS expert Dr. Howard Weiner in Boston, and recommended that I pay him a visit. Dr. Weiner wrote the presumptively titled book *Curing MS*. Midway through my year of Novantrone treatments, I landed an appointment with him at Brigham and Women's Hospital. I hoped he would know things my neurologist didn't, and he would give me the ammunition I needed to fight back. With little fanfare, he confirmed my diagnosis of primary progressive multiple sclerosis. No surprise there, but I had wanted to hear it from him. Next, he suggested I try his drug of choice called Copaxone—the same drug Dr. Muscat had dismissed as ineffective. Like Novantrone, Copaxone was in a clinical trial for use with primary progressive MS.

When I requested that Dr. Muscat begin treating me with Copaxone, he resisted. But I was persistent, and he indulged me. While still undergoing Novantrone infusions, I added this second powerful and expensive treatment regimen (both of which we successfully lobbied my insurance company to cover). Copaxone required a daily self-injection, and I wasn't crazy about needles.

I received my Copaxone kit in the mail, which included pre-filled syringes and an autoinjector device that did the dirty work for me. I loaded the syringe into the autoinjector, selected a spot on my thigh, and pushed the button. All the literature I had read and patient reports I had received on the Internet led me to believe that Copaxone injections would be easy. I was sorely disappointed. It felt like a nasty bee sting. Over the months, the injection sites—which rotated between my thighs, belly, and butt—often bruised any number of colors for days. I felt betrayed by the medical community and by my fellow MSers. Either nobody had mentioned the discomfort that came with the shots, or I had somehow ignored this fact when researching Copaxone.

I've since learned that pain at the injection sites is hit or miss. Many folks experience no discomfort, but a few of us do. (I've been hanging around doctors too much—referring to pain as discomfort.) On rare occasions I felt little or no pain. I wanted more days like that, so I built a detailed spreadsheet for tracking my shots, with date, exact location on my body where I injected, and how the injection felt. I failed to identify any pattern that would predict the pain associated with a given shot. Despite the difficulty I had with Copaxone, I remained optimistic this treatment would slow the progression of my MS.

One morning, about six months after beginning my Copaxone treatment, I read online that the Copaxone trial for PPMS had been discontinued due to poor results. This didn't sway me.

Just because the drug failed to meet certain statistical criteria for the test population doesn't mean I'm giving up on it. I'm conducting a trial of one. I'll stop taking Copaxone if and when I determine it's not working for me.

I loaded the syringe into the autoinjector and lifted my shirt so I could inject into my belly. According to my spreadsheet, it was a belly day. Those were the worst. This time, though, for some reason the autoinjector would not discharge. Was it the spring mechanism? No. Was the syringe incorrectly loaded? No. The problem was in my head.

I had made the commitment to myself that I would use Copaxone for a year before assessing its effectiveness, just like with Novantrone. But the news of the failed trial, coupled with my continued disease progression and a growing disdain of the painful shots, led to a change of heart. This was impetuous Mitch, making one of his rare appearances. I shifted from fully committed to completely done with this drug, right then, forever.

Over the ensuing days I came to realize that giving up on Copaxone meant temporarily giving up on the fight against MS, and that wouldn't do.

No, that wouldn't do at all.

CHAPTER 20

Paradise

The old-timers say that the town of Paradise, Kentucky, situated on the banks of the Green River, lived up to its name until the 1950s when coal was discovered underneath the houses. By 1959, the Tennessee Valley Authority had built a coal-fired generating station nearby and began strip-mining the area indiscriminately. The town became so polluted from the mining and the boiler emissions that everybody moved away. In 1969, TVA demolished the last buildings and homes, and Paradise was lost forever.

From 2001 until 2003, Paradise was my home away from home. I served as the project manager for an environmental compliance venture at the aforementioned TVA generating station, now called the Paradise Fossil Plant (meaning it burns fossil fuel as opposed to nuclear fuel). We were part of the team that designed and built a scrubber to treat the air emissions from one of Paradise's mammoth coal-fired boilers. Pollution from this plant affected not only the local area but also cities and states well to the east and northeast. After the new scrubber went online, everyone breathed a little easier.

Our consulting/engineering firm was a subcontractor of a subcontractor of the general contractor hired by the pseudo-governmental conglomerate that is the TVA. While each organization jockeyed for a larger share of the project budget, waste and redundancy became commonplace. I like to think my company was the exception. From our spot at the bottom of the food chain, we produced real engineering designs with minimal overhead. As the project manager, I was the minimal overhead.

Regularly traveling the same route from Portland to Kentucky had its benefits. I came to know the airline ticket agents, some of the flight attendants, the hotel staff, the waiters and waitresses, and the bartenders. I learned the locations of the Nashville Airport gates and where to catch the rental car shuttles.

Someone even showed me a dirt road shortcut from the hotel in Bowling Green, Kentucky, to the power plant. The road weaved through forest and swampland, occasionally interrupted by a trailer or rundown shack. Local men in pickup trucks with gun racks glared at my team and me as we cruised down the shortcut. It saved 10 minutes each way, however, so we took our chances. Because the power plant maintained the dirt road in top condition, we flew along at 60 miles per hour or more, kicking up dust in hot weather or mud in wet weather. Oh, the looks we got when we returned our rental cars in Nashville.

In those days, airlines offered more generous frequent flyer rewards than today. With my high mileage count, I upgraded to first class more often than not, and always for no extra charge. I learned that the front seats on a plane aren't occupied so much by the wealthy or the top corporate executives as they are by overworked salespeople, consultants, and other business managers. These folks bounce around the country every week, intent on maintaining their upper-middle-class status, and I had become one of them.

I didn't allow the Novantrone treatments to interfere with my business travel. In fact, I never missed more than a few hours of time in the home office for each treatment. I scheduled the infusions for Friday afternoons, just in case I had some fatigue or nausea afterward, which I never did.

Similarly, for the six months I injected myself each morning with Copaxone, I carried the appropriate number of prefilled syringes with me on my business trips. Copaxone could only remain unrefrigerated for a few hours, so I called ahead to each hotel and confirmed that I would either have an in-room refrigerator or access to the kitchen refrigerator. Before heading out each morning, I would ice the injection site for five minutes, inject the drug, and ice the site for five more minutes.

In January of 2003, at the end of a long week at the TVA plant, one of my clients and I decided to visit downtown Nashville. I learned two lessons that night—one about my MS and the other about the Nashville music scene.

Jeff, the client, and I walked along a chilly 2nd Avenue looking for a place to get a drink. As I grew cold, an unfamiliar stiffness gripped my legs, enough for Jeff to notice and ask me about. He knew of my diagnosis, so at least I didn't have to go through that rigmarole. I explained spasticity to Jeff, which I was experiencing for the first time.

"Our extremities have opposing pairs of muscles, flexors and extensors, which usually operate in a coordinated fashion. When spasticity occurs, however, both muscle groups fire simultaneously, and the affected limb becomes rigid."

I knew this because my mother had suffered from spasticity. Although she had no conscious control of the muscles below her trunk, her legs routinely decided on their own that all muscles, flexors and extensors, would fire, and would fire for a long time. In her later years, these spasms grew so intense that her seated body could become as straight as a board, from head to toe. Eventually, she lived with a pump surgically implanted in her abdomen. The device supplied her spinal cord with a muscle relaxant called Baclofen—straight up, no chaser. Today, I take oral baclofen and expect one day to need my own Baclofen pump.

Jeff and I happened upon a dive bar and dove right in. The bar surface was unfinished plywood. The area behind the bartender wasn't stocked with top shelf liquors but with decorative cowboy boots. Our shoes stuck to the floor, and the air tasted stale. The few regulars in attendance regarded us with suspicion.

I ordered two Budweisers, which seemed the appropriate brew for the venue. A band had set up in one corner, but there were no musicians in sight. It was only 7 o'clock, and I didn't reckon we would get to hear them play. Based on everything else about this bar, I felt confident we didn't want to.

A few minutes later, as we stood up to leave, four men in Western duds materialized. They mounted their instruments as smoothly as a cowboy would mount his trusty old steed. Giddy-up. Jeff and I fell back in our seats. The quartet of musicians surveyed the crowd of maybe seven patrons and one bartender, and they started playing.

In most cities, we wouldn't have had front row seats for this quality of music unless we paid a cover charge or even purchased tickets. I'm not a country music fan, but I appreciate good, live music of any genre, and these people delivered. When the electric fiddler played the obligatory "The Devil Went Down to Georgia" riffs, I was transported back to my high school days. We stayed and drank a couple more beers.

Because they were in Nashville, these four outstanding musicians considered it worthwhile to play for a smattering of people on a weeknight. They did so on the off chance somebody important in the music industry would drop by and discover them. Given that we were in the saddest bar in the downtown area, I assumed most bands playing in the city at the time had to be even better. *There must be no bad music in Nashville*, I concluded, an observation I still share today whenever the subject comes up in conversation.

"My company's corporate headquarters are in Nashville."

"You know, there is no bad music in Nashville."

"My great aunt Eunice lives in Nashville."

"That's nice. You know, there is no bad music in Nashville."

"I adopted this stray dog that was picked up on the streets of Nashville and flown all the way to Maine by a charity. His fur is so soft, and white, and fluffy. I think I'll name him Snowball. Go ahead, pat him."

"Sure, whatever . . . did you know that there is no bad music in Nashville?"

Given that our company had multiple, large projects with TVA, we set up a satellite office about a mile away from their mega-corporate headquarters in Chattanooga, Tennessee. If we had a meeting at their campus, we walked to it, because walking is an essential part of a healthy lifestyle.

Later that same winter of 2003, I spent a couple of days at this satellite office. The TVA project manager summoned me to a meeting. I was joined by Tom, the manager of our Chattanooga office; Jim, a project manager for our company on another TVA project; and Paul, from our client company. By the time we arrived at the TVA office building, I struggled to put one foot in front of the other. I stopped and rested on a bench outside the entrance—odd behavior for an apparently healthy 39-year-old.

"What's the matter?" asked Paul.

"Oh, it's nothing."

"It looks like more than nothing. Did you injure yourself?"

Although I had a liberal disclosure philosophy about my MS, I had not informed all my co-workers and clients. Doing so was tiresome. But when my symptoms were laid bare, like they had been that day, rather than fashion a lie or some lame excuse, I disclosed on the spot. Sometimes this didn't turn out well, because when I revealed my diagnosis in a state of even temporary physical compromise, I elicited sentiment that smelled more like pity than empathy.

"Well, I've got a problem I might as well explain to you. I've told some people in the Maine office. It's no secret."

"Sounds serious."

The team huddled around me like the quarterback on a football field, waiting for me to call the next play.

"I've been diagnosed with multiple sclerosis. It hasn't affected me much, and with any luck, it never will. But when I walk, I don't know, about as far as we just walked, I have to stop and take a break."

Paul was an engineer, so he needed some facts. "How does that work, if you don't mind me asking? Do you get winded, or do your muscles get tired, or what?"

"My muscles get tired, although that's not where the problem is. The signal from my brain to my muscles is messed up. It's a malfunction in my central nervous system." *Malfunction* was a good engineering term.

"Are there any drugs you can take for it?"

"Yes, I'm in a treatment program right now. I'll tell you all about it later. You guys ready? We're going to be late for the meeting."

"I feel sorry for you. Let me know if there's anything I can do."

"I will," I responded. But I knew I wouldn't.

Tom, the manager of our Chattanooga office, was a traditional southern gentleman. On the day after my troubled walk to the TVA office, he asked me in a serious tone of voice, "How are you?" This confused me at first. Then I realized he must have been referring to the MS.

We sat down, and I gave him the whole story. I had become proficient at telling it. He admired how well I was dealing with my challenges and praised me to the point of embarrassment.

I felt frustrated because I didn't know who in our company was aware of my diagnosis and who wasn't. I thought about sending a general email to all my co-workers. For reasons that escape me today, at the time I considered that such an announcement would be unprofessional. I hoped the momentum from the gossip mill would take over, and everyone would know.

The next day another employee of ours at the Chattanooga office, a kind, soft-spoken gentleman, stopped by my cubicle for a chat.

He stood there with his hands clasped in front of himself, and said with confidence, "I'm sorry to hear about your MS. But I believe everything happens for a reason."

I understood he meant to provide comfort, yet I found his statement to be absurd. The man had his view of the world, and arguing with him would be fruitless.

I forced a smile and said, "It's kind of you to stop by, but I'm late for a meeting." I didn't have a meeting.

I suppose, in the strictest sense, everything does happen for a reason. Rain falls when clouds become saturated with water. So, rain happens for a reason. These same storm clouds sometimes spur a tornado. I don't understand how that happens, but meteorologists do. So, tornadoes happen for a reason. This same tornado may rip through a town, leaving some homes and their residents intact, while bringing great harm to others. The tail of the tornado whips around in a path which is too complex for even meteorologists to explain or predict. When something becomes so complex as to fall beyond our capacity to understand it, some individuals ascribe the phenomena to forces such as God, the universe, or karma. They confuse complex causes for supernatural causes.

I've learned to accept that things happen—the good, the bad, the insignificant, and the life-changing—for no discernible reason. Complexity, randomness, and unpredictability play a critical role in our lives. The fact that some of us find this disquieting doesn't render it any less true.

I've heard, "Mitch, maybe you got multiple sclerosis so you could help other people with MS through your advocacy and writing."

My response is, "If this were true, what is the reason all these other people got MS? So I would have someone to help?"

If I don't believe my suffering is part of a bigger, unknowable plan, then how do I cope? It's like this. When everything doesn't happen for a discernible reason, there is no false expectation of fairness in life. There is no asking, "Why me?" There is only, "Why not me?" or better yet, "So what do we do now?"

There can be no divine or karmic justification for our worst suffering. Please don't try to convince me otherwise.

* * *

Around the same time I experienced walking problems in Tennessee, I encountered new difficulties in my own home. Everywhere I turned I found stairs, stairs, and more stairs. Getting around in house number three had become a chore. After living there for a little over a year, Kim and I realized that, though we loved our house, we would have to sell it.

It wasn't only the house. We saw the benefits of relocating to the next town over—Cape Elizabeth. Kim worked there, and both of our kids attended school there. We had finally sold our house in Lincoln (house number two), giving us some money to play with in the more expensive Cape Elizabeth market.

A real estate bubble had formed that summer, and we sold our Scarborough house without a realtor, in one weekend, for 40 percent more than we paid for it 16 months earlier, having sunk almost no money into it. We found a beautiful home in Cape Elizabeth (house number four) and moved in shortly after selling house number three.

Given our history, I knew my routine sentiment—we will never leave this place—was unreliable, but I couldn't see what the problem would be. I hadn't looked very hard.

CHAPTER 21
Dead Man Walking

When I returned to Maine from Chattanooga, my boss Kevin pulled me aside and asked how I was doing. He had heard about my walk to the TVA headquarters.

"My disease is still progressing," I answered. "I won't be able to walk around plants and job sites at will for much longer." We both agreed I could compensate in other ways, such as confining myself to plant conference rooms and relying on blueprints instead of my eyes.

By all accounts, I did an outstanding job for this company. I had found my sweet spot in the business world—manager of large projects. I possessed a well-rounded engineering mind and a natural ability to monitor and oversee complex, interrelated activities. I had a knack for facilitating compromise when two parties found themselves in disagreement, and disagreements occurred every day on large engineering/construction projects.

The TVA executive in overall charge of the Paradise project praised me to my bosses. At a companywide meeting our CEO recognized me for my outstanding leadership, and he handed me an envelope with a cash bonus inside. I had worked hard, and I was pleased to know that my contributions were valued.

A couple of months later, in the spring of 2003, my TVA-Paradise project began wrapping up, and the backlog of new projects had run dry. I didn't know what I would do next. This made me only slightly uncomfortable. Something would come up. It always did. In April, Kevin asked me if I could assist another project manager with some air emissions testing at a paper mill in Woodland, Maine. Our company was struggling for business, so I knew the importance of accepting this assignment. As I browsed through the project documents, I became concerned that the job might involve a lot of walking, but I had to give it a try.

The next day, a co-worker and I drove to the Woodland mill. I walked for 10 hours on Tuesday, 13 hours each on Wednesday and Thursday, and four hours on Friday. The level of activity was too much for me. I felt compelled to share my conclusion with Kevin when I returned to the office on Monday.

There I was—a project manager without a project to manage; a chemical engineer without legs to get around a chemical plant; and a 39-year-old who, for the first time in his life, was in danger of being let go.

I had heard gossip for weeks about an impending general layoff. I put my odds of survival at 50/50. One day, just before lunch, Kevin invited me to a meeting in the main conference room at 1:15. I didn't ask for the agenda, and he didn't offer.

During lunch I organized the documents on my desk. I gathered the names and contact information of those with whom I wanted to stay in touch. I ran through the various scenarios in my head. Was this the end for me?

In the conference room, Kevin sat with three other unfortunate souls. One of them, Karen, who had worked as a coordinator on my Paradise project, said, "Oh, you're involved in this?" The administrative people knew the purpose of the meeting. They always knew.

Kevin gave a short speech about the reason for these layoffs—a sharp downturn in the workload as the TVA projects reached completion. The other team leaders delivered similar speeches to small groups of their people throughout the building. Kevin handed us each an envelope with a modest severance package, shook our hands, and indicated that we should exit the building sooner rather than later. I returned his handshake, but I gave him no sign I was okay with it. I wasn't. No amount of preparation, no careful consideration could have readied me for that moment.

In a daze, I returned to my office and filled a box with my personal items. As I lugged the box down the hallway on my way out, two co-workers, by then former co-workers, stared at me with their jaws agape. Without missing a beat, I channeled the prison guard from *The Green Mile* and declared to nobody in particular, "Dead man walking."

Whether I had done anything to deserve the layoff, I felt a deep shame. What would people think of me when they heard? I worried about the reaction of other professionals, but also of my parents, siblings, wife, and kids. Not least of all, the layoff would vindicate those who questioned my decision to leave Lincoln for other opportunities, if indeed anyone did (I may only have imagined this).

As my situation came into focus over those first few days, I reminded myself that job performance was not the issue. Only a few months earlier I had earned a bonus and special recognition for my outstanding leadership. I had made no significant missteps after that time. So, if it wasn't performance based, that left two possibilities: business conditions or MS, both of which were out of my control, but only one of which might ever improve.

When a company learns of an employee's MS diagnosis, they have three choices. One, they can look for the first opportunity to rid themselves of the employee without getting sued, because even though he may still be productive, he will only ask for more and more accommodations over time. He will increase the company's medical premiums, and his work output is bound to decrease as the disease progresses. Let another company, maybe a bigger company, shoulder the burden. If it becomes bad enough, there's Social Security. The company is a business with fiduciary responsibilities to its stockholders, not a charity.

Two, the company can go to extra lengths to keep the employee on the payroll because of genuine compassion or to appear compassionate (different motivations, same result). After all, it would be heartless to put a sick person out on the street.

Three, the company can disregard the MS, other than meeting the requirements of the Americans with Disabilities Act and any other applicable laws. If he performs, keep him. If he can't perform with reasonable accommodations, let him go.

I'll never know how it went down in the boardroom. But I had a lot of idle time during the period of my unemployment, and I ran different scenarios through my mind. On bad days I thought the company took advantage of the opportunity to get the guy with MS out the door by including me in a broader layoff. The bastards!

On good days, I realized the only value I could add to this company was as a manager of large projects, but there were no more of them to manage. The best solution for all parties was for me to secure employment elsewhere—someplace where my skills would be in demand and my physical limitations would not be an issue.

I had about an equal number of bad days and good days.

After I returned to the workforce, I had to lay people off due to poor business conditions. On those occasions, I always thought back to my experiences in 2003. This rendered me a compassionate executioner, but did that make the experience more palatable for the people I had to let go? Probably not.

Knowing MS played at least some role in my job loss concerned me because I expected things would only get worse down the line. I had to re-enter the workforce when I was unsure of my capabilities, how fast my disease might progress, and what ethical obligations I had to prospective new employers.

Even in the best of times, the great State of Maine doesn't offer a chemical engineer with an MBA a wealth of opportunities outside the paper industry, and I refused to go back. Because I wouldn't relocate to where the jobs were, I had to be patient.

One evening my wife and I had dinner with our dear friends Mark and Carrie. We met them at a restaurant carved out of the first floor of a massive, abandoned, turn-of-the-century textile mill preserved by one of those urban renewal projects. Of course, in the early 1900s when men, women, and children labored long hours there, the place never looked this respectable, and the workers never ate this well.

"How's the job search going?" asked Mark, a vice president of a high-tech manufacturing company.

"My MS complicates things," I said.

"Really? I don't understand why."

Mark is a smart guy, so this naïve statement caught me off guard. "I'm afraid if I reveal my condition too early in the interview process, they will find some excuse to take a pass. Yet I feel an obligation to let them know. I don't want anyone to regret hiring me."

"You're over-thinking this. If someone revealed that fact to me in an interview, I would be more inclined to hire him or her, not less."

If only there were more executives and friends like Mark, this would be a better world.

As my quest for employment dragged on, my disease steadily progressed. I began to wonder how I would have functioned in my previous job as a project manager if I hadn't been laid off. As the months went by with no promising opportunities, I entertained the possibility that my working days had come to an end. I knew the statistics—fewer than half the people with MS were fully employed. I had purchased a COBRA long-term disability policy when I was laid off. But it didn't feel right, yet. I still had more to give.

I could find another engineering management job, or I could open a business. I even considered returning to college to learn a new profession. I sat for the Law School Admission Test, and I scored high enough to be a strong candidate for acceptance.

But before I could even apply to law schools, an opportunity came along with a local environmental engineering firm called Vortechnics. I interviewed, and it seemed a great match—except for one thing. The job required no less walking than my previous one. In every other way, Vortechnics represented the best opportunity since I'd been laid off. I had grown tired of sitting at home and looking for jobs, and I worried about my financial solvency. I needed to get back in the game. I had looked around for six months and had found no better way to make a living.

I wondered what my obligation was to Vortechnics during the hiring process. Should I tell them about my MS up front? Should I only describe my physical limitations and not overtly discuss the diagnosis? Should I do either of these things in the first interview, the second interview, after receiving the job offer, my first day on the job, or never?

The offer came in. We negotiated a bit, and I visited the office to formally accept the position. My new boss, Ted, seemed pleased to have brought me onboard. I capitalized on his positive feelings and chose that moment as the perfect time to talk about MS—thirty seconds after solidifying our employment agreement.

"There's one thing I want to make you aware of," I said. "I have MS, and it affects my ability to walk long distances. I have to rest now and then."

"No problem. You can stop and take a rest whenever you need to at these plants and job sites. When can you start?"

Good man, that Ted.

CHAPTER 22
I Gotta Fly

My ideal winter used to consist of frigid temperatures, heavy snowfall, and no "January thaw." Such conditions kept the snowmobile trails set up nicely from early December until April.

My favorite snowmobile trail system circled Maine's largest body of water, Moosehead Lake. On one ride in that region, my friend Mark pulled over to the side of the trail. I parked behind him, and we shut off our machines. We had put a little distance between ourselves and Kim. We knew she would be along soon, though. Kim was the best female rider I ever knew. She could keep up with most men, but Mark and I were not most men.

A few snowmobiles had parked just off the trail ahead of us. One machine lay on its side, and everyone stood around it. A member of the group walked up to us, and before he could say anything, I asked, "Is everybody okay up there?"

"No. One guy is dead," he stated, matter-of-factly. "He missed the turn and hit a tree head-on. He was wearing a helmet, but it didn't matter. His 20-year-old son was on the snowmobile right behind him and saw everything. My friends and I were the first ones to arrive on the scene."

I asked, "Is there anything we can do?"

"No. Someone has already gone to call the game wardens. We'll stay here until they arrive."

When Kim caught up with us, I briefed her. We stood around feeling awkward for a while and then Kim said, "If there's nothing we can do to help, maybe we should just move along, right?"

Mark and I looked at one another and put on our helmets. The three of us started up our snowmobiles and crept past the fatal accident.

I intended to stare straight ahead, but I peeked at the grieving son who sat beside his father and wept. I wish I hadn't.

Five minutes later we pulled into Kokadjo Trading Post—a famous gathering place for snowmobilers on the east side of Moosehead Lake—and stopped to collect ourselves. During the busy snowmobiling season, the husband-and-wife owners worked all day, every day. They operated a small grocery store, restaurant and bar, and a group of rental cabins, but their biggest moneymakers may have been the two gas pumps. Snowmobiles lined up to pay well over market price for gasoline. Kokadjo was the only refueling opportunity between North East Carry and Greenville. The three of us arrived around 9 o'clock in the morning, a couple of hours before the place would become a madhouse.

We ordered breakfast and sat in silence, stirring the food around in our plates. Mark spoke first. "This puts things in perspective. I have a wife and two kids at home who depend on me."

"Yeah, maybe it's time we start driving more responsibly," I offered. Two heads nodded in agreement, if ever so slightly.

"I can have just as much fun at half the speed," said Kim. "It would be nice to enjoy the scenery."

More nodding.

Although MS had only been in my life a short time, it had impacted many of my recreational activities, but not my ability to drive a snowmobile. I hesitated to self-regulate a skill, a talent, which had so far eluded MS. But I knew the right thing to do.

When we resumed our ride from Kokadjo to Greenville, I took the lead and set a more relaxed pace. The haunting look on the face of the dead man's son kept me in check. The trails leading out of Kokadjo were perfect—wide, well covered with snow, and freshly groomed. After a few minutes, we found ourselves on a familiar straightaway, a place where we would typically run our machines wide open. I increased my speed ever so slightly. I still felt in complete control.

That's really what it's all about. As long as I maintain control.

The more distance I put between myself and the accident scene, the more I slipped into my old, familiar habits. Gliding through the countryside, I achieved a sense of flow. The machine's engine, suspension, and skis became as much a part of me as my arms, hands, and legs. On each successive corner, I carried a bit more speed and leaned a little harder, inducing those elegant changes in direction reminiscent of a bird in flight.

Ten minutes out of Kokadjo, I succumbed to my urges. I only knew one way to ride.

Who am I kidding? I gotta fly.

And I did. We all did, and we never looked back.

* * *

The next winter, 2004, my friends Marco and Mark joined me for what would be a landmark snowmobile ride. As always, the three of us expected to overtake plenty of people on that day. We didn't enjoy passing other snowmobilers; the process of finding a safe place to do so slowed us down, and we didn't like slowing down. But we knew one thing with certainty—nobody would pass us.

The lead snowmobiler in our group assumed extra duties, so we rotated the responsibility. He had to watch for any obstacles in the trail, like moose or fallen trees. He also had to signal his buddies if he came upon other snowmobilers traveling in either direction. The leader was expected to accomplish these safety-related tasks while setting an aggressive pace for the riders behind him. The last thing you wanted to do was slow down your buddies (other than, I suppose, lead your buddies off a cliff).

Although we drove aggressively, I didn't feel that we were a menace to the more casual riders. We only attacked the trail if it was empty. When cornering, we assumed there was an oncoming snowmobile just out of our line of sight, and so we worked hard to stay on our side of the trail. This was our goal, anyway. Can I say, truthfully, that we *never* infringed on other snowmobilers' enjoyment or safety? I wish I could.

On this day, for the first time, I couldn't keep up with Marco and

Mark, and I didn't take my turns in the lead position. They waited for me at intersections like I would wait for Kim when we rode together.

I didn't give up easily. I tried my best to keep the pace until I blew a corner and careened into the woods. I missed every tree, and because I never completely lost forward momentum I didn't get stuck in the deep powder. After maneuvering back on to the trail, I shut down the engine, brushed the snow from my clothing, and removed branches from the windshield. Marco and Mark were so far ahead that I couldn't even hear the whine of their engines.

Sitting alone in this vast, frozen wilderness, I realized I was no longer an elite rider, and I had to stop pretending to be one. For the rest of that day, I slowed down and took the corners with my butt firmly planted in the center of the seat. When I encountered bumps on the trail, I backed off on the throttle so the snowmobile's suspension didn't bottom out. We covered a respectable 270 miles that day, and I was a physical wreck by the end. To top things off, for the first time in my life, a group of snowmobilers caught up from behind and passed me.

The deterioration of my riding skills had the potential to crush my spirit, but that didn't happen. Although I had dreaded this day, when it came, I felt a lightness. Sometimes the anticipation of loss is more stressful than the loss itself. "There, that's done," can be a most liberating sentiment. I could still ride, just not at high speeds, and maybe that was a good thing for safety reasons. And I finally could take in the scenery.

I saw little scenery. For the remaining two years I owned my snowmobile, I rarely took it out. It just wasn't the same.

Operating snowmobiles at high speeds had been addictive. Today, I know with certainty I won't be dragged out of the woods on a stretcher with a cracked vertebra, like my friend Preston, or, worse yet, wrap myself around a tree, like that guy outside of Kokadjo. The natural high that came with riding on the edge always muffled the little voice in my head telling me this approach was selfish and irresponsible. Although I rarely heeded that little voice, it haunted me at times. It haunts me no more.

CHAPTER 23

Coming Out

For a time, I occupied the nether-land between healthy and disabled, and my plight was invisible to the casual observer. I wondered if being in a wheelchair would be preferable. My condition didn't yet warrant one, but the concept held a certain appeal. People in wheelchairs don't live in a state of ambiguity. They don't constantly question their capabilities. There are a set of activities they clearly can do, and a set they clearly can't. Also, people in wheelchairs don't have to describe or justify their level of disability. It's visible and obvious. "Oh, he's in a wheelchair. I won't ask him to join me for a jog after work." Or, "Oh, he's in a wheelchair. I guess he does have a serious illness after all. He's not exaggerating his disability."

I didn't wish to be in a wheelchair. I had to work my way through a few other devices first. I had become so frustrated with my situation, however, that I entertained the idea well before it's time.

* * *

In Maine, the schoolkids get a weeklong April vacation. Kim and I decided to take our children to Washington, D.C. during that break in 2004. None of us had ever done the tourist thing in D.C., so we looked forward to the trip.

"I've been thinking," I said to Kim. "One day, hopefully far in the future, I may need a scooter or a wheelchair. This trip to Washington would be the perfect opportunity for a trial run, for me to experience what it's like to be disabled in public. Nobody would see me except you guys."

"That's a great idea, and it will keep you from being worn out and having to rest all the time."

119

I found a company in D.C. that rented scooters, but not the cool, two-wheeled type like Kim's Vespa. I needed something along the lines of the "Rascal" scooter George Costanza drove in that classic Seinfeld episode where a group of geriatric badasses chased him down in their scooters.

We spent two full days in Washington—one each at the Municipal Zoo and the National Mall. I used my rented scooter in both venues and learned a few things in the process. First, I found out about curb cuts. I hunted for these sidewalk transitions because, it turns out, scooters don't go up over curbs. I confirmed, however, that if you don't mind a jolt to your spine, they will go down over curbs. I also learned that ramps and elevators are often well hidden in buildings, especially old ones like those in the capital. These are issues only a disabled person or an architect would ever care about. I wish more architects were disabled (or the kinder version: I wish more disabled people were architects).

I also learned that using a mobility device has unintended benefits. A scooter helps with the long lines outside tourist attractions. I, and everyone with me, skipped right by all the other people—no waiting required. Best of all, the folks I passed in my scooter smiled at me politely, without a single complaint about how I cut in line. I suppose this, as with handicapped parking placards, is one way society attempts to equalize the fates of its members—redistribution of happiness.

On the drive home from Washington, Kim asked me, "What did you think of your little scooter experiment?"

"I guess I hadn't realized how much mobility I've already lost. I've been avoiding sporting events and shopping malls—"

"Even the grocery store," she offered.

"Yes, even the grocery store. I thought this experiment would provide a peek into the future, but the future is already here. Without the scooter, I wouldn't have enjoyed this vacation."

Kim didn't exactly gloat, but she had a look on her face that let me know she was well ahead of me, and I was still catching up. "That's quite an admission. How do you feel about it?" Kim, the counselor, asked.

"Good and bad. It's one thing to walk with a limp. People might think I suffered an injury. But when I start using a scooter, I announce to the world that I'm broken, probably forever."

I continued, "On the other hand, any assistive device will send a signal. It will tell people that I'm not lazy or drunk. It will announce that I have a medical condition, and that's why I don't move so well."

"Anything else?"

"Yeah. It sure would be nice to do all those things again, go to all those places. I gotta get back out in the world."

I gotta fly.

A few weeks after we returned home, I paid $31.50 for a wooden cane, the first, and least expensive, of many mobility devices I would purchase.

The Washington trip felt like a preseason baseball game—not the real thing, but good practice. The true challenge would be when I introduced my new cane to the people I saw every day or the people I cared about the most. As I thought about this unveiling, it brought back the horrors of seventh grade when I went to school wearing glasses for the first time. As soon as I walked through the doors, I saw a cute girl named Terri, and she said, "You look good with those glasses."

A sense of relief washed over me. "Thank you," I said.

"Just kidding. You look stupid."

That one still hurts.

On the evening of July 4th, 2004, I mustered the courage to take my cane on a trial run when a small group of us attended the fireworks celebration in Portland. Because of the large crowd, I knew we'd have to park a considerable distance away from the optimum viewing area and walk in. I don't compromise when it comes to fireworks. Ever since childhood, I've made it a priority to watch fireworks celebrations from Ground Zero. I want my breastbone to vibrate from the explosions. I want the smell of burnt powder to fill my nostrils. I want my neck to be sore from the acute angle I hold it for the duration of the show. On a related note, I also like bonfires and thunderstorms, and I would probably walk toward an erupting volcano if I ever saw one.

I only bumped into one acquaintance at the fireworks show, a work associate of Kim's, and I didn't feel self-conscious at all about using my cane. I had passed the first test. That didn't open the floodgates, however. I kept the cane tucked away at home for a while longer. If I remember correctly, I took several weeks to wear the glasses full time in seventh grade, too.

In August we hosted a weeklong reunion in Portland with about 20 close friends from our days in Cleveland. I used the cane for the entire week, traipsing about downtown Portland in broad daylight— much bolder than my little jaunt at the fireworks celebration. One day as we strolled down Commercial Street, I noticed a piece of trash paper lying on the sidewalk. In one deft motion, I plucked the paper from the ground with the tip of my cane and placed it in a dumpster, without even breaking stride. My friends were impressed with my new superpowers.

Of all the groups I faced for the first time with my cane, I felt the most trepidation about my co-workers. To draw the analogy one more time, they were my seventh-grade classmates: people I spent lots of time around, but with whom I felt neither intimate nor comfortable. Only about half the people at work knew I had MS at all, even though I hadn't kept it a secret.

In October an opportunity presented itself. Our CEO scheduled a weekend retreat for the entire company. We would participate in those silly team-building activities that required feats of strength, balance, and coordination. As always, there would be lots of drinking, too. Time to introduce the cane.

Sixty or seventy of us took the train from Portland, Maine to the University of New Hampshire, in Durham, New Hampshire. I boarded with cane in hand. I'm sure everyone noticed. How could they not? Some people politely ignored me. Others asked me if I had injured myself. A few folks looked at me with a knowing glance. These were the people who understood my MS had progressed to where I needed a mobility aid.

I couldn't participate in some of the more physically-oriented teambuilding activities, so I had two new experiences that weekend. I used a mobility aid in the presence of my co-workers. Also, for the first time, I sat on the sidelines and watched other people enjoy activities I couldn't, with a smile on my face so as never to let on that it troubled me. That was difficult in 2004. Today, after years of practice, it's much easier.

I still hadn't revealed this mobility aid to my extended family— my parents and brothers. They understood the seriousness of my diagnosis, and I'm sure they expected developments like this, but it was still a big deal. Once again opportunity knocked, this time in the form of moose hunting. That's right, Maine has a lottery system for a limited number of moose permits, and after 20 years of trying, I finally got one.

I used the cane in front of everyone that week, and I shot a big bull moose. Things worked out well. I had my mobility aid to make life easier, and I had full disclosure—no more secrets. I had forever changed my identity, and although it came with some sadness, I mostly felt relief.

I got a lot of miles out of that $31.50 purchase. The cane sits in my attic now, having outlived its usefulness. Barring a medical miracle, I'll never need it again.

CHAPTER 24

On Human Experimentation

I held the phone up to my ear, and the questions came rapid-fire.

"When were you diagnosed with MS?"

"October of 2001."

"Has your neurologist told you that you have primary progressive multiple sclerosis?"

"Many times."

"Are you able to walk, even a few steps?"

"Yes."

"Do you experience claustrophobia, for example, when you are in an MRI machine?"

"A little. It's no big deal. I get through it."

"Thank you for your interest. Unfortunately, you're not a suitable candidate for this clinical trial. Have a nice day." Click.

Damn.

In October of 2004 Dr. Muscat learned of a clinical trial for PPMS. I hadn't been on any treatment for a while, so I couldn't let a minor issue like claustrophobia stop me. That problem could be solved by a washcloth over my eyes and a little Valium I had stashed away from a previous medical situation.

Two additional hospitals in the Boston area were involved in the same trial. They listed their own screening phone numbers. I called the Worcester, Massachusetts, number first. She asked all the same questions and then the big one.

"Do you experience claustrophobia, for example, when you are in an MRI machine?"

"No, I do not."

The interview went on for a few more minutes, and at the end she said, "Congratulations, you qualify as a candidate for our trial. Questions?"

"How soon can we start?"

The experimental drug, Rituxan, a potent immunosuppressant and mild chemotherapy agent, had a long track record with other diseases such as non-Hodgkin's lymphoma, but almost no history with MS. I felt modestly optimistic. The pharmaceutical company planned to throw a lot of money at this trial, and they don't spend their money frivolously. But I also knew that no trial in the history of clinical trials had ever produced a treatment for PPMS.

Various factors delayed the start, but in May of 2005, the call finally came with instructions to report to the University of Massachusetts Memorial Hospital in Worcester for my initial evaluation.

The trial protocol would be placebo-controlled, double-blind. Placebo-controlled, at least in this case, meant two-thirds of the participants would receive Rituxan and one-third would receive a placebo. Double-blind meant neither the patient nor the treating physician (and his/her staff) knew whether the patient received Rituxan or a placebo. Only a few nameless, faceless data analysts would know who was who.

Each trial participant would report to UMass Memorial between one and three times a month for treatments and examinations. I lived two hours from Worcester, so this represented a significant time commitment. But I had a bigger concern—foregoing all other MS treatments while perhaps receiving a placebo for two and a half years. Dr. Muscat and I had a list of potential treatments we hadn't yet tried and, while none of them seemed promising, information could change, or new options might become available. If left untreated, I feared what the next two and a half years might bring.

I needed to find out if I was on the placebo or the experimental drug. Knowing I was on Rituxan would keep me motivated, making it likely I would stick with the trial until the end. Knowing I was on the placebo would give me options. If I found another opportunity to fight the disease, I might leave the trial to pursue it.

I had a friend in the medical field, and I briefed her on my situation. She conducted some research and learned of a routine blood test she could administer before and after my first infusion to determine if I had received Rituxan or the placebo.

In late May of 2005, she drew a blood sample from me. On June 2, I received my first trial infusion. A few days later she drew my blood again. Not long afterward she told me, "The blood tests indicate a high likelihood that you received an infusion of Rituxan. Congratulations, you're not in the placebo group."

During this trial I entrusted my healthcare to complete strangers, but they didn't remain that way for long. Over the ensuing years, I saw more of the team at UMass Memorial Hospital than I did of anyone other than my wife, kids, or co-workers, and certainly more than my local medical team.

Every six months I received a pair of Rituxan infusions, each two weeks apart. I experienced no side effects from the medicine except a low-grade fever and headache on the first infusion, a typical reaction to Rituxan, and further evidence I had not received the placebo. Between treatments, I visited UMass Memorial Hospital to be tested, have blood drawn, and undergo MRIs. Despite the four-hour round trip, I looked forward to my visits to Worcester. Doing something, anything, to fight back against the disease buoyed my spirits.

After a year, things looked promising. The clinical testing showed that my disease had not progressed at all. Kim and I agreed that the ease with which I could execute my tasks of daily living supported the clinical assessment. Something good was happening. But I managed my expectations. It was much too early to claim victory over MS.

According to my trial physician, Dr. Riskind, these positive results continued in the second year of the trial. In every area his group tested, I showed no disease progression. By evaluating my tasks of daily living, however, Kim and I observed modest disease progression in that second year, better than we had seen before Rituxan, but not a total cessation. As the end of the trial approached, I wondered what would happen next. In October of 2006, I sent the following email to Dr. Muscat:

> I get my last two infusions on 10/18 and 11/1. I am uncomfortable with the concept that I'll not be getting another pair of infusions in six months.
>
> I know the trial neurologist is not the trial sponsor. He is blinded, and he can't promise me anything that costs anybody money. However, it appears that the sponsor will be content to study what it is like for me to come down off the drug for one year after my last infusion. This is borderline unethical. If I am getting the drug, and it has benefited me and many others, isn't extending the trial the right thing to do, and isn't it even more interesting data-collection-wise than studying how my body adjusts to coming off the drug?
>
> Mitch

Dr. Muscat sympathized, and he shared my frustration. On October 18, 2006, I received my seventh trial infusion, and on November 1, my eighth and final one.

In the two extreme cases of a clinical trial, the endgame is straightforward. Often it becomes apparent, even before the scheduled completion date of a trial, that the treatment has not worked or has done harm. In those situations the experiment is stopped early or simply considered a failure at its conclusion. Everybody packs up and goes home. "Nice try. Good effort. We'll get 'em next time." This trial didn't seem to fall in that category.

On the other extreme, a clinical trial may be a rousing success—high fives all around. When this happens, the participants often continue with the treatment in what is called an "open label" phase. After all, it would be cruel to snatch a miracle drug away from long-suffering patients who experienced relief. Plus, this gives the trial sponsors, usually the pharmaceutical company, an opportunity to study the longer-term effects of the treatment. This is how trials worked out for several of the relapsing remitting MS drugs that currently have FDA approval.

With the Rituxan trial's endgame in limbo, I grew uneasy. Being a pragmatist, I worked two parallel paths. Maybe the trial would have an open label phase. In case it didn't, I consulted with Dr. Muscat about setting up my next Rituxan treatment outside of the trial. Since the FDA had not approved Rituxan for MS, my insurance company would not cover it. I assumed the cost to be $5,000 per infusion, for an annual cost of $20,000. I didn't want to pay that much, but I would consider it.

In April of 2007, five months after my last infusion, I had a routine appointment with Dr. Riskind, the trial neurologist. I learned the trial's sponsor continued to pour over the data, with some hope of an open-label study in about a year. I was appalled. They planned to take their sweet time watching and thinking and graphing and pondering. With no treatments, I expected my disease progression to resume with vigor. What amount of disability would I accumulate while they contemplated?

With PPMS, the symptoms don't come and go. The damage is slow and steady, irreversible and permanent. Every smidgen of disability remains with me forever. Given this reality, time was of the essence. Waiting a year for an open label study that may or may not materialize was not an option.

Approximately eight months after my last infusion, the disease progression returned to the pretrial rate, as measured both by Dr. Riskind and by my personal experience. This didn't surprise me, but it frightened me. It frightened me into action.

I asked Dr. Muscat to prescribe Rituxan for me. I would pay the $10,000 cost out-of-pocket for this first pair of infusions. I only needed to bridge the gap until Rituxan got approved for treatment of MS, at which time my insurance company would take over the expenses, or so I thought.

Then I got more bad news. I had the wrong information on the cost of Rituxan, by a factor of two. A pair of infusions cost $20,000, not $10,000. This changed everything. The extra $10,000 meant the difference between feasible and not feasible, go and no-go.

Dr. Muscat and I turned our focus to my insurance company. The crux of our case with them would be a letter from the clinical trial administrators indicating they had treated me with the trial drug and not the placebo, coupled with the positive clinical data from my examinations.

Through Dr. Riskind, I asked the trial administrators for such a document, an email, some hen scratching on the back of a napkin, anything to prove I had been on the trial drug and not the placebo. They ignored me. Although the infusions had long since finished, the study remained blinded, which meant the information stayed under lock and key. The months ticked by. I made phone calls. I wrote letters. While I waited to hear from the trial administrators, more irreversible damage occurred to the myelin sheath around the nerves in my spinal cord. While the administrators hoarded the data I desperately needed, I accumulated more permanent disability. Walking any distance became increasingly difficult. But, the more important consideration was the trial protocol. That's what I'll always remember about this experience. The damn protocol was preserved.

In July of 2008, the administrators finally unblinded the data, and I received this note from Dr. Riskind:

> Mitch - We have learned that you WERE on
> Rituximab (Rituxan). I am happy to write a letter of
> support on your behalf. Please let me know what you need.
>
> Peter

Based on my clinical results during the trial and based on the fact that I had received the drug rather than the placebo, the insurance company granted the appeal. I began receiving infusions again, after an absence of nearly two years. However, we fought with the insurance company for each Rituxan infusion I received—a total of six. The infusions each went flawlessly, and I waited to see if Rituxan would once again stop or at least slow down my progression.

By August of 2009, with the insurance company again refusing to pay for more infusions, I took an objective look at my situation. I had to admit Rituxan had provided no benefit since the clinical trial had ended. I had fought so hard for the six post-trial infusions I received. But the drug just didn't work anymore. Had I lost momentum with all the delays? If I had stayed on the trial schedule, with no missed infusions, would the Rituxan have continued slowing my disease progression? I'll never know. Reluctantly, I told Dr. Muscat I'd had enough.

Thus ended my foray into the bizarre world of clinical trials. I use the term *bizarre* because, under what other circumstances would a doctor ask a patient to accept an infusion of a drug, the contents of which neither of us can be certain. What taker of the Hippocratic Oath would dare ask patients with a chronic disease to endure permanent damage to their central nervous systems for years so that this damage could be measured and compared to that of other trial participants, in the name of furthering science but also of maximizing profits? In what alternate universe might I respond positively to the trial drug, yet it could be withheld from me at the end of the trial so that scientists could study me as I came down off the drug? What mad men devised this draconian method of sorting through which treatments work for which diseases? I want names!

To be clear, I never met the people who screwed me over in this trial. I don't know what they look like. I just know they screwed me over. The people I dealt with personally, the doctors and nurses and technicians, were all wonderful people. They just weren't holding the cards. Neither was I.

What about my behavior? I lied about my claustrophobia, and I went behind the trial administrators' backs to find out whether or not I was on the placebo. Did I behave unethically? Perhaps. But I looked at it from a practical standpoint. I understood that because there were hundreds of trial participants, nothing I did could affect the trial findings. I took those steps to potentially save myself from two and a half years of irreversible disease progression. That's how I justified it. Would I behave differently today if a similar situation arose?

The answer is no. For someone with an incurable, chronic, progressive disease, it's just too much to ask.

Over a period of four years this drug had been my focus, my obsession, and now it had disappeared. Despite my attempts to keep expectations low, when I finally gave up on Rituxan, some frustration and even fear crept in. This didn't stop me from fighting the disease, though. It motivated me to do better. In my next treatment experiment, I wouldn't put myself at the mercy of nameless, faceless people.

When the pharmaceutical company eventually released the results of the trial, Rituxan did not prove to be a viable treatment for PPMS, and of course there was no open label phase to the trial. It was all for nothing, and when I heard the news, I felt nothing. I had already moved on.

I recently learned that it wasn't *all* for nothing. Despite the trial's official findings, Dr. Riskind observed improvements in me and other patients and has used Rituxan successfully in an off-label manner since then. Repeated denials from insurance companies, however, have frustrated him.

In 2017, years after my clinical trial experience, a revised version of Rituxan, called Ocrelizumab, became the first drug to obtain FDA approval for treating primary progressive multiple sclerosis. I began treatment in the summer of 2017. As of this book going to print, I've experienced no positive results.

Kathy, the Rituxan trial coordinator, and I became friends and stayed in touch after the trial. We once took in a Red Sox baseball game with our spouses, and today we still chat on Facebook. A few years ago, Kathy wrote me to say she had been diagnosed not only with MS but with the primary progressive form. The disease she treated for years, a rare condition, turned around and visited upon her. The thing is, PPMS is in no way contagious. Weird stuff.

CHAPTER 25
Judy, the Physical Therapist

"Why the cane?" asked Judy.

"Multiple sclerosis," I answered.

The physical therapist's face lit up. "Let's talk about your MS."

"But I'm here today about tendonitis in my left shoulder."

She ignored me and asked a thousand MS questions, finishing with, "Have you ever seen a physical therapist for your MS?"

"No."

"Never?"

"Never."

"You're long overdue."

Judy had me perform various feats of strength and dexterity, to assess how well everything worked. When our time was almost up, I reminded her, "My shoulder?"

"Right. Sorry I didn't get to your shoulder today, but we can take a look at it next visit. I'm more interested in your MS issues. I think I can help in several areas. I'd like to see you twice a week for a month or two."

She never did look at my shoulder, and it got better on its own.

At the next appointment, while Judy stretched my legs, she asked, "Did you drive yourself here today?"

I understood where this was headed, and I became defensive. "Yes, I drove myself. I drive myself everywhere."

She didn't back down. "Based on how weak your legs are, I'm surprised."

"Thank you for your concern. My driving is fine." She went back to stretching my legs, but with the raised eyebrows of someone who knows they are right.

For the next few days, I paid closer attention to my driving. I had no difficulty with the highways and major roads. City driving, however, was a different story. I had to move my foot from gas to brake and back so often I found myself grabbing my right pant leg just above the knee to help with the transitions. I hadn't even realized.

The next week I said to Judy, "You were right about my driving. But what can we do? I *need* to drive."

She didn't gloat even a little. "Let's get you some hand controls. We can start the process today."

First, Judy evaluated me for the most common type of controls, where a lever is attached near the steering column. I would push the lever down with my left hand for gas and forward for the brake. She measured my hand strength and dexterity and found them acceptable. Next, she conducted a coarse visual screening, and I passed. The last step was a cognitive test to make sure I had the mental capacity to drive. *Seriously?*

"I'll read you a paragraph taken from a novel. When I'm finished, I'll ask you to repeat it back to me as closely as possible. You won't get it word for word, but don't let that bother you."

I couldn't have been more confident. She recited the hundred or so words, and I began to speak them back to her. Before long I lost my way. I couldn't remember what she had read to me. I botched the test.

"That was, um, unexpected," she said.

"No kidding. I'm not sure what happened. You want to try it again?" I asked.

"No, I don't have another paragraph. But don't worry. I've interacted with you enough that I can vouch for your cognitive abilities."

Although she wasn't concerned, I was. Most of my lesions were in my cervical spine, but my brain had a few, and apparently they had affected my memory.

This was not my first problem with memory recall. A couple of months earlier, I received an email from one of my company's salespeople detailing a back charge from a customer for almost $12,000. I read the email and took offense. I felt he only sent me these details to accuse my department of the errors leading to this back charge. I fired a defensive email to him, and he replied similarly.

Never having had a disagreement with this gentleman before, I shared my dilemma with a co-worker and asked for her opinion. After studying the correspondence, she said, "You sent him an email last week requesting the details of this back charge. He only did what you asked him to do." The email didn't even look familiar when I read it, but I was its author. I apologized to the salesman, and I wondered if I was losing my mind.

Next, came driving lessons. Using my hands instead of my feet felt awkward at first, but I simply needed to practice enough so the impulses in my brain that had previously traveled to my right leg for gas and brake control were rerouted to my left hand. After a couple of weeks, it became automatic.

I found a company to install the controls in my two vehicles, at $1,400 per vehicle and no insurance help.

At about the same time I had the controls installed, I received a letter from the State of Maine indicating my license would be forfeited in one month if I didn't pass a driver's exam with my new hand controls. Judy had forewarned me an exam would be required, but I hadn't expected a threatening letter. Whose business was it anyway how I chose to drive?

It turned out to be the State's business. Once Judy evaluated me for hand controls, she informed the State, as required by law, and I became subject to an impersonal relicensing procedure. The Department of Motor Vehicles treated me as if I had committed some offense, and I needed to come back into compliance or suffer the consequences.

Why do you have to act like such dicks? Can't we just talk about this like adults?

I showed up at the DMV a few minutes before my scheduled driver's exam and sat down among the nervous 16-year-olds and their nervous parents. My parents didn't come with me.

At age 15, I had failed my first driver's test. I either made a critical error, or the examiner was a lunatic egomaniac who lived for the power he wielded over our young lives. I'm going with the latter. But on this day, some 27 years later, I dealt with a friendly gentleman who quickly put me at ease.

The examiner shared a story as I drove around the streets of Portland, more deliberately than I had ever driven those streets before or since. A few weeks earlier, a person who had lost his license due to mental illness but had undergone successful treatment took the driver's exam to get his license reinstated. The examiner asked the driver to parallel park, easily the most stressful part of the exam. The driver struggled and began to argue with himself in two different voices as if the examiner wasn't even there.

"You idiot! Can't you park a car correctly?"

"Shut up. Leave me alone. You're not helping."

"You're going to fail this test, aren't you?"

"Shut up!"

And so on.

The examiner had no choice but to fail the driver. He hated to break this news to somebody who had already been through hell and back (or not quite all the way back). Like my mother's account of the roommate who blinked to spell out her desire to die, this story reminded me that things could be so much worse than they were.

I passed my driving exam without difficulty, and I never again operated a vehicle without hand controls.

Judy didn't like my $31.50 cane. She showed me how relatively unstable a single, traditional cane was when compared to two forearm crutches. She let me try them out. Wow, what an improvement. Even when I used only one forearm crutch, the fact that it connected to my arm in two places instead of one made all the difference regarding stability. And when I added a second forearm crutch, there was no comparison. In February I ordered my own set.

As soon as I began using the forearm crutches at home and in the office, I gained new confidence. My movements felt controlled and stable. I decided to try a more substantial outing. We went to the

Maine Mall, a place I hadn't visited in years because of all the walking involved. Kim wanted to check out a sale at JCPenney. Dutiful husband that I was, I maneuvered around the aisles with Kim and gave her my input on various ensembles. Although not my favorite activity, I reveled in my newfound mobility.

Next, I needed to purchase some rewritable CDs at Best Buy, at the other end of the mall. By the time we got to Starbucks, about the halfway mark, I had to sit on a bench and rest. That's when I realized the forearm crutches gave me stability, but they didn't solve the problem of leg fatigue.

Damn.

CHAPTER 26
Little Indignities

In the spring of 2005, my employer, Vortechnics, based near Portland, Maine, merged with our biggest competitor, Stormwater Management from Portland, Oregon. To adjust our attitudes from those of hated rivals to trusted partners, our CEO arranged for a group hug at a neutral location. He expected every employee from both coasts to attend. This gathering was ostensibly for team building exercises during the day, but stronger connections were made in the evenings when we consumed a staggering amount of alcohol together.

In the days leading up to the retreat, I became concerned with mobility issues, so I spoke to the meeting coordinator. Callaway Gardens, a private resort in Pine Mountain, Georgia, was a sprawling complex. The coordinator assured me my mobility issues would be taken into account. I was still new enough at the disability game that I accepted his assertion at face value.

Based on my positive experience with the scooter in Washington, I decided to rent one for some of the longer walks at the resort. One other employee, Margo, had mobility issues, so I volunteered to coordinate the rental of two scooters for the weekend.

On a Friday night in October of 2005, we descended upon Callaway Gardens as two disparate groups, highly suspicious of each other. After a banquet and an open bar together that first night, though, we became one backslapping, inside-joking, harmonious group, at least for the rest of the weekend.

After breakfast on Saturday, we gathered at the front of the main building to board buses that would take us to the other end of the resort for the day's activities. Although the meeting coordinator told me the buses could accommodate scooters, the bus driver felt otherwise. Being the troopers we were, Margo and I said we would drive our scooters down the road and meet everybody at the destination. That was a mistake on my part. I should have been more insistent on some means to transport the scooters.

The meeting coordinator handed maps to Margo and me and instructed us on where we would reunite with the others for a group photo. We set out down the private, paved roads in our scooters. Before long, the buses passed us. Everybody waved. I felt foolish crawling along at five miles per hour in my scooter while everyone else rode together on buses, like normal people. But I said nothing. Let's call this Indignity Number 1 of the weekend.

When we came to a fork in the road, I said, "Margo, my map doesn't show this intersection. Which way are we supposed to go?"

"I'm not sure. I seem to remember them saying something about staying to the left."

"Or was it stay to the right?" I wondered out loud. "No, I think you're right. It was left. Let's go to the left." So we did.

The road gained elevation as it weaved through an ancient hardwood forest. After a few minutes we came upon a lovely park with open spaces and a covered picnic area. It seemed the perfect place for a group photo, except for one thing. There was no group. I pulled my scooter up to the edge of the hill and looked down. Below, on the road we should have taken, sat the buses and our co-workers.

"Margo, come see this."

"Oh my goodness. We took the wrong road. Let's go back."

"I don't know. They seem to be assembling for the picture right now. I don't think we'll make it in time if we backtrack. Look at this path that goes down the hill. If we follow that, we may have a chance of getting there in time."

"If you think so."

I started down the path, and Margo followed. I liked our chances, but halfway down the hill, the path ended. Margo pulled up beside me in her scooter. Together, we watched as the group assembled below us, posed for pictures in front of a professional photographer, and then disassembled.

Eventually, someone noticed us and waved. I motioned for them to help, and a group of people climbed up to our location. I pulled out my forearm crutches and picked my way down the hill. Two people helped Margo navigate the steep slope. The rest of the folks wrestled our scooters to the bottom. Let's call missing the group photo and being assisted down the hill Indignities Number 2 and 3.

Today, this group photograph is a revered and sentimental reminder of that magical weekend. It serves as proof of who attended the now legendary meeting, and who made up the original members of the merged company. Only Margo, me, and a couple of people nursing hangovers are missing. The photo still hangs in a special place at the office. I have little doubt that one day it will be displayed in the Smithsonian Museum, in Washington, D.C. The caption will read— *The Most Awesome Corporate Retreat Ever.* My future grandchildren will exchange knowing glances when Grandpa points to the picture in the glass case behind the velvet rope and claims he was there. "Just didn't make the photo."

"Sure, Grandpa, did you walk on the moon, too?" Nudge, nudge, chuckle, grin.

Little shitheads.

Back at Callaway Gardens, we broke into our scavenger hunt teams—maybe six or eight people per group. Special boxes had been hidden in the immediate area. Once I realized the boxes couldn't be found in the middle of the road, I retired to the location where everyone would meet afterward. Also present were twisted-ankle-guy, way-too-hung-over-guy, and eventually Margo. Let's call not being able to help my team out in the scavenger hunt, Indignity Number 4.

After the scavenger hunt and some kumbaya time, everyone took the afternoon off to explore Callaway Gardens. Margo and I and a few others visited the Butterfly Conservatory and an exhibit of live birds of prey. They were nice attractions, but if they had placed the birds of prey inside the butterfly Conservatory, now that would have been something to see.

By late afternoon, we needed to return to our cabins and prepare for dinner. Shuttle buses zipped around the campus and gave rides to our co-workers. Margo and I grabbed the maps and set out for home in our scooters. Before long, both of our battery warning lights came on. About 100 yards shy of our cabins, Margo's scooter ran out of juice. I positioned my scooter behind hers and pushed her the rest of the way—Indignity Number 5.

We both recharged our batteries and had no more mobility problems that weekend, and no more indignities.

I have grown accustomed to suffering these embarrassing moments. When my mother came upon an uncertain mobility situation, like me, she might elect to avoid it. But if there was no way around, she kept her cool and helped her caregivers solve the problem. Once they had dealt with the mobility situation, she appeared to give it no more thought and enjoyed herself. I'm the same way. Either I observed her in action, or she passed along her genetic predisposition toward remaining calm and positive, or both. Either way, thanks, Mom.

CHAPTER 27

Our Housing Carousel

K im and I are fairly bright, disciplined people. Given this, I can't understand why we made such bad decisions on houses. Each time we set out to find a more accessible home, we fell in love with something else. We had told ourselves that the Cape Elizabeth house was suitable because we could always move to the first floor if I became unable to climb the stairs to our second-floor bedroom.

One day, a few years after we moved in, Kim watched me struggle to ascend the stairs, and she spoke up.

"Is it time for us to switch bedrooms with Amy?"

"We could, but is that really our only problem with this house?"

Kim thought for a moment, then shook her head. "Nope, not even close."

I had recently purchased a scooter like the ones I had rented in Washington and in Georgia, and I wanted to use it in the house, but the layout didn't support that, even on the main floor. I could no longer access the backyard because of its steep slope. I could no longer walk to the mailbox at the end of the driveway, again, because of the slope. I couldn't get from the car to the house without climbing steps.

I wasn't in denial about having a serious illness. We had purchased these houses because I felt optimistic that I could control the disease through one or another medical intervention, and I could make any house accessible with clever modifications. Neither of those assumptions turned out to be true.

This Cape Elizabeth house represented transitions. I had entered the home without so much as a cane to assist me. I left five years later in a scooter. The first summer we lived there I cut down dead trees in the back yard with my chainsaw and processed them into firewood. Five years later I couldn't walk among the trees without assistance. When we moved in, I was the person in charge of most home improvement projects. Five years later, out of necessity and because of her can-do attitude, Kim had become a carpenter, plumber, landscaper, and electrician. She laid tile and hardwood floors. Sometimes, she dove in over her head, but she always found a way back to the surface.

We scoured Cape Elizabeth for an accessible ranch house but didn't uncover many candidates. When we expanded our search to nearby Scarborough, we found a suitable home. Within a short time, we sold our Cape Elizabeth house and closed on the one in Scarborough. After a few months of renovations, we had a wheelchair accessible home in a lovely suburb of Portland. We were more confident than ever that we had found the perfect living situation.

We were close—so close.

With the move came options for the kids. Zach would be starting eighth grade. Because Kim worked in the Cape Elizabeth school district, he could continue attending school there. We preferred that he switch to the Scarborough schools, but we didn't tell him that. We didn't want to bias his decision (as long as he made the right one). Cape Elizabeth is a small, affluent district filled with kids who tend to fit a certain mold. Zach was an individual, and had cultivated few friendships in Cape. We knew there would be more social diversity in Scarborough, and, because it was a larger school district, more kids to choose from.

"Zach," his mother began, "you can continue attending school in Cape Elizabeth if you want. You'll have to ride back and forth with me. Or, you can start attending school in Scarborough, and take the bus."

"I'll just go to school in Scarborough. That will make things simpler."

Zach was a boy of few words, so I'll never know if he had the same feelings we did about the suitability of Cape versus Scarborough, or if he cared only that the logistics would be simpler. If he had selected Cape, we would have gently pushed back and made sure he considered all the issues, but we would have let him make the decision.

Amy, who was entering her senior year at Cape Elizabeth High School, had an easy choice. She drove her car to classes in Cape from our Scarborough home each day, and graduated with her friends.

Kim and I had similar parenting philosophies, but she executed them much better than I. Kim was a professional when it came to dealing with adolescents, and she possessed more patience and empathy. I wanted to have a better relationship with our children than my father had with me. Despite my shortcomings, I largely achieved this goal.

Our kids couldn't have been more different. Zach was mellow and accepting. When unsuccessful, he would shrug it off. This served him well in terms of managing stress, but it drove Kim and I crazy when it appeared to us that he was lackadaisical. Amy approached life with intensity and drive. We were proud of her many accomplishments, but when things didn't go well for her, it became unpleasant for everyone.

Both kids had big hearts and did the best they could with the strengths and weaknesses they possessed. They each grew up to be responsible and well-adjusted adults. I'm glad we didn't break them somehow.

CHAPTER 28

Carnage in Our Wake

In 2004 the Boston Red Sox won their first World Series championship of my father's lifetime. At 74 years old, he put it in perspective
by telling me, "Now I can die in peace." Dad wasn't the only Red Sox
fan of that generation to utter those words. Red Sox baseball was that
important to us.

In 2007 I took my scooter to Fenway Park in Boston for the
first time. We decided to save on parking fees and use public transportation. I checked their website, and the Green Line subway system
described itself as wheelchair accessible. When we got to the boarding
area for the Green Line, we noticed four steps leading up on to the
trains. As we pondered the inaccessibility of this accessible train, an
attendant came along with an archaic device in tow.

He instructed me to drive up on to this portable lift. When I
did, he cranked a huge wheel, leaning hard into the task, not unlike
how a medieval dungeon master would have tightened the rack to torture a witch or a heathen. But my limbs were not stretched. Instead,
every time he turned the ratcheted wheel, I rose a little higher until I
reached the level of the train, no worse for the wear, physically anyway.

By this point all the busy people on the train had been delayed,
and I was the obvious reason. As I attempted to drive from the lift
on to the train, everyone had to squeeze out of my way. I learned the
Green Line trains are filled beyond capacity before and after Red Sox
games. Wonderful. If this train had a designated wheelchair spot with
safety equipment such as tiedowns, I would never find it in this sea of
humanity. I didn't even try.

When we arrived at Fenway Park, we reversed the process. My
level of comfort with poor accessibility is not unlimited. So, I vowed

that I wouldn't subject myself to the Green Line again, and I haven't. On the way back from Fenway Park, we walked over to Northeastern University and boarded the Orange Line instead, which is a legitimately accessible train.

Today, we drive to Fenway. We know all the accessible parking spots in that part of Boston, and those spots are always free.

* * *

In 2007, as the year wore on and my disease progressed, I graduated from occasional to frequent scooter use, and we needed some upgrades. We purchased a full-fledged wheelchair accessible van, with an automatic door and ramp system—no more manhandling that portable ramp every time I wanted to load or unload the scooter.

Wheelchair vans are expensive, a cruel irony because there is a strong negative correlation between level of disability and income. Often times Medicare will supply a disabled person with a heavy, power wheelchair, and then they will have no means to transport it. In 2007, a new van started out at about $45,000. But, by a stroke of luck, we found a used model with low mileage for only $18,000. I wouldn't be so fortunate when I bought my next one.

As soon as I had the van, I decided to bring my scooter to work for the first time, and I sent this office-wide email the evening before:

> This is fair warning for everyone that I'm going to start using my electric scooter when I come into the office. I'm sharing this with you because I like most of you and think you deserve to know a few things about me and my scooter:
>
> 1. It goes faster than you walk, and it is quite stealthy. I apologize in advance for anyone whose toes I run over. It has a horn, but I've disabled it, so you won't have any warning.
>
> 2. Please do not call "shotgun" and jump on the back of the scooter for a free ride to the coffee machine or copier. A couple of folks have tried that, and yes, the

front tire of the scooter can come up off the ground. And if you abscond with my scooter for some sort of cross-office trek, you do so at your own peril. It's not as easy to maneuver as you might think.

3. Yes, you may still see me use the forearm crutches from time to time, but I must tell you that the thrill of moving faster than everyone else, instead of slower than everyone else, usually results in more scooter use and less crutch use.

4. Louie, please do not don a mask, grab a machete, and do donuts with my scooter in the parking lot. It will only scare the children next door – again.

Thank you,
Mitchell Sturgeon, P.E.
Operations Manager

A note of explanation: a couple of years earlier, as we arrived at work on the morning of Halloween, Louie rode on a small motorcycle around the parking lot, with a machete and a full monster mask on. It was amusing until the Day Care Center next door called the cops.

My boss, Rob, in Ohio responded:

Your note is funny . . . but I am concerned about your health.

And I wrote back:

I appreciate your concern.
As long as the symptoms stay in my legs, I'll be good to go. I'm lucky to have a job that suits my ailment well. The office environment with occasional travel is very manageable for me. However, if the MS starts spreading to the rest of my body, I'm screwed. There is no way to predict if it will stay south of the belt or migrate up.

We all have uncertainty about what our futures hold. Any of us can be stricken with a disease, hit by a delivery truck, or killed by terrorists at any moment. The primary

cause of my uncertain future is just there for all to see.
That's the only difference.

* * *

I didn't find it intimidating to fly all around the country as a disabled person. I valued the travel opportunities my job afforded me. In February of 2008, I took my first major scooter trip, flying solo from Portland, Maine to Portland, Oregon to visit our West Coast office. For a couple of years, I had managed certain East Coast Operations, but I had recently taken over the *Left Coast* too. I had no interest in reducing my workload. I still considered career advancement a high priority.

For the first time I made use of a wheelchair accessible taxicab. In this case, I was transported from the airport to my hotel in Portland, Oregon. Until then, I hadn't even known all large cities had such taxis. Our office sat across the street from the hotel. Therefore, I didn't need a rental car. I spent two nights in Portland and took the same taxi back to the airport so I could fly to Denver.

In Denver I rented a wheelchair accessible van with hand controls. I spent three days at an enormous trade show and conference and put a lot of miles on my scooter. I encountered no problems. From there I flew to Las Vegas to spend the weekend with my childhood best friend, Dave.

Dave owned a pickup truck, so we disassembled the scooter into three pieces and loaded it into the back of his truck whenever we drove from point A to point B. I learned that Vegas is a highly accessible city if you have a power wheelchair or scooter—not so much if you are a slow walker. There's too damn much territory to cover.

Dave had earned his Electrical Engineering degree with me at the University of Maine but chose to make a nice living from his love of music instead. Vegas is an ideal place to create music and enjoy the single life. Dave had never married but tended toward serial monogamy. Because he was always involved in a serious relationship, he avoided falling victim to the more self-destructive temptations in Vegas.

On this visit I learned that Dave was finally going to get married. One evening we met up with his fiancée, Teena, and walked the Vegas strip to see what kind of fun we could stir up. A couple of times during the evening, being the consummate gentleman, I offered the lovely Teena the opportunity to sit on my lap and enjoy a ride on my scooter. She always accepted. The last time I made this offer, I took my hands off the steering tiller and put her in charge of the driving. That may have been a mistake.

Teena drove like a maniac. The fact that she had matched me beer for beer all evening probably didn't help. I had only a slight buzz, but I outweighed her by about 100 pounds. We zipped through the crowded casinos, Teena in my lap and her hands on the controls, with total disregard for the safety of anyone in our path. People dove out of the way to keep from being run over.

If any two groups of people are given a free pass for reckless behavior, it is beautiful women and cripples (and if anyone is given a free pass for using the word cripple, it's a cripple). Even though we were completely out of control and laughing so hard we could barely stay in the seat, nobody said a cross word to us. I'm sure we left carnage in our wake, but we never looked back. I still smile every time I recall that ride.

It might seem that my travels in a scooter and using a wheelchair accessible van could be a huge burden. In fact, it was the opposite. Here I was, a guy with MS, who traveled all over the country for business and pleasure, like an ordinary person. These trips made me feel engaged in life.

Sometimes, when I traveled alone in my scooter, and later in my wheelchair, airline attendants, hotel clerks, or car rental agents would ask me, "Are you traveling alone, sir?" I hoped to hear that question because I loved to deliver the response.

"Yes. Yes, I am."

* * *

By the spring of 2008, I had become a proficient scooter pilot. I drove the Blue Streak almost everywhere I went, indoors and out. I always carried the forearm crutches on the back, but I used them less and less as my leg strength continued to deteriorate.

The scooter was a flawed device, however, and I, its flawed driver.

Our longtime friends Marco and Jean, regular weekend drinking buddies of ours back in Lincoln, came to visit us in April of 2008. We started the evening at a Portland sports bar called Rivalries, a 10-minute drive from our house. April is the only time of the year when the Boston Red Sox, Bruins, and Celtics each play regular-season games, and all three teams were on TV that night. Because Rivalries has an abundance of screens, we kept tabs on all the games from our table.

Everyone felt nostalgic that night, and we wanted to drink until we got drunk—except Kim, the designated driver, and maybe Jean because she's an adult. Marco and I conceived a game where we would do a shot whenever the Red Sox or Bruins scored. We couldn't think of a way to incorporate the Celtics game into our drinking without suffering alcohol poisoning. It turned out to be a great night for the Boston teams and a memorable evening for all of us.

We eventually tired of Rivalries, and Rivalries tired of us. We slid into an Irish pub called Ri Ra, which had the Red Sox on their bar TV. We continued our drinking game until we could drink no more. It had been a while since I consumed so much alcohol, and things got away from me. We stepped out of Ri Ra and found ourselves on the sidewalk of Commercial Street in Portland, Maine—the heart of the Old Port District where all the cool bars, fancy restaurants, and beautiful people can be found.

I steered my scooter down the wide, brick sidewalk, in front of Kim and our friends. I dodged imaginary obstacles, carving a path like a blindfolded slalom skier. A solitary man stood in the middle of the sidewalk ahead of me. I became inspired to cheer him up by demonstrating just how merry my band of followers and I were.

I moved the speed dial on my scooter from turtle all the way up to hare and locked in on this unsuspecting pedestrian. I planned to run circles around him until he smiled, and then I would continue down the sidewalk and seek out another forlorn soul to sprinkle with my magical happy dust. About halfway through my loop-the-loop around this man, however, the laws of physics asserted themselves.

According to Wikipedia, centrifugal force is "the apparent outward force that draws a rotating body away from the center of rotation." Well, away I went. I spilled my three-wheeled scooter on its side. The hard brick surface broke my fall, but because I was inebriated, I felt no pain. Instead, I considered my predicament to be about the funniest thing I had ever experienced. I laughed with such intensity that I began gasping for air.

Mine was only one perspective on these events. The innocent, unsuspecting soul whom I had targeted—he had another. He saw a drunk, handicapped man, who had tipped over his scooter on to the pavement and injured himself so severely he seemed to be laboring to take his last breaths.

My posse ran forward and assessed the debacle for what it was. They attempted to put the pedestrian at ease, but he had not signed up for this. Although he soon understood the situation, he remained traumatized.

When a larger-than-average disabled man falls down drunk, it's not easy to raise him. Somehow my team of three people plus the pedestrian, with scant cooperation from me, gathered me up and poured me back on to my scooter. I had only a few minor scratches and bumps to show for it. I should have been embarrassed beyond consolation, but I wasn't (and oddly, I still am not).

Kim didn't take me directly home, though she did cut me off from drinking for the rest of the night. They worked some food into me, and I said some funny, but not creepy things to a waitress. I never fell off my scooter again that night, or ever.

That was the last time I became drunk. Although I find intoxicated behavior to be boorish and immature, it feels like a loss to no longer have the option to be boorish and immature.

CHAPTER 29

iBot

There is no relationship between human and machine more intimate than that between a wheelchair and its user. The chair serves not only the function of legs, but also couch, recliner, dining room chair, car seat, chaise lounge, dog walker, coat rack, drink holder, getaway vehicle, and shopping cart. It is, therefore, ironic that the customary term for such a condition is *confined to a wheelchair*, when, in fact, the more accurate term is *empowered by a wheelchair*.

Even so, it's an absurd proposition to commit oneself to a wheelchair voluntarily. Isn't a wheelchair supposed to be forced upon its user? Shouldn't there be a made-for-TV moment, set in a hospital, that unfolds something like this:

> "What the hell is that doing in here?"
>
> "It's a wheelchair, Jimmy, and you've got to learn to use one."
>
> "I won't, Pa! I can't! I refuse to leave this hospital in a wheelchair. I can walk just fine. Watch me."
>
> "No, Jimmy!"
>
> Jimmy takes one step and crumples to the cold, hard floor, tearing out his IVs.
>
> Ma glares at Pa. She lays her hand gently on Jimmy's cheek and says, "It's okay, Jimmy. You don't have to sit in that chair today. We'll get you back up in bed, and you just rest."

With a progressive disease, however, there is no dramatic scene. You wrestle with the idea for months or even years. Some days you're almost sure it's time, and other days the concept of a chair with wheels seems ridiculous. Then, at least in my case, unexpected events bring a new perspective.

I saw my first iBot wheelchair on a television commercial in the middle of the night. Marketers must know insomnia is common among the disabled. I perused their website, and I began to see things differently. This wasn't a mobility aid to fight but a life-changing tool to embrace. The iBot was not my mother's wheelchair.

The website demonstrated the versatility of the iBot. In standard mode, it performed similarly to most power wheelchairs. In four-wheel-drive mode, the iBot could navigate rough terrain and climb sidewalk curbs. In balance mode, the iBot would rise onto two wheels and operate almost like a Segway, placing the operator at eye level with standing people. The fourth mode? Stairclimbing. Yeah, this freaking wheelchair could climb stairs all day long.

If I had to be in a wheelchair, I wanted it to be the most advanced one ever made. I signed up for a demo and received a phone call a few days later from Independence Technology, the manufacturer, to schedule a home test drive.

On April 10, 2008, Darcy showed up at my house. She unloaded the demonstration iBot from her van and drove it into my house. Mounting the iBot for the first time felt like boarding a roller coaster. I knew I would be in for the ride of my life. Darcy pushed some buttons to calibrate the iBot for my weight, and I began the test drive.

I can't count how many times people have asked me if I was frightened when I first used the iBot in balance mode, there in my living room. My typical response is, "Maybe I should have been freaked out, but I wasn't." Although I can understand why people ask such a question, I felt safe and comfortable in every iBot configuration, right from the beginning.

Given that there were no stairs in my house, we used the two steps from the back deck to the ground for a less than satisfying stairclimbing demo. I got a better feel for that mode by watching videos at their website.

In Maine, we refer to April as mud season. The recently melted snow had left my lawn soft and spongy. At Darcy's urging, I put the iBot in four-wheel-drive mode and slogged all around the yard without getting stuck. I was at once impressed with the iBot and concerned for my lawn. Everywhere I drove, I left two deep, parallel ruts in my wake. They disappeared after a few weeks.

After Darcy left with her iBot, Kim said, "You looked like you enjoyed yourself."

"That was one of the most incredible experiences of my life. Can you believe what that chair will do?"

"I didn't know something like that was even possible."

"For months now, when I've thought about a wheelchair, I worried about how others might perceive me. But if I went out in the world in an iBot, I could turn the tables. Healthy people would almost be jealous or at least wouldn't pity me."

The next step in the process required me to spend a few hours at Northeast Rehab Hospital in Salem, New Hampshire. A two-way interview ensued. I further evaluated the iBot (enjoyable but unnecessary). An independent consultant—a physical therapist named Jean— ran me through the paces to make sure I met all the criteria, mental and physical, for operating this complex device.

Jean spent a lot more time than Darcy had teaching me all the features of the iBot. This facility had a set of practice stairs, so I got a better feel for that function. Jean scrutinized my every move and asked me a slew of questions about my condition and about how I intended to use the iBot.

Ever since I fell in love with the iBot during my home test drive, a lingering doubt had nagged at me. Toward the end of our session, I felt comfortable with Jean and impressed by her knowledge and professionalism, so I spoke up. "Can I ask your opinion on something?"

She stopped scribbling notes on a clipboard and gave me her full attention. "Please, go ahead."

"I love the iBot. But I can still function using my scooter and forearm crutches. Am I jumping the gun by going with an elaborate power wheelchair right now? Am I just so intrigued by the technology that it's clouding my judgment?"

She paused for a moment, and then said what I wanted to hear.

"No, it's not too early for you to get a wheelchair. Your condition warrants it."

"Thanks. I'm glad to hear you say that—"

"On the other hand," she interrupted, "I'm not sure the iBot is the right wheelchair for you."

"Really? I thought I operated it pretty well today."

"It's not that you're unable to use the iBot in your current condition. It's that I worry about how long it will be suitable for you, due to your worsening MS. You may soon need a different kind of wheelchair."

I hadn't seen this coming, and I found her statement absurd. "What do you mean?" I blurted out. "What could possibly prevent me from using this wheelchair?"

Jean looked down for a moment, gathered herself, and continued. "Well, since you asked . . . " She spoke in detail for several minutes, spelling out the declines in function I might experience in the coming years, and how the iBot was not as adaptable as other wheelchairs. It had inadequate head support if my trunk and neck weakened. It was not ideal for skin ulcers if I became unable to adjust my position throughout the day. If I developed vision problems or my hands became so weak I couldn't control the joystick or the other knobs and buttons, this wheelchair would no longer work for me. It had a minimal recline function and no leg raise functions, which might become important later, she explained. Before long, I got her point and didn't want to hear more, but I sat there politely while she finished.

No medical professional, not even Dr. Muscat, had given me as thorough a worst-case scenario as this one, and it was sobering. True to my nature, however, I compartmentalized the negative comments and focused on the positive—I no longer had to wonder if I was disabled *enough* to proceed with the purchase of an iBot.

I said to Jean, "I hadn't thought about it that way. Thanks for sharing your concerns with me, but I'm willing to take that chance. I've got to have one of these chairs. What's the next step?"

"As long as you understand the financial risk you're taking, that this expensive chair could become obsolete for you, it's your choice to make. I'm going to approve you for the purchase of an iBot. I'll let Darcy from Independence Technology know, and she can walk you through the ordering process."

Although I had made the wheelchair decision, my insurance company categorized this device as *not medically necessary*. Medicare, and, therefore, most private insurance companies, don't consider themselves in the business of improving the ability of disabled people to get out in the world. They're only responsible for helping us move from bedroom to kitchen to bathroom, perpetuating our miserable existence, not elevating it.

With no reimbursement forthcoming, I did what any red-blooded American would. I charged the whole damn thing, a little over $24,000, to my credit card. Then, my brothers agreed to sell a piece of property the three of us owned. Our dream had been to someday build a hunting camp there. Year after year had passed, however, with no progress. The time had come to put the asset to use. Andy and Tom gave me a generous cut of the proceeds, and I paid off my credit card debt, but not before accumulating hundreds of dollars worth of reward points.

A few weeks after placing the order, I received notification that my iBot would be ready for pickup and training on July 11, 2008. I had already learned through my procession of assistive devices that, although the day I adopted each new mobility aid marked a milestone in my disease progression, the days prior were some of my worst, and the days immediately afterward were some of my best. When I resisted a new aid, because of embarrassment or guilt about admitting defeat, I missed out on life. When I accepted help, the world opened up for me. I couldn't wait for July 11.

Kim and I arrived first thing in the morning at the same rehab hospital where I had been evaluated for the iBot a couple of months earlier. This time both Darcy and Jean stayed for the entire day.

Kim accompanied me so she could learn to be a stair-climbing assistant. If a set of stairs had an adequate hand railing, I could tackle them solo. Otherwise, I needed an assistant. Kim trained four hours that day to become qualified.

I once read a book that described the training regimen for Navy Seals. I noticed similarities between Seal boot camp and iBot boot camp. Sure, my training only lasted a single day, and although Darcy and Jean sometimes used their *serious* voices, they rarely made me do push-ups and almost never shot live ammunition over my head.

But, as with the Navy Seal training, my instructors crammed oodles of information into my head in a short period and made me practice and practice until I could operate my wheelchair in my sleep. At the end of the day, they tested me to make sure I had mastered the necessary skills. And, as with Seal boot camp, I came out of iBot boot camp a changed person. In my case, I emerged as a Cyborg that iBot users morph into—an organism with both artificial and biological systems.

The iBot had several maximum speed settings, configurable only by an authorized therapist. I don't know if Jean was messing with my head or not (drill instructor that she was), but early in the day, she made it clear that new users never leave her training sessions with the fastest speed enabled. I accepted the challenge. Later in the afternoon, when she agreed to configure my iBot for maximum speed, I felt badass.

Near the end of the day, Kim and I watched a short film graphically demonstrating what could happen when operating the iBot improperly. The actors were trained stuntmen. So far, I've not emulated any of the spectacular crashes shown in that video, even though I have pushed the iBot beyond its stated capacity many times.

After the final exam I signed a pile of papers and took ownership of my iBot. Smiles and high-fives abounded as we posed for group pictures. I reflected on what wonderful jobs Darcy and Jean had. At the end of each training session, they knew they had changed someone's life. I rarely enjoyed that feeling at the end of my workdays.

On the drive home Kim and I found ourselves alone with the iBot. Our trainers were no longer there, approving or disapproving of every move. This reminded me of the drive home from the hospital so many years earlier with our first child, wondering if we were ready for the added responsibility, but excited about the future.

* * *

A couple of weeks later, Kim and I drove up to visit my parents and show them the iBot. They had seen me in the scooter on several occasions, but I usually left it out in the van and used my forearm crutches when I went inside their house. I worried how they would react when they saw me in a wheelchair.

I immediately noticed that, although the design of their kitchen and living room accommodated one wheelchair, it was a little tight for two. My mother and I had to be careful about who went where and when. I demonstrated the various iBot modes for them. We went out on their back deck to show off the stair-climbing mode. Both my parents found the iBot fascinating.

I can't know how they felt about me showing up at their house in a wheelchair for the first time, but they appeared to take it in stride. They didn't put on one face for me and another face for my brothers, like when I told them of my MS diagnosis seven years earlier.

It had been a few months since I had seen my mother, and on this visit I noticed Mom looked older and frailer than ever. I now know that she suffered from repeated urinary tract infections and constipation. She battled age-related macular degeneration and was slowly going blind. Earlier in the year, her muscle spasticity became so problematic she had a Baclofen pump installed in her abdomen, feeding the muscle relaxant directly into her spinal cord. The doctors had difficulty adjusting the dosage from the pump. It seemed always to deliver too much or too little Baclofen. I wondered how much more she could bear before becoming distraught.

At the same visit where I introduced my iBot, my mother told me she had been evaluated for a new wheelchair. All her chairs up to that point had been simple—no recline, no leg lift, no other advanced features. This new wheelchair was well overdue. Its functions would help with her weakening muscles and growing spasticity. I was thrilled for her.

But the wheelchair never came.

CHAPTER 30

Vernice

In 1908, when Cataldo Battaglini turned 18, his parents kicked him out of their home in Pofi, Italy. There wasn't enough food to go around. Southern Italy was suffering from widespread corruption, rebellion, and starvation, not to mention several natural disasters including earthquakes and mudslides. He and his 22-year-old brother, Joseph, boarded a ship and sailed to the United States.

Cataldo earned his citizenship by enlisting in the United States Army during World War I. After an overseas tour of a little over a year, he became a lumberjack in Maine where he met and married his American-born wife, Helen. In 1925, she gave birth to my Aunt Vivian, and in 1934 to my mother, Vernice. Sometime after his honorary discharge from the military, he felt compelled to shed his lyrical name of Cataldo Battaglini and become Carl Batleno, morphing from butterfly to caterpillar. Because of "Grampy Carl," my brothers and I and our descendants have some Italian blood, and we're proud of it.

In 1945, the dashing James Bayley swept Aunt Vivian off her feet, married her, and moved her across the country to Santa Barbara, California. One year into their marriage, Aunt Vivian gave birth to Jimmy. She lobbied her parents to allow her little sister Vernice to spend her eighth-grade year in Santa Barbara. She needed help with the new baby. To everyone's surprise, Carl and Helen allowed it.

The only accounts I have from that year are conveyed by the photographs my mother left behind. If the images can be trusted, young Vernice had a magical year in California. In one picture with three other classmates, somebody wrote the phrase "the Four Musketeers" on the back. In another photo, she stood beside a brash young man named Wesley. He stuck his tongue out at the camera and Mom rolled

159

her eyes, yet she leaned toward him, not away. In other photos, she posed at vineyards, oceanfront vistas, and sandy beaches.

The Maine to Santa Barbara connection has remained strong over the years. In 1964 Paulana, Vivian's daughter, spent her sophomore year of high school living with us in Lincoln. Vivian, her children, and her grandchildren have made the trip to Maine numerous times. Twice after her accident, Mom visited her sister in California. (Dad never went.) My brothers or I find ourselves in Santa Barbara every few years.

Because she had spent time in exotic California, when Vernice returned to Maine and began her freshman year at the high school in Lincoln, she had acquired a certain mystique. For example, she came to school that autumn carrying a purse. None of the other girls had purses yet. They did soon afterward.

Carl was a strict, traditional father. Once, in high school, Mom's friend Debby teased her when she wasn't allowed to go to a party. "Just because you can do anything you want doesn't mean that I can," Vernice snapped, in a rare moment of anger.

Debby introduced Vernice to Theodore Sturgeon, three years older, who became the lucky man to catch her eye. Ted and Vernice married in 1951, the same year she graduated at age 17. Although salutatorian of her class, Mom never seriously considered going to college. She had fallen in love, and her parents approved of the groom and the marriage.

* * *

In October of 2008, Mom was admitted to the hospital in Bangor when she became delusional and agitated, classic symptoms of Baclofen withdrawal. The doctors suspected problems with her Baclofen pump.

Andy, who lived near the hospital and saw Mom daily, told me what to expect when I visited. Her normally sweet personality had disappeared, replaced with an angry, accusatory, and paranoid one—a different person altogether. But that's not what Kim and I found when we drove the two hours north to see her. Instead, Mom smiled and spoke with the same upbeat tone she always had, just like my visit with her after the accident in 1969. Although sick and in the hospital, she maintained her good spirits. I didn't mention the horror stories I'd heard about her behavior. I'm sure she had no memory of them.

As I looked upon my mother, not zipping around in her wheelchair, but in a hospital bed, old and frail, I felt a sense of urgency. Although she seemed well on her way to recovery from the Baclofen withdrawal, at 74 years old, having been a quadriplegic for 39 years, she was wearing down. I had so many questions, but I didn't ask them. I'm left only to imagine such a conversation. It might have gone like this:

"Mom, do you mind if I ask you about a few things?"

"Of course not, Mitchy. Anything."

I gathered my courage and inched closer. My foot pedals clanged against her bed frame, a metal-against-metal reminder of the difficulties of physical intimacy in a wheelchair. I rehearsed the question in my head, and began. "Has Dad always been this difficult, or did your accident make him that way?"

"I wish I could say he changed after the accident, but he's always been a challenge to live with. You shouldn't be too hard on your father, though. He's a good man."

"I know. I know."

My confidence grew, and I fired off the next question without hesitation. "You and Dad are so different, though. How did you end up together? Why did you choose him?"

"He tried hard to get my attention. I was flattered. And I loved being around him. He had boundless energy and always wanted to take me fishing or for walks in the woods where he could show off everything he knew about plants and trees and animals. And the way he talked about family and friends, I could tell he was a decent man. Even if he had occasional problems with his temper, he never scared me. We spent a lot of time together during my senior year in high school, and eventually, we fell in love. Back then, girls weren't encouraged to go off to college. Grampy Carl was traditional. He wanted me to get married, and I liked that idea too."

I moved on to the deeper topics. "Mom, how have you done it all these years? What's your secret to staying strong and living such a positive life, despite your challenges?"

"My challenges? Everyone has something. What I've faced is not nearly as bad as what others have had to contend with, even people who appear healthy and happy."

Unsatisfied, I pushed back. "That's true. Still, I'd like to know your philosophy of life. I'm facing some of the same difficulties as you, and I'm scared as hell. I need to understand how you stay so positive."

"What are you scared of, exactly?"

"I don't think it's the disease so much as I'm afraid of not living up to your example."

"Oh, don't be silly, Mitchy. You're already there. You and I are cut from the same cloth. We stay positive because, well because what other choice is there?"

What other choice is there? Can it be that simple?

Emboldened, I asked the unthinkable question. "Can you tell me about the night you got hurt? Dad didn't give us many details."

She paused, lowered her voice, and said, "I suppose it's time I gave you the whole story." She moved her hand toward the edge of her bed. I leaned over, reached as far as I could, and managed to touch the end of my middle finger to the end of hers. She spoke in detail about what transpired that night in 1969, and for the weeks and months afterward. When her voice trailed off, I looked up at her face. She had closed her eyes and fallen into a peaceful slumber.

Regrettably, this conversation never took place. I didn't possess the wisdom or courage to ask those questions. It was not in my makeup. Stoicism and restraint, those were the twin pillars, or emotional crutches, of my character.

Mom didn't tell me what attracted her to my father, but I feel my made-up version is close. She never gave me the pep talk about finding my way to happiness, although I'd like to think the conversation would have gone as I wrote it. And she never told me, or anyone else as far as I know, the compelling story of the night she got hurt and how she survived that first year.

Instead, I asked her about the hospital food and the quality of the nursing care. She inquired about my kids and my job. I so wish the conversation had been more like the one I imagined because it was the last conversation I would ever have with my mother.

When we got home from the hospital a few hours later, I called Tom and said, "Andy told me that Mom was disoriented and paranoid, but she seems to have pulled out of it. She was her regular old self today. I think she's on her way to recovery."

There was silence on the other end of the phone, and then Tom said, "I'm surprised to hear you say that. We got there about an hour after you left, and she acted exactly how Andy told me she would. I had never seen her like that before."

My heart sank. I shook my head. *Fucking Baclofen pump. Can't those people do their jobs and get that running correctly?*

"Maybe she'll come around," I said.

"Based on what I saw today, I'm not hopeful," Tom said.

Andy called me the next evening, Saturday night, to let me know Mom had taken a turn for the worse. She had contracted pneumonia and could only breathe with the assistance of a respirator. When Kim and I arrived at the hospital on Sunday morning, we found Mom in an induced coma in the intensive care ward. It didn't look good. Tom's daughter, Kaitlin, a nursing student at the time, had stayed in Mom's room and attended to her for days on end.

My father, brothers, and I met with Mom's medical team in a conference room. The lead physician gave us the bad news. We faced two problems. First, Mom had a Do Not Resuscitate order, and it had been violated. In the heat of the moment the night before, when it looked like they would lose her, the medical team installed a respirator, and it remained in place. Second, she had grown so weak she almost certainly wouldn't survive this illness, respirator or not. Even if she did somehow recover, she would have suffered considerable damage to her health. The lead doctor told us we needed to decide whether to keep her on life support or let her go. The doctors left the four of us alone to discuss the options.

It occurred to me that this might be Mom's best *opportunity* to die. She had been a quadriplegic for longer than she hadn't and had fought the good fight. Now, she was nearly blind from age-related macular degeneration. Her body had grown weak and tired even before entering the hospital. She had severe bouts of spasticity that the Baclofen pump could not control. Even if she recovered enough to leave the hospital, her quality of life would be horrible. We all want to live vivaciously until the end, and then die quickly, don't we? This was perhaps her only chance to do that. *What would I want my family to choose if I were in this situation?* That settled it for me, because I would not be surprised if, like so many things in my life, the circumstances of my death mimic my mother's.

But I kept those thoughts to myself and made my argument based on medical factors like the doctor had done. We didn't rush to a decision. We talked. We sat in silence. We talked some more. In due time, we reached unanimous agreement. We would let her go.

We told the medical team of our decision. They outlined for us how things would likely play out and then left the room to set the process in motion. We prepared ourselves for what would be a difficult 24 hours or less; Mom's new life expectancy.

The medical staff removed her respirator and adjusted the drugs so she would wake up from her induced coma. We worried about which Vernice we would see—the real one or the imposter. Soon, she became alert and appeared comfortable, although soreness from the respirator prevented her from speaking. She didn't need words to let us know that the authentic Vernice had returned. We gathered around her bed and enjoyed our last moments with her.

I held her hand, the most distinctive part of her body, for a few minutes. Both of her hands curled up unnaturally. She could open them slightly, but never all the way. If not for these contorted append-ages, you might temporarily forget about her paralysis and consider her a healthy person who simply preferred to sit in a chair with wheels.

After a couple of hours, Mom fell asleep and never woke up. We all went home except Tom and Andy. They stayed with her into the early morning hours when she took her last breath. More than once I had breached the childhood contract my mother and I made—our silent promise never to be apart. Now the agreement had expired; it died with her.

Being part of the decision to let my mother go and spending time with her as she faded away that evening—those were the most trying times of my life. As devastated as I was, I accepted that she had gotten everything out of her broken body that she possibly could have. This provided me, and I suppose all of us, with some consolation.

My father's greatest fear was that he would pass away before my mother, leaving her helpless and destitute. So, although I don't believe he wanted her to go so soon, he surely took consolation in the fact that he hadn't failed her in this way.

For years my brothers and I had discussed which scenario would be better for everyone involved—if Mom died first or Dad. We agreed Mom could handle Dad's passing better than he could handle hers. We thought Dad would be lost without Mom's guidance. For those first few days, however, he held up well. He became a mess only after everyone went home and left him alone.

Sometimes when a loved one passes away, even during the height of grief, thoughts creep in like *I need to secure such and such a possession.* Often the prize is coveted by more than one survivor. But in my case, nobody—not my brothers, not my father, not anyone I knew—had an interest in the same item I did. I wanted my mother's wheelchair. Not the old clunky one she had used for the last ten years. I needed a backup for the iBot, like the beautiful, fully loaded, power chair she had ordered through Medicare and had not yet received. So, two days after she died, I called Black Bear Medical and instructed them to deliver the chair to me instead.

"Why would your mother not take delivery?"

"Because she passed away on the 28th."

"I'm sorry for your loss, but Medicare has rules about these things. I'm afraid we need to cancel the order."

"There's no way around—"

"No, we can't deliver a deceased person's wheelchair to somebody else."

I thought about explaining the special circumstances, about the silent promise between my mother and me, about what happened to each of our cervical spines in the summers of our thirty-fifth years, about what she would have wanted. Instead, I felt stupid for even having asked.

* * *

After attending my mother's funeral service and reception, I went to bed early at my father's house. Kim wasn't tired, so she joined a group of friends and relatives to commiserate at a local bar. It was Halloween night, 2008. The subject of Mom's accident came up, and two of my cousins told Kim a story different from the one my father had told Andy, Tom, and me. I later determined they didn't have the details correct, but their version was closer to the truth than Dad's.

When Kim came to bed, she spoke to me about the rumors she had heard, assuming I would have an interest. I didn't. I considered this story settled, off-limits, and even sacred (in my atheistic way). Over the years Kim brought the subject up on occasion, and I continued to ignore her each time. I wasn't ready.

Kim did find an interested listener in Andy's wife, Karen. In fact, a couple of weeks after my mother died, when we all got together at the house to go through her things, Kim heard Karen ask my father, "So, Ted, what really happened the night Vernice got hurt?"

"I didn't talk about it when she was alive, and I'm damn sure not going to talk about it now that she's gone."

CHAPTER 31
The Cardholder

In 2008, a couple of months before my mother passed, Kim and I sat down with her parents to play nickel-ante poker. On my first deal, I shuffled the cards overhand a few times then split the deck and placed half in each hand. I dovetailed the two half-decks together and performed the flamboyant, yet surprisingly easy, cascade finish. I repeated the overhand a few more times and dealt the cards. For most of my life, I had followed this shuffling routine, but on this day something didn't feel right.

A *dullness* had crept in, like what I experienced in my legs years earlier. I wouldn't call it a *numbness*. My sense of touch remained unaffected. My fingers just didn't move as precisely as I needed them to for such an intricate activity. The subtlety of the deficit, however, made me wonder if I had imagined the whole thing. I didn't assume MS had moved to my upper body, but I put myself on notice, and I paid closer attention.

Several times a day, I evaluated my hands by holding them out in front of me and running them through a series of tests. Each time I did this, everything checked out. After a while, my concern diminished, and my hand testing stopped.

A few weeks later, while taking notes in a meeting, I felt that dull sensation again, and it didn't go away. I experienced it every time I held a pen. Within days, I noticed it when I typed.

From the moment of my diagnosis, I assumed MS and I had reached a gentlemen's agreement. MS could have my legs, but I would maintain control of the rest of my body. As it turned out, no such deal existed. I didn't have any leverage in this negotiation.

It felt like being diagnosed all over again, but with another, more horrible disease. Paraplegics, people with paralysis only in the lower body, still have so many options in life. Quadriplegics, people with paralysis in all four extremities, lead a more limited existence. Paraplegics can drive and type and feed themselves. Quads often can't. With my new upper body symptoms, it seemed more likely than ever I would end up a quad like my mother, or worse.

Until the disease moved north of my waistline, I could envision life as a paraplegic, and it didn't scare me. The game had rules, and the field of play had boundaries. I couldn't participate in certain activities anymore, but with adaptations, the important things in life—enjoying time with friends and family, eating, breathing, moving—would still be possible. When my upper body became vulnerable, the game changed. My future became ill-defined and frightening.

Still, I had already faced so many disappointments, had been told so many worst-case scenarios, that I didn't fall into despair. My emotional defense mechanisms performed admirably—a well-oiled machine if there ever was one. Like my mother, I never asked, "Why me?" I only wondered, "What can we do now?"

One day, about a year after my mother passed, I looked down at my hands as they rested in my lap. I opened and closed them. The fingers didn't lie flat anymore. They appeared almost claw-like.

Yes, I've seen this before.

And then it struck me. These appendages were no longer my own. MS had stolen my hands and replaced them with my mother's.

Today, given the manner in which my physical condition has grown to mimic hers, in more ways than just our hands, I sometimes wonder if my disability is only a psychosomatic emulation of my beloved mother. Could my paralysis be nothing more than a subconscious yearning for the days when we were inseparable, when we existed almost as one? I wish it were so, because then I could be cured with a handful of visits to a shrink. Unfortunately, the lesions on my spine are not simply in my head.

* * *

When my mother came home from the hospital in 1970, talented friends and relatives devised homemade aids for her. They built a cup holder for her wheelchair and poles with hooks or other attachments on the end to help her reach things. Junior Bowers, a family friend and the carpenter who built the Edwards Street house, fashioned a wooden cardholder for Mom.

Mom played Bridge at a high skill level. Later, she used the cardholder to enjoy games like UNO with her grandchildren. She used the holder so often over the years that it became worn and smooth, but it held up well.

While going through my mother's things after she passed away, Kim came across Mom's cardholder and held it up for me in a questioning manner. I said, "Sure, let's take that. You never know." I noticed the name "Vernice Sturgeon" etched on to the front, just in case anyone wondered to whom it belonged. This was my childhood handwriting. I remembered personalizing the cardholder for Mom when she first got it.

After the funeral, we took the cardholder home, and it sat in our attic for a few years. During that time, my hand function slowly deteriorated, and one day I asked Kim to dig it out of storage. I assumed something as ancient and simple as this device wouldn't be sufficient for my needs. I was wrong. We tried a couple of store-bought models, but they proved inferior to my mother's. Today, I use her almost 50-year-old cardholder exclusively.

If I were a religious man, I might say that when I'm playing cards, Mom is looking down on me with a big smile on her face. I have two problems with this. First, I'm not a religious man. Second, even if I were, she obviously isn't watching over my card playing because I don't win any more often than I did before I started using her cardholder.

The decline of my upper body impacted more than my card playing and typing. Only a year after purchasing the iBot I began to have difficulty with solo iBot stair climbing. Solo climbing requires moderate upper body strength and hand dexterity, two things I was steadily losing. I went out in style, though.

I had an appointment on the second floor of a medical building. As we finished up the therapy, all the lights went out. I'm not sure why. But I wasn't bothered since my appointment was over anyway. My therapist, Kristen, pointed out, "I bet the elevator isn't working. You're stuck until the power comes back on."

I smiled and asked, "Do you want to see something cool?"

I had used the stair-climbing mode many times before, but never when I had been stranded on an upper floor.

Because of the power outage, the stairwell bustled with activity. By the time I descended from the second floor to the first, a large group of people had formed to watch me, and another group waited for me to get out of their damn way. I'm glad the power went out, though. It made my day.

Although I still climb stairs in the iBot with Kim's assistance, I never again went solo.

CHAPTER 32
The Evangelist

I've heard it said that bad news comes in threes. As I grieved my mother's death and began fearing the migration of MS to my upper body, one more disappointment came my way in 2008. In December, less than six months after I purchased my iBot, I received this letter from Independence Technology:

> Dear Customer:
>   We're writing today to inform you that Independence Technology L.L.C. is ceasing sales and marketing of the iBot® Mobility System in January 2009. This is a difficult announcement for Independence Technology because we believe that the iBot® Mobility System has spurred innovation in the mobility market and has helped people with disabilities see and experience the world in a new and unique way . . .
> Independence Technology, L.L.C.

From the time I took delivery of my iBot until the moment I read this letter, I had been an evangelist. Everywhere I went, I spread the good word about this life-changing device. Nobody with a progressive, crippling disease had ever been more delighted than me to obtain a wheelchair, not only because it improved my life, but because I became part of something bigger than myself. I felt proud to be one of several hundred people in the world to own an iBot, and I wanted anyone who needed one to have that same opportunity. Few causes come along in an individual's life that are this deeply personal, this rewarding, this freaking awesome.

And, poof! It was gone.

After the letter I still showed off my iBot's capabilities, but I said things like, "Look at the cool tricks this chair can do," instead of, "This chair will redefine what it means to be disabled." To make matters worse, each time I saw the excitement on the faces of these onlookers, I felt obligated to extinguish it with the truth. More than once I couldn't bring myself to do that, and I left them thinking they could buy one of these chairs for Grandma or their husband or their 18-year-old who had broken his neck after being hit by a drunk driver.

I suffered a loss, and I grieved. I'm still grieving. Today my iBot remains operational, but I live in constant fear of it going into alarm mode or breaking some irreplaceable part.

The iBot program failed for two primary reasons. First, the FDA considered it to be a Class III medical device, subjecting this chair to much more oversight than all other wheelchairs, which are typically Class II medical devices. Any modifications or improvements Independence Technology tried to make to the iBot were, therefore, expensive and burdensome. Recently, the FDA reclassified the iBot as a Class II medical device. Too late for this version of the iBot, but helpful for any future reincarnations.

The other reason the iBot failed is that Medicare didn't consider it medically necessary and wouldn't reimburse patients for its purchase. If Medicare won't reimburse patients for a company's wheelchair, the company won't sell many of them.

Our government, which presumably exists to serve the needs of its citizenry, imposed these conditions for failure. Technological progress that improves the lives of some of the most disadvantaged people in our society should move only in one direction—forward. It shouldn't make an appearance and then vanish because of red tape, because of fixable bureaucratic problems. But it did. Our society has advanced further in terms of technology than compassion.

Despite all this, I still appreciated my good fortune in purchasing an iBot before production ceased. If I no longer had a cause to promote, at least I owned one of these chairs myself, and that provided some consolation.

Since obtaining this wheelchair, I had become an iBot exhibitionist. I loved to show off. Whenever someone saw me in balance mode, for example, or spied me climbing stairs, they couldn't look away. They would try not to stare, and it was hilarious for me to watch their struggle.

The situation with mothers and children was different. If a mother saw me coming down the grocery aisle in balance mode, she would typically grab her child and hold him close. Mothers are hardwired to protect their children, so I didn't blame them for a first reaction of that sort. But I think they also pulled their children close to give me plenty of room, to make sure the children didn't bother me.

Small children blurted out questions like, "How come you're in a wheelchair?" This always threw their mothers into a fit of apology, but I let them off the hook quickly. I appreciated the blunt honesty that comes from children not yet fully socialized. Depending on my mood, and my read of how advanced the child might be, I varied my responses from "It's a magic chair" to "I have this disease called multiple sclerosis, and this is a cutting-edge wheelchair called the iBot."

Of course it wasn't only the optics I liked. The iBot gave me a level of mobility I would not have otherwise achieved. Once, I visited a nearby McDonald's restaurant, enticed on a hot summer day by the siren song from their ice cream cone machine. Two sets of heavy doors guarded the main entrance, with no other patrons nearby who might help. When a pickup truck pulled up to the drive-through, I got an idea.

I put my iBot in balance mode, raised myself up to the height of a standing person, and pulled in behind the pickup. When it was my turn, I eased up to the microphone, and the attendant asked for my order. I requested one ice cream cone. She couldn't see my mode of transportation and instructed me to pull my car around to the first window. I waited a safe distance behind the guy in the pickup as he paid for and received his food. This time, he noticed me in the rearview, and I behaved as if this was the most natural thing in the world to be doing.

When I pulled up to the window, I surmised that the cashier was embroiled in an internal battle. Part of her wanted to gush all over me and say, "Oh my God that's the coolest thing I've ever seen." Another part of her, perhaps the result of McDonald's customer service training or just good parenting, compelled her to carry on like nothing strange was happening.

"I bet you don't get many wheelchairs in the drive-through, do you?" I asked.

"No, sir, you're the first one."

Another time, the iBot salvaged an evening out for Kim and me. Every holiday season we try to enjoy a Christmas-themed show in the greater Portland area. One year we scored tickets to the hip-cool Nutcracker Burlesque at the St. Lawrence Arts Center, located in an old church that had been converted to an intimate, and on this occasion erotic, 110-seat theater.

When we arrived at the playhouse, me in my iBot and Kim in her sexy, high-heeled boots, the theater manager led us to the wheelchair lift. We jumped on board. This option looked quicker and easier than having Kim guide me up 20 or so steps.

"It's better if I close the door at this level and operate the lift from upstairs. Is that okay?" asked the manager.

"Absolutely," I said. "Whatever you need to do."

With the benefit of hindsight, I now realize she seemed uncomfortable with the lift from the get-go, hoping for the best, but fearing complications.

She appeared in the glass window of the door one level up, smiling and waving. When she turned the key, we inched up the elevator shaft. Soon, the lift stopped. "Don't worry," she lied, both to herself and us. "Everything is all right. Just one second."

The seconds turned into minutes. Kim said to me, "This isn't good. I'm afraid they don't know what they're doing."

The manager shouted, "I'm so sorry, Mr. and Mrs. Sturgeon. This lift can be a little testy, but we'll get you going in no time."

She called upon other employees to look over the situation. Each of them apologized to us and showed sincere concern for our state of mind—essentially trapped in an elevator. We tried to put everyone at ease so they could concentrate on the technical challenges. As any wheelchair user can attest, when you leave the confines of home and venture out into the disabled-unfriendly world beyond, shit can happen, and you can't let it ruin your outing.

"How are you holding up?" Kim whispered to me.

"I'm doing fine. If you're wondering about my claustrophobia, this isn't the kind of situation that triggers it. I only freak out when I feel squished—when something is pressing against two sides of me."

A couple of minutes later Kim observed, "I bet I could climb to the second-floor landing. Maybe the reduction in weight will be enough so they can restart the lift."

"Good idea," I said.

I let the others know what Kim was about to do. They didn't like it—a patron climbing an elevator shaft—but they didn't know my wife. So Kim, sexy high-heeled boots and all, shimmied up to the next level. The lift still wouldn't move.

We heard the master of ceremonies announce that the show would begin in a few minutes. Kim looked down the elevator shaft at me and frowned. Then she made a critical observation. "You know, you're only about two feet off the bottom floor. If we could somehow get you out that way and use the iBot to climb the stairs, we might still catch the start of the show."

"But how would we get me . . . "

Just then, a plan formulated in my head. "I need a barstool, and I need Kim to climb back down here and help me transfer to it. While I'm doing that, send your two strongest men to the bottom floor so they can lower the iBot off this lift." Everyone became soldiers in a military unit, with me as their general.

They found a stool. When Kim rejoined me, she whispered, "I have to wonder, if this wasn't a burlesque show, would you be so inspired to find a way off this lift?"

"It is? I didn't know that."

"You're a terrible liar!"

"No time for chit-chat. Let's get me on to the stool."

The theater manager, desperate to be useful, had climbed down with Kim. Together, they transferred me from the iBot to the stool. We powered down the iBot and put it in freewheel mode. Kim, the theater manager, and two stagehands carefully lowered the 290-pound iBot from the lift on to the main floor.

After examining the situation, I decided that if I executed an assisted slither half-twist or maybe a compound free-fall 180, perhaps I could transfer from the stool and stick a landing squarely in the waiting iBot. It worked. Greg Louganis, Shaun White, or Nancy Kerrigan would have been proud.

"Quick, get me up those stairs!"

Kim guided the iBot up the staircase with ease, and we found our spot in the front row just in time to see the curtain rise. The manager comped our tickets, but we enjoyed the show so much that we left a donation on our way out. As we exited the theater, a crowd of patrons gathered around the stairwell while Kim expertly directed me and the iBot down the stairs to a chorus of oohs and aahs. Because of the capabilities of the iBot, and our positive attitude, that evening was nothing less than a pleasant night out on the town.

* * *

As this book is going to print, the inventors of the iBot, DEKA Research and Development, a company led by the incomparable Dean Kamen, are partnering with Toyota to produce the next generation of iBot wheelchairs. I can't say for sure if there is another iBot in my future—I certainly hope so—but even if there isn't, this is great news for the disabled community.

CHAPTER 33

Risky Business

The iBot proved invaluable on my business trips. I loved that I could still complete travel assignments, often by myself. My trips were uneventful from the time I got the iBot in July of 2008 through the end of the year. Then the winter of 2009 happened.

In January I flew back to Maine from who-knows-where. For the last leg home to Portland, I boarded my US Air flight in Philadelphia. A winter storm pummeled the Northeast corridor that night, dropping ice, snow, and rain. Not long into the flight, the pilot announced that the Portland Jetport had closed—the runway was a sheet of ice.

The airline rerouted us to a rainy Logan Airport in Boston to wait out the storm. Not long after landing, they terminated our flight. The flight attendant announced that US Air would charter a bus from Logan Airport to the Portland Jetport. I summoned the flight attendant.

"Is this bus wheelchair accessible?" I asked.

"I'm not sure. Let me check."

After a few minutes, he returned and said, "I'm afraid it's not wheelchair accessible." He paused as if it were my turn to speak.

"Then you need to provide me with a cab ride to Portland. I know Boston has lots of wheelchair accessible taxis."

It didn't take long for the airline to confirm they would supply me with a cab ride home—a drive that takes an hour and a half with no traffic or weather issues.

The water falling out of the sky didn't turn to ice until we were about half an hour from my home. Anyone I know, including myself, would have slowed to a crawl on the slippery highway, but not this cab driver. I didn't admonish him, though. After all, he was a professional, and that would have been insulting.

When we arrived at my house, I unloaded from the cab directly into our warm, cozy garage. My head hit the pillow around 3:30 a.m. That was a long day, and it was about to get longer.

We had slept for only a short time when we heard a loud crash from the other end of the house. Kim jumped out of bed to investigate.

"What the hell?" she screamed to nobody in particular.

"What is it?" I wanted to know, but not so badly that I would get up, transfer to my wheelchair, and go out into the living room.

Kim came into the bedroom. "A branch fell right through our kitchen window. There's glass everywhere—in the sink, on the counters, all over the floor, and there's the better part of a tree laying in the kitchen."

Amy's boyfriend at the time, now her husband, Nick, had been sleeping on the couch. He and Kim cleaned up the glass, removed the offending branch from our kitchen, and boarded up the window. What a night.

I often flew out of the Manchester, New Hampshire airport, about a 90-minute drive from my house, because of better connections. A month after my ice storm trip, I flew back into Manchester on a snowy evening. If all went well, I would be home by 10:00 p.m.

It snowed so hard I couldn't differentiate the passing lane from the driving lane on the highway between Manchester and Portsmouth. It was challenging enough to stay between the snowbanks. Every few miles I saw another car off the road. Sometimes emergency vehicles and tow trucks had already arrived. Other times they hadn't, but I never stopped to help. What good would I have been?

Eventually, common sense prevailed over my natural desire to sleep in my bed, and I decided to find a place to spend the night. While I drove in the snow with my hand controls, I worked my smartphone, googled some hotels, called a couple of them, and found a room in Portsmouth. Ninety minutes into what should have been a ninety-minute ride, but only halfway home, I pulled into the hotel parking lot. I transferred from the driver's seat to my iBot, grabbed my suitcase, and put the iBot in four-wheel-drive mode. I opened the side door to the van, lowered the ramp, and drove out into the unplowed parking lot.

As I made my way toward the hotel entrance, my feet acted like a plow in the deep snow. The snowbank I produced in front of me became so high that several times I had to back up a little, and go around it, and start a new snowbank. I'm not sure how I would have managed if not for the four-wheel-drive ability of my iBot. The next morning, I finished my 45-minute drive home in about 45 minutes. In the Northeast, we are well practiced at cleaning up after snowstorms.

But I still had more winter to get through. A month later, I traveled by myself to Houston for a conference. When I arrived at the Portland airport to catch my departing flight, I drove up and down the parking garage several times, looking for one of those coveted handicapped van spots near the elevator. The only one I could find was on the roof. I parked my wheelchair van in the open air, without much thought.

The business trip was fruitful, and the return flight uneventful. However, the plane didn't touch down until just before midnight. I took the elevator to the top floor of the parking garage and surveyed the situation. With my left hand, I pulled my large piece of luggage on wheels, and with my right hand I operated the joystick on my wheelchair. This left me one hand short to open the door from the elevator lobby to the roof of the garage.

I required so much handicapped stuff that I couldn't manage with only a carry-on bag like most business travelers do. An unspoken competition exists among seasoned travelers—a badge of honor. How lightly can you pack, or how long a trip can you go on without checking a bag? This was another indignity I had to suffer on the road. I had become a *bag checker*.

After a couple of tries, I squeezed myself and my bag through the door from the elevator lobby to the parking garage roof. This was the coldest night of the year. It may have been the coldest of the decade. It felt as if I had jumped into an ice bath. Here I sat, in extreme weather, in the middle of the night, all by myself in my wheelchair. If I had become stuck there for any reason, I wonder how long it would have been before I froze into a solid block.

The first challenge was to wheel across the icy roof of the parking garage to my van. Again, thanks to the four-wheel-drive mode of my iBot, I had no difficulty. Next, I needed the automatic side door on my van to open and the ramp to extend. The little motors responsible for those actions groaned and creaked but came through despite temperatures well below zero and wind chills even lower. Once I entered the van, I pushed the close button for the ramp and the side door, and they complied. Although the inside of the vehicle was an icebox, I knew that being out of the wind made me safer.

I transferred from my wheelchair to the driver's seat, inserted the key, and turned it. The engine did not make a comforting sound. It struggled. It protested. "You've got to be kidding," it muttered under its breath. Just when I thought it would never turn over, the engine relented and did what engines are supposed to do. What a relief. I set the heater on high and began the 15-minute drive home. Another late night. Another victory for me over forces that would try to prevent me from doing my job.

After the adrenaline wore off, however, I made a more sober assessment. I had been fortunate on these trips, and I was taking too many risks.

Yet, I had little choice but to continue. My job demanded year-round travel.

CHAPTER 34

Long Overdue

At a routine appointment, Dr. Muscat asked, "How is work going? Have you given any more thought to what we discussed last time?"

"Going on disability? No. I'm still doing fine," I responded.

"Like I said before, I think you will have no difficulty qualifying. When you're ready, I'll do everything I can to help you."

"Thanks. I'm just not there yet."

I meant what I said, but after I left the appointment, I continued to mull it over. I weighed the travel challenges, the recent disease progression in my upper body, cognitive and fatigue problems, and the effort needed to get through each workday carrying the burden of this disease. And I would never feel better. Each year would bring only more difficulties.

In the days and weeks after my appointment with Dr. Muscat, I warmed to the idea of disability retirement. I saw obstacles, however. I had never been good about maintaining separation between my work and personal lives. If asked, I would claim to be a father and husband first, and an engineer and businessperson second. But the time and effort I put into these roles didn't reflect that prioritization. I worked all day, and I kept up with my emails on nights and weekends. I always made myself available.

This would be such a dramatic life change. I worried. *If I eliminate this part of me, what might be the unintended consequences? What if I don't like who I become? If I stop working, will I be giving up on more than my career?*

I also faced practical obstacles. The disability systems, both private insurance and Social Security, are designed for people who get run over by a truck, struck by lightning, or suffer a massive heart attack. They are not designed for people who have a chronic, progressive disease.

In a perfect world, I would have ramped down my hours from 40 or more per week to maybe 30, and then after some period down to 20, and so forth, as my MS progressed. A proper disability insurance system would have provided some level of compensation for lost wages each time I decreased my hours. But that's not how these programs work. Instead, I would have to pick a single moment in time, before which I was a fully functioning employee and after which I was permanently and completely disabled—an arbitrary and absurd requirement.

To further complicate matters, I couldn't request preapproval of these benefits. The disability model assumed something catastrophic had already happened to an employee, and that person sat at home or in the hospital with no paycheck. If I stopped working—a requirement to initiate the process—and one of the organizations rejected my disability application, I would be screwed. How could I get my job back when my physician and I had already made a strong case that I was unfit for it? How difficult would it be to find employment somewhere else when I left my last job because I said I couldn't work anymore?

This would be one of the most important decisions of my life, and I had to get it right. Having weighed all the issues, I considered myself *ready* for disability, but I decided I would wait for some impetus, either having to do with my job or my health. I wanted one more reason to leave—something to help push me out the door.

In April of 2009, my boss invited me, on short notice, to a meeting at corporate headquarters in Cincinnati. The information conveyed in the meeting turned out to be the push I had been looking for. As I waited to board my return flight at the Cincinnati airport, I called Kim.

"I've made a decision," I said.

"Have you?"

"You know how I was waiting for some sign from the universe, even though I don't believe in signs from the universe, to tell me when to stop working? Well, it couldn't have been more clear today. I'm ready."

"Good. I think. What happened?"

"My boss, Dan, outlined a major reorganization where I'll have all new responsibilities. I just don't have the energy or the drive to do this anymore. I made my decision before the end of that meeting."

"This is a big deal for you. How are you feeling?"

"I don't know. Excited. Relieved. Guilty. Overwhelmed. But I'm convinced it's the right time. Oh, and I'm going to need professional help—a lawyer."

"I'll ask around at work, confidentially."

Kim got a recommendation for a lawyer, a good one. I consulted with him to evaluate the strength of my disability case and to help me navigate the complex application procedures. He indicated I was a strong candidate for my company's long-term disability policy and Social Security disability. The lawyer, Dr. Muscat, and I made up the team that would run this bureaucratic gauntlet.

On the evening of May 1, 2009, I set the process in motion when I called my boss in Ohio. After exchanging pleasantries, I said, "Dan, as you know, I like to stay positive and carry on as if my MS is not getting worse, but it is."

"I'm not surprised. I worry about you all the time."

"The advice I've received from my doctors, for a while now, is to stop working so I can focus on my health issues, and I've come to agree with them."

"A leave of absence?"

"No. This will likely be permanent. I'm applying for long-term disability benefits."

"Is there anything we can do to help you stay on the job longer?"

"The company has given me every accommodation I've asked for. You guys have been so helpful. But it's time."

"Okay, Mitch. I'll support you in any way I can."

We picked an end date a few weeks out and talked about how I would transition my responsibilities. As the conversation wound down, I said, "I have to tell you, Dan, I've given it a lot of thought, and I've consulted with some smart people, but walking away from my career at age forty-five is about the scariest thing I've ever done."

"I'm sure it is, but I'm confident you'll make it work. Hey, I'll check my schedule and find a time in the next couple of weeks to fly to Maine and say goodbye in person. You pick the restaurant." True to his word, Dan and his boss, the president of our division, took Kim and me out to dinner at the nicest restaurant in Portland, Fore Street; a place I will only go when someone else picks up the tab.

The day after my telephone conversation with Dan, I began to inform those who needed to know and those who ought to know. It felt similar to disclosing my MS diagnosis eight years earlier. In this case, however, I worried not only about upsetting people, but also about whether some folks would think less of me, would question my motives. Might they accuse me of playing the system, giving up, or any number of similar indictments?

To the best of my knowledge, these concerns were unwarranted. My friends, family, and co-workers provided me with only empathy and support. The most common sentiment I heard was "this is long overdue." No second-guessing. No judgment.

The process dictated that I file for short-term disability with my employer first, which would provide me with six months of benefits while I worked on permanent disability applications. I received approval almost immediately, as expected.

Next, I applied for Social Security disability benefits. I knew it could take up to five months to process my request, with a chance that the decision could be negative. After only two months, I got my answer. Not only did I qualify for benefits, but the Social Security Administration wouldn't reevaluate me until five years down the road. This meant I was a no-doubter, a slam-dunk. It's been nine years now, and I've still heard nothing about a reevaluation.

After that, I applied for my employer's long-term disability benefits. The fact that I had already qualified for Social Security benefits made my application stronger but gave me no guarantees. Just over a month later, I received my approval letter. Again, this was better than my most optimistic estimates.

I didn't qualify for Medicare, however. Individuals who are approved for Social Security disability have a two-year and five-month waiting period before they can receive Medicare benefits. For me, this amounted to a minor burden, since Kim's medical plan covered me anyway. But what about disabled individuals who don't have a spouse with a medical plan? Until the Affordable Care Act became law, they had no good options. Even with Obamacare, there can be significant costs for these individuals who have suddenly stopped working, often for the rest of their lives, and who have higher than average medical bills.

Why the 29-month wait? When Medicare expanded in 1972 to include individuals on Social Security disability, Congress instituted this two-year waiting period, in addition to the five-month waiting period for Social Security benefits. Lawmakers structured it this way to make the package less costly for the federal government and more likely to gain passage in Congress. But this waiting period places an undue hardship on disabled individuals, and it needs to be eliminated. I hold out little hope, however, that Congress will do the right thing in the near future.

As for me, both the government and private insurance agencies took one look at my applications and threw money at me. While reading each approval letter, I felt relieved, exhilarated, and troubled, in that order. Relieved and exhilarated are self-explanatory. I was troubled because nobody even put up a modest fight. These organizations see a lot of sad stories come across their desks, and mine must have been among the saddest. As with the iBot evaluation, I went into this process concerned that I may have been acting prematurely and emerged having absorbed a shot of reality, straight up, no chaser.

CHAPTER 35

An Inconsistent History

The concerns I had about losing my identity if I stopped working, about becoming someone I didn't want to be, never came to fruition. My mind, although affected by MS, remained intellectually curious. I found plenty of ways to pass the time, including quality television, reading, and sampling free online courses. However, an activity called blogging, where I wrote weekly essays and posted them on a website, became my passion.

I met Marc Stecker at an online chat room when we both were contemplating a $25,000 outlay for a dubious stem cell treatment in Israel. Thankfully, neither of us followed through on that idea. Marc is a famous MS blogger, better known as the Wheelchair Kamikaze, a moniker he earned by producing highly entertaining videos zipping around Manhattan with a camera mounted on his wheelchair. Marc helped me set up my blog in 2009.

First, I had to choose a name. "Enjoying the Ride" immediately came to mind. This spoke both to my positive attitude and to the fact that I had an incredible ride in my iBot. But I assumed someone would have already snatched up such a common phrase for their motorcycle website or, well, use your imagination. Nobody had, so I became the proud owner of a URL, all rights reserved, etc., etc.

I loved writing, and I basked in the glow of positive feedback on my first few blog posts. Even better, I established a network of people interested in my story and my struggles. Many of these readers felt supported by me, and I by them. This virtual community has grown over the years, and I don't know how I would survive without it.

It's not a pretty word—blogger. A more appealing name for what I do is *writer*. But I'm hesitant to self-identify with such a lofty moniker. Writers are the ultimate intellectuals. They are, despite how poorly they sometimes manage their own affairs, the group of people who understand and articulate the nuances of life better than anyone else. I'm more than a little insecure about placing myself in their company. Yet, here *you* are, reading what I have written, presumably by choice as opposed to coercion, so perhaps I need to rethink this.

I have an inconsistent history with writing. I caught the bug in second grade when I stumbled upon some poetry well beyond my understanding. Inspired, I scribbled down a poem for my teacher, forsaking the "roses are red, violets are blue" form popular in my demographic. I so impressed Miss Andrews, with whom I was in love, that she called me to her desk and asked if I could explain my words. Based on the advanced verses I had discovered earlier, I considered poetry to be nothing more than a collection of beautiful sounding, random phrases strung together—*the soft wind blew down on the bright green grass until it sang to the clouds delicately.* I didn't know poems were supposed to mean something.

"What does the poem mean?" she asked.

I shrugged.

"It is beautifully written. What is your poem about?"

Miss Andrews smelled so nice. She wore makeup and jewelry, and a tight sweater. Standing this close to her, I realized I was in over my head, regarding both love and poetry. My brain and mouth seized, and I stopped breathing. Just before I would have passed out from lack of oxygen, she said, "Never mind. You can go back to your seat."

Oh, the disappointment she must have felt as she accepted that this quiet boy who sat in the back of the class wasn't a prodigy after all, and that this would be a day like all the others at Ella P. Burr Elementary School, ordinary and forgettable. The little Sturgeon kid had merely strung together a collection of beautiful sounding, random words and phrases.

I redeemed myself in fourth grade by winning a writing contest sponsored by the school. They awarded me a thick, hardcover, American Heritage School Dictionary with the inscription "Presented to Mitchell Sturgeon, Grade 4, for his short story, 'Measurement of

Manhood,' winner in the Ella P. Burr Pulitzer Project, June 7, 1974."
That massive, blue dictionary sat prominently on bookshelves at my
parents' house, in my college rooms, and in my adult homes. Our
children even used it until the Internet rendered such a book obsolete,
other than to prop up my computer monitor.

Having received so much notoriety at such a tender age—winning a big, blue dictionary—all the little boys wanted to be me. All
the little girls wanted to be with me. If not for my highly-developed
sense of humility, I might have become a snob and a bully. I could
have surrounded myself with hangers-on, and we could have ruled the
fourth-grade hallways. But alas, I chose not to flaunt my stardom, and
in doing so, enjoyed a normal childhood. Close call.

My high school creative writing teacher, Mr. Reed, inspired me
to do my best work. In one assignment I considered the silent lives
of brook trout, the role of grandparents in society, and the utter fool-
ishness of wearing neckties, all in one essay. He read it aloud to the
class—his highest form of praise.

I recently reread my valedictory address for the first time in
about 30 years. What a disappointment. I made no effort to keep the
hundreds of people in attendance from falling asleep. The message
I tried to send was admirable for such a young man. I advocated
for environmental protection, preservation of animal species, setting
lofty personal goals, and keeping all things in perspective. Not bad
stuff. The product, however, the words and sentences I delivered from
the podium, made for a dreadfully boring speech. But at the time, I
thought it quite well done.

During college, I enrolled in the only English class required of
engineers—Freshman Composition. I considered myself an excellent
writer, and I awaited confirmation of such from my instructor, a
grad student who smelled nice, wore makeup and jewelry and a tight
sweater, and whom I lusted after. I received neither acknowledgment
of mutual attraction nor confirmation of my advanced writing skills.
She possessed a critical eye in both regards. I barely managed a B in
the class, and I didn't write creatively again for 25 years.

CHAPTER 36
New Hope—CCSVI

On March 17, 2010, Kim and I arrived at Kings County Hospital Center in what could only be described as a tough part of Brooklyn, New York. She helped me change from my street clothes into a blue surgical gown that seemed scarcely better than being naked. Here I was on St. Patrick's Day, not wearing a stitch of green.

The operating room impressed—spacious and packed with high-tech equipment. The surgical team hooked me up to various monitors and prepped the area in my groin where the catheter would be inserted. When Dr. Sclafani arrived, everyone stopped what they were doing and gathered around me.

The doctor began. "First, we will go through some formalities required by law. My name is Dr. Salvador Sclafani. I am an interventional radiologist and Chief of Radiology at this hospital."

The others in the room—a second physician, two nurses, and two technicians—gave their names and job functions. Although they went through this exercise as a legal requirement to minimize medical errors, it felt like good manners and a nice way to start things off.

Dr. Sclafani then motioned to me and asked, "And you are?"

"Mitchell Sturgeon."

"And what procedure will you be receiving today, and for what purpose?"

"Balloon angioplasty as a treatment for multiple sclerosis."

About a year earlier, my friend Marc (Wheelchair Kamikaze), had introduced me to a radical new theory of the root cause of MS and a treatment protocol to address the problem. This idea, and the patient-driven movement that resulted, turned the MS world upside down, and I was right in the thick of it.

As early as the middle of the twentieth century, researchers had identified a connection between the vascular system and MS lesions. For a variety of reasons, these observations never gained traction in the MS world. Then, in 2008, an Italian vascular surgeon named Paolo Zamboni found most MS patients had restrictions in the veins that drain the central nervous system. He coined the term Chronic Cerebrospinal Venous Insufficiency, or CCSVI, to describe this condition.

Angioplasty, inflating tiny balloons in a patient's blood vessels, is typically used to treat clogged arteries in the heart. Dr. Zamboni employed a similar procedure, venoplasty, to open restrictions in the neck and chest veins of MS patients, with apparent success. People stopped getting worse and started getting better.

I spoke to, called, emailed, blogged, private messaged, Skyped, tweeted, and Facebook chatted with hundreds of people about CCSVI. A group of MS patients in New England had formed a loose coalition with the goal of recruiting a doctor in the Northeastern United States to diagnose and treat MS patients for CCSVI. They also wanted to create a science-based organization to advocate for this newly found condition, and they needed help building a website. That's where I came in.

Randi, who lived in Boston, reached out to me after she read my blog and saw my name on some of the CCSVI message boards. She said her group could use help writing copy for their new website, and, oh, by the way, she might be able to help me find treatment too. I warned Randi I had taken disability retirement earlier that year, and the last thing I needed to do was overburden myself with charitable work. But yes, I would love to help.

I became close friends with Randi, her partner Al, Michelle, Sharon, Joan, and a few others from the organization. I relished the opportunity to contribute to something bigger than myself—a feeling I missed after having left the workforce and having been disappointed by the iBot program. I took care not to get sucked into more than a few hours a week.

Early in 2010, this group put me in touch with Dr. Sclafani, whom they had recruited. Most of these folks had already been treated by either Dr. Sclafani or by a Stanford University physician, Dr. Michael Dake. In March of 2010, Kim and I packed up the wheelchair van and drove to Brooklyn.

A couple of days before the procedure, we enjoyed dinner in Manhattan with Michelle, the lady who recruited Dr. Sclafani into the CCSVI world; Marc (Wheelchair Kamikaze) and his wife, Karen; Barbara, who would be treated the same day as me; and Dr. and Mrs. Sclafani. I'd never socialized with a personal physician of mine, especially days before I would be in his operating room. But it heartened me to spend time with a group so dedicated to the cause of helping people with MS. Marc and Michelle had already been treated by Dr. Sclafani, so they were able to comfort Kim when she learned I would be his eighth CCSVI patient. She didn't like that I was in the single digits.

And that's how I ended up in a Brooklyn operating room on St. Patrick's Day. I remained awake and alert throughout the procedure, and the only pain I experienced was in my ass after lying perfectly still on the operating table for over an hour. I felt nothing when Dr. Sclafani threaded the catheter from my groin, through my femoral vein, into one side of my heart and out the other. I did hear the *whooshing* sound as he released test dye into the veins in my neck, and I felt odd sensations when he inflated the tiny balloons. It was all good, though. That was where I wanted to be, and those were the experiences I wanted to have.

The next morning, we met with Dr. Sclafani to go over the previous day's images in detail. He showed us how the venoplasty had improved blood flow in several of my veins. But that's where he stopped. He couldn't know whether the blood flow would remain improved, and he couldn't know if I would see any changes in the course of my MS. This met my expectations. I told him how grateful I was for doctors like him who were willing to work with patients like me—patients who couldn't wait ten years for approval of this treatment.

Kim and I arrived home in Maine on Thursday evening. I posted this on my blog:

> How am I doing? Just fine, thank you. Ask me again
> in six months or a year, and I may be able to tell you
> if this procedure had any positive effect on my disease
> progression. Wouldn't that be something?

As a show of support for this emerging therapy, I ordered a vanity license plate for my wheelchair van that read, simply, CCSVI.

MS patients are a frustrated group. We not only suffer from our disease every day, but many of us continually pile up new, irreversible damage. So, when a potential blockbuster like CCSVI treatment wasn't immediately made available to everyone, it was understandable that we became angry, vocal, and resourceful.

On the other hand, medical practitioners and scientists are a cautious and logical group. So, when people demanded a treatment that had not been proven through a series of blinded, placebo-controlled studies, they exhibited skepticism and resistance. These professionals had seen so many prospective treatments fall by the wayside under close scrutiny.

Few mainstream neurologists advocated for further research in this area, and even fewer supported the vascular surgeons, interventional radiologists, and rogue neurologists who were already diagnosing and treating CCSVI. Some neurologists spoke out about what they considered to be a crackpot theory. They accused the doctors who supported CCSVI of wasting research money, falsely raising the hopes of MS patients, profiteering, and worst of all—risking patients' health.

Not to be outdone, leaders in the patient community criticized the vocal, mainstream doctors and accused them of being in the pockets of the pharmaceutical companies. Thanks to freedom of information laws, patients had data to support these accusations. The rhetoric became heated.

My neurologist, Dr. Muscat, expressed skepticism about the theory. But since he couldn't provide me with any better alternatives, he supported my exploration of CCSVI. His biggest contribution was successfully advocating on my behalf with my insurance company. These procedures were not inexpensive.

In response to the controversy, and to further advance our understanding of the possible connection between vascular health and MS, my friends and I formed the CCSVI Alliance and launched the website CCSVI.org.

Our mission statement read:

> CCSVI Alliance is dedicated to educating patients with research-based information, providing tools for patients to advocate for themselves, and supporting medical professionals' exploration of Chronic Cerebrospinal Venous Insufficiency (CCSVI).

In the weeks following my procedure, I tried not to dwell on it. I had already learned it takes at least six months to determine if a treatment is effective or not. If I attempted to make an assessment before then, I could misidentify the normal ebbs and flows of life as a change in my disease course. Yet, it is human nature to seek immediate answers. Well-meaning MS patients and my friends and relatives kept asking if I felt any improvement. I kept explaining to them about the ebbs and flows of life.

When the six-month mark arrived, my conclusion was certain. I announced through my blog that CCSVI treatment didn't work for me. I hadn't expected improvements in my symptoms. I only hoped I would stop getting worse. But after this procedure, my MS continued to progress at the same slow, steady rate it had since my diagnosis nine years earlier (except for some period during the Rituxan trial).

This weighed on me for several reasons. First, my friends and loved ones hoped the treatment would work, and I hated to disappoint them. Second, I appreciated that the larger MS community craved good news from those of us on the forefront of new treatments. Every success story brought hope, and I didn't like extinguishing hope. Third, I thought this might work, and I became deeply disappointed when it didn't. This represented yet another in a long line of dead ends, and I was growing weary of them.

Despite my negative results, I remained confident that in the end, CCSVI would be considered the most important discovery, ever, for the larger population of people with MS. And if a relatively simple procedure could help so many patients, instead of pumping toxic, exorbitantly expensive drugs into their bodies day after day, year after year, so much the better.

I stayed close to the CCSVI community, continued to post on discussion boards, and helped out as much as ever at the Alliance. Eventually, all the positive stories I read about and all the YouTube videos I watched began to wear on me. I knew I should have felt only joy for each person who apparently benefited from CCSVI treatment, and yes, I was happy for them. Sometimes feelings of resentment crept in, however, because I didn't benefit myself. I wasn't proud of this, but I acknowledged these emotions and dealt with them.

Also, I worried that a small minority of the MS community, some of the most fervent supporters of CCSVI, would have preferred I remain silent about my poor outcome. I felt they only wanted to hear the good news because they feared admissions like mine emboldened the CCSVI detractors. I believe the vast majority of MS patients, however, wanted us to relate our treatment experiences no matter the outcome, and that's what I did through my blog. Those were some of my most widely read posts.

In early 2011, I still hadn't given up on CCSVI. In fact, I attended a conference on the subject, hosted by Dr. Sclafani in Brooklyn. There, I heard a talk from Dr. Gary Siskin, the chair of the Radiology Department at Albany Medical Center. He had performed hundreds of CCSVI treatments, and he broke down his results this way: one-third of his patients showed significant improvements, another third saw modest or only temporary improvements, and the remaining third saw no improvements.

I decided to give Dr. Siskin a try. Why? Because I was desperate. A power wheelchair, especially my iBot, was an elegant adaptation for people who could not walk. My quality of life had not greatly diminished for having been in a chair. However, I worried my arms and hands would soon be in the same condition as my legs. I didn't know of any assistive device that replaced the function of arms and hands as well as a wheelchair replaced the function of legs. I felt my quality of life, my enjoyment of life, might not endure this next assault. I had to do something other than sit and wait for brilliant researchers to study, debate, verify, and eventually agree on a treatment or cure for this disease.

In March of 2011, I visited Dr. Siskin's operating room for my second CCSVI treatment. He found narrowing similar to what Dr. Sclafani had a year earlier, and he ballooned those restrictions. Apparently, Dr. Sclafani's work had not provided a permanent fix.

Again, I felt normal within a few hours of the procedure. No side effects. No improvements. This double-edged sword felt all too familiar. I had undergone so many treatments and had ingested and infused countless drugs over the years. On the one hand, I rarely suffered any of the side effects. On the other, I seldom experienced any of the benefits.

Six months after my second CCSVI procedure, I visited Dr. Siskin's office in Albany to follow-up on my March treatment procedure, knowing how the appointment would go. Dr. Siskin and I agreed I was one of those MS patients who showed no benefit from CCSVI treatment—the bottom third. I had seen zero impact on my disease progression in the 18 months since my Brooklyn treatment or the six months since my Albany treatment. Dr. Siskin reluctantly discharged me from his care. Soon afterward, I changed my vanity plate from **CCSVI** to **MS**, two letters representing both my disease and my initials.

Thus ended my personal CCSVI saga. I thought I might continue to monitor the progress of this treatment and research, and, if new information came to light, I wouldn't hesitate to revisit treatment a third time. Instead, this theory fell off my radar. I resigned from the Alliance and stopped receiving updates from the various researchers.

For a few more years, a dwindling group of patients and professionals still advocated for CCSVI research and treatment, but the excitement generated in 2008 through 2011 subsided over time. The focus moved from diagnosing and treating CCSVI to establishing broader relationships between the vascular system and certain diseases, especially neurologic disorders. I sincerely hope their persistence will result in useful, actionable discoveries. But, the CCSVI world that I was part of, where thousands of patients were diagnosed and treated with venoplasty, has become a thing of the past.

To be clear, I have confidence that all the people I worked with, both patients and medical professionals, had the best intentions, and I don't regret my participation in this effort. If nothing else, the CCSVI movement challenged researchers to take another look at the potential vascular components of MS and other diseases. And, perhaps most importantly, we sent a message to the medical industrial complex that we won't sit quietly, waiting for treatment decisions while our central nervous systems melt away.

I also experienced personal growth from this CCSVI advocacy experience. I learned more than I ever thought I would about the anatomy of the human vascular system. I gained experience building a charitable organization. I made some lifelong friends. Most importantly, I learned what it feels like to take control of my own healthcare, whether successfully or not. I tasted empowerment.

Patient-driven movements like this one will only become more common in the future. Because of technology, we have unprecedented access to information (both good and bad) and so many ways to organize ourselves. I have little doubt that one of these times, one of these miracle MS treatments will turn out to be the cure.

Won't that be a wonderful day?

CHAPTER 37

Belonging to the Woods

When my father grew up in the 1930s and 1940s, his father always had a deer hanging in the shed during the winter. For dinner, my grandmother would go out and cut a piece of meat off the carcass. When they shot deer in warmer weather, they canned the meat. They didn't hunt to preserve tradition and to commune with nature so much as they hunted to put food on the table, to survive.

In the 1950s and 1960s, homeowners started to buy electric freezers, even in rural northern Maine. Most families enjoyed a standard of living that no longer required the killing of game for food. Nevertheless, the hunting tradition endured in our family and many others. It still produces a special feeling, and it scratches an evolutionary itch, to pull a package of deer steak out of the freezer, prepare it, and eat it. I find that meat my family shot and butchered ourselves is more satisfying to consume. (Gardeners who take pride in eating their harvest know what I mean.)

The common stereotype depicts hunters as a bunch of heartless, drunken idiots wandering around the woods in orange clothing, brandishing high-powered rifles. These people do exist, and most television and movie writers paint all hunters with that broad brush.

In my generation, hunting was about family. November served as a time to catch up with one another. Male bonding, I suppose. Yes, we consumed alcohol, but we had a strict rule—we never, ever had our first drink until we put the guns away for the day. And we *almost* never, ever allowed hangovers to interfere with the next day's hunting plans.

My hunting experiences were not all that different from my forbearers' over the past couple of hundred years—power wheelchairs,

ATVs, and precision optical scopes aside. More than anything else, the essence of hunting was and is about disappearing into the woods for a few hours at a time, belonging to the woods to the extent humans can.

I still harken back to those Saturday mornings in November with my father:

We are so well practiced at the predawn launching procedure that conversation is unnecessary and unwelcome. I hold the 20-foot aluminum canoe steady while my father waddles down its length, turns, and plops on to his seat. He nods, and I heave the canoe into Passadumkeag Stream and jump aboard. I am 16 years old.

My father cranks on the six horsepower Johnson outboard, establishing a rhythmic cadence. The sounds from the engine inform us which pull has been successful. I listen with anticipation, because if the process takes too long, I have to paddle the canoe clear of the downstream rocks. I would rather not deal with the rocks or my father's cursing.

But the Johnson fires after a few pulls, spewing a pungent, gray cloud of exhaust into the air. The little motor sputters and chugs and settles into a monotonous hum. Dad pulls the gearshift lever forward, opens the throttle, and points the canoe upstream. I can tell for certain when we prevail over the force of the current only if I pick a spot on the shore and verify which way we move relative to it. If I instead look down at the water rushing by, we are going a hundred miles an hour.

We launch early in the morning to land the canoe near our prime, upstream hunting locations before the deer bed down for the day. Even before dawn, the glow from the eastern sky outlines the stream and the surrounding woods. In such low light, no colors exist, only shades of black and gray.

Once we gain speed, the November wind cuts through our heavy wool clothing. I pull my knit hat down as far as I can. The shell ice which formed overnight clings to the shore. To avoid underwater obstacles, Dad navigates the center of the stream, driving a wedge through the black, glassy surface. The wake reaches shore 30 or 40 feet behind us, shattering the thin ice and the morning quiet.

Sunlight leaks over the horizon and paints the water deep blue, the tall grasses green and yellow, the autumn leaves burnt orange. The natives take exception to our trespass. A pair of wood ducks explodes into a flurry of wings and water as they take flight. A beaver slaps his broad tail on the surface of the stream and withdraws, presumably to the comfort and safety of his lodge.

For the first few minutes of our upstream voyage, the trees rooted to the shoreline lean over the water in their life-or-death struggle for sunlight. As we round the first bend, Ayer Brook Meadow drives a wedge between the stream and the forest until the treeline is a mile from us. I rise to my feet at the bow of the canoe and survey the open landscape for deer, using my naked eyes and the scope on my rifle. I rarely spot deer in this way but feel obligated to try nonetheless.

Meandering brooks bisect the larger meadows. Their incessant flows carved these paths, are still carving these paths, over thousands of years. Islands of higher ground hold out against the advancing wetlands, often with a solitary tree standing guard. Behind the meadows sit rolling hills of hardwoods mixed with ancient spruce, pine, and hemlock. I should conduct my upright survey of the meadows expeditiously because canoes are tippy by nature. Instead, I linger—more enchanted by the beauty than committed to the hunt.

After we pass by Oak Point, the meadows fade from view, and I take my seat. A gaggle of Canada geese honks overhead, laboring together in a perfect V-formation, compelled by the innate urge to migrate thousands of miles. My father maneuvers our canoe by Scalp Rock and navigates Rocky Rips with only a couple scrapes against submerged boulders. We pull ashore near Big Island and tie the canoe to a tree. Silently, separately, my father and I fade into the woods to execute the hunting strategy we mapped out over breakfast. We, too, are compelled by innate urges.

At the agreed-upon time, we meet at the canoe and motor back downstream to the boat ramp. Sometimes we bring home a deer, but our appreciation of the day does not depend upon it.

The stream is our portal from civilization to wilderness, from necessarily complex lives to temporarily simpler ones. Although the water is inanimate, the Passadumkeag lives—breathing, moving, mysterious. It will swallow you up if you make a mistake. But if you engage the stream, it reveals secrets and inspires wonder.

* * *

Every fall, deer hunting brought together my two older brothers, my father, and me. The consummate sportsman, Dad ran the show when we were young. As we became adults, however, my brothers and I took over the operation of the six horsepower Johnson, and we shot the deer. Dad continued to draw up the strategies. Occasionally we followed them. Over the years Dad went up the stream less and less but always waited for us at the hunting camp. We enjoyed giving him the details of the hunt, successful or not, and he devoured our stories.

Dad often followed up with one of his own tales. Although he possessed a considerable number of stories, repeat performances were inevitable. His consistent and enthusiastic delivery left my brothers and me wondering whether he didn't remember having told us the stories before, or if he didn't care that he had.

As the years passed, the deer population up the stream dwindled, although Dad argued this point. We spent more time hunting in other parts of the state. My brothers and I, and our growing families, all migrated away from northern Maine. We sold the hunting camp near Passadumkeag Stream. I relied on the telephone to keep Dad informed of my hunts in central and southern Maine. We both cherished these conversations. Nobody will ever care about anything I do more than Dad cared about my hunting.

In 2003, two years after my diagnosis, I harvested a deer, and then I went on an extended dry spell. I still hunted regularly, but I used an all-terrain vehicle, which served as a warning siren to all the deer I might have otherwise encountered. By 2009 I could no longer operate an ATV. I became relegated to hunting from automobiles and wheelchairs, and that brings me to the fall of 2010.

Tom had secured a hunting spot for me not far from his house in Bowdoinham, Maine. I decided I would sit in my wheelchair van on one brilliant November afternoon. I didn't want to brave the cold in my iBot, although I had done so several times earlier in the season. As a disabled person in Maine, I had a special permit to shoot from a parked vehicle, an otherwise illegal activity. I positioned the van so I could aim my Browning 30-06 at a spot in the corner of a field where I hoped a deer might show up. I couldn't hold a rifle properly, so I rested it on a supportive stand.

Dad didn't raise me to do this type of hunting. Until I couldn't walk in the woods anymore, I crept along, ever so slowly and quietly, often in remote areas where I would not be bothered by other hunters. That approach provided a unique view of the forest after each and every step taken. The constant change of scenery kept things interesting. Having been demoted to sitting and waiting, I sometimes slipped into a daze.

I had stared at the same group of trees for hours, waiting for a deer to reveal itself. That's what they do most of the time. You look one way, then back, and a deer has materialized as if it had been there the whole time, as if you had been looking straight through it.

In this waning autumn daylight, I closed my eyes for just a second, then scolded myself. *Come on, Mitch. Stay alert. This is the best part of the day.* With only ten minutes of hunting time remaining, I checked an area to my left, and there stood a doe. A surge of adrenaline wiped away my grogginess as if someone had doused me with ice water.

I tried to get the deer into my scope but couldn't swing my gun far enough to the left—the shooting stand restricted me. I summoned all my strength, tossed the stand aside, got the deer in my crosshairs, and pulled the trigger. She bounded into the trees where the nighttime darkness had already taken hold.

I had fired this rifle, or ones like it, hundreds of times in my life, but never from the confines of a vehicle. The amplified noise startled me, and spread throughout the immediate area, marking the boundary between two distinct time periods that day—the solitary and quiet hunt versus the hectic series of events that followed.

Before cell phones, our communication system consisted of a series of gunshots. Dad would say, "If you shoot a deer, or need one of us to help you track a wounded deer, wait ten minutes after your original shots and fire one shot. Then wait a few seconds and fire two quick shots. I'll do the same if I need you."

Those days were gone. I started texting people instead, beginning with Tom and his son, Brad, who were at work about 20 minutes away. I asked them to bring their flashlights and come search for the deer. I knew they had looked forward to receiving such a message as much as I had looked forward to sending it. The terrain between me and where the deer stood was not navigable by my iBot. So I sat in the driver's seat of the van and waited.

Next, I phoned the landowner to let him know the shot he had heard was mine. Then I called my father in Lincoln.

"Dad, it's Mitchell. I just shot at a deer."

"Is that so? Did you hit it?"

"Hard to say. Tom and Brad are on their way to look for her." I gave Dad the details. He always insisted on details.

Before hanging up, he said, "Even if you missed the deer, I'm so happy you had a genuine hunting experience."

"Me too, Dad. I'll call you when I know more."

Then I gave Kim the news that I would be late for dinner. I could hear the delight in her voice.

The landowner showed up a few minutes later on his ATV. By then, it had become pitch dark even in the open spaces. Two of his friends joined him, and I directed the three of them to the spot where the deer had stood. I could see the beams from their flashlights moving in every conceivable direction, but I couldn't determine the nature of their conversation. When Tom, Brad, and our friend Mark showed up, I watched from a distance as now six flashlight beams bounced through the woods. Finally, Mark yelled and said, "We found her, Mitch!" I tooted my horn twice as acknowledgment.

I had already reconciled with the idea that I would never again shoot a deer. I had worried my afternoon hunts represented nothing more than a pathetic refusal to accept the truth—my body was too damaged to continue this charade. Yet, I had driven my minivan to the site myself. I had loaded the rifle, aimed, and shot. And now I had downed an animal for the first time in seven years. Although I received a lot of help, nobody handed this deer to me. By some measure, I earned it.

I called my father. "Dad, we found the deer. A nice, big doe."

"Well, I'll be damned. Congratulations." Then silence.

"Are you still there?" I asked.

"Yes, I'm still here." His voice cracked. "I can't tell you how happy I am. I know I've shot my last deer, and I was afraid you had too."

Through the silence on the other end, I knew my father was crying.

He wasn't so stoic on that day, the day when his broken son shot a deer.

CHAPTER 38

Two Great Oaks

As we had expected, my father struggled after my mother passed away. He had never lived alone before, and he didn't like it one bit. So, at 78 years old, he plunged into the world of online dating. Dad possessed rugged good looks when he was young, but the years had taken a toll on him. On top of that, he behaved in an off-putting way—grumpy and inflexible. Because of these shortcomings, I didn't expect him to attract many women. I was wrong. Given the female-to-male ratio in that age group, a man who drives a car, owns a house, and has a pulse is a freaking rock star.

Not only that, but I learned my father could charm the ladies for short periods of time, and they lined up to meet him. After an online chat and a phone call or two, they would set up a date. He preferred Applebee's and Friendly's as meeting spots. Before they even placed their food orders, he would make a speech along these lines:

"As you know, I'm not interested in someone to go out on dates with. I live alone, and I'm looking for a woman to move in with me at my house in Lincoln. Purely platonic. You will have your own bedroom. You'll pay no rent, but you'll take care of the cooking and cleaning. We'll split the cost of utilities. If we find we're compatible, is that something you could consider?"

More than once, Dad gave me the following post-date assessment: "She was just after a free meal."

Several women took the bait and tried out the arrangement for a few days. All but two of them never came back. His expectations rarely aligned with the lady's, and he wasn't as charming over a longer period as he was for an hour at a restaurant. Susan became the first to move in for an extended stay. She lasted a couple of months. My father told us she was so challenging to live with he asked her to leave. I suspect it was the other way around, but I'll never know for sure. He went through a couple more short-timers until Beth came along. A sweet lady in difficult circumstances, she had no better place to go. Beth threatened to move out more than once, but my father talked her into staying.

Dad remembered Susan as a good-looking woman, much more so than Beth. (I didn't notice the difference.) He would say to someone, often in front of Beth, "Beth is a nice person, but she's no Susan. She's got a belly on her." Beth must have found his playfulness just charming enough because she never left.

* * *

Growing up, we looked forward to one special family activity several times a year. After the sun had gone down, we closed the drapes in the living room. One of us dragged the projector and screen out of the spare bedroom closet. We kicked the legs out into a tripod and unfurled the screen like an upside-down window shade. Dad set up the projector and loaded the newest box of slides into the feeding tray. Mom and one of us made the popcorn and slathered it with melted butter. Sometimes only our immediate family attended. Other times friends or relatives joined in, especially if they might be subjects of the photos. When everyone took their place, Dad turned off the lights, and the show began.

Today, when I watch slideshows on my computer monitor, I miss the mechanical sounds of the slide box advancing and the individual slides feeding in and out. If I close my eyes, I can see the dust in the beam of light and smell the hot projector bulb. I can hear my father's narration and my mother's comments. But what I remember most fondly is the anticipation I felt sitting in the dark and waiting for the next image to appear.

This tradition ended in the late 1970s when Dad converted from slides to prints. He filled up albums instead, which people could look at any time of the day without a big production. The boxes of slides gathered dust in the back closet for over 30 years until early 2011 when I volunteered to digitize them.

This proved a massive undertaking. The collection contained more than 1400 slides from 1953 to 1977. I didn't have sufficient dexterity in my hands to work with the slides, so my son Zach scanned them for me. I organized the digital files and applied Photoshop repairs where I could. We ended up with over 1200 quality images. I gathered the most meaningful ones and produced a video where Andy, Tom, and I discussed our favorite slides and our memories associated with them.

My most meaningful slide was a family photo taken on Mother's Day, 1972, almost three years after my mother's accident. The five of us had assembled on the back deck of our Edwards Street house. Starting from the left, a 15-year-old Andy sat on the bench with a confident smile, wearing a blue sweatshirt and blue jeans. We called them dungarees. He held his dog, Tarr, between his legs. Tarr stared intently at something off to the photographer's right.

Our 41-year-old father sat on the bench to Andy's left. An undersized, brown ball cap rested on his head, and he wore a plaid, long-sleeved shirt. I have never seen this facial expression in any other pictures, and I can't remember him exhibiting it in person. He was neither happy nor sad. His look says to me: *look how well we survived.* But I'm not sure it's that benign. Other times when I consider the same photograph, his eyes say: *if you harm my family, I will find you.* Maybe it is both sentiments at once.

My 37-year-old mother sat in her wheelchair in front of and to the left of Dad, with her full head of black hair combed back away from her face. She sported her outlandish cat's eye glasses (not so out-landish in 1972) and exhibited a genuine, broad smile. On a chilly Sunday in May, she was the only person to wear a short-sleeved shirt. A bouquet of red roses sat on her lap—her Mother's Day present. She wasn't so much holding the vase as it was propped up in her hands. The flowers rested on her crumpled apron, which she wore almost all the time. Someone had the good sense to pull it down off her upper body before the picture was taken. Mom wore a light blue skirt that stopped just below her knees. A one or two-inch gap exposed the tops of her shins before her long, white hospital-issued socks took over. She looked lovely for all she had been through.

As an eight-year-old, I leaned on my mother's left armrest. I wore a green ball cap, a pink, long-sleeve shirt buttoned to the top, dungarees and a large watch on my left wrist. I sported a genuine smile, and why not? I was young, and healthy, and summer was on the way.

Eleven-year-old Tom stood behind me and off to my left. He had on a purple and orange ball cap, red and gray pullover, and red pants. He tried his hardest not to smile, but a smirk escaped, if only for the millisecond it took the shutter to open and close.

I don't think there's a better portrait of the five of us. We looked good individually, and we had a synergy that day. Together, we had been tested. We survived, even flourished. This picture will always be my reminder of that.

Zach and I completed the digitizing project in May of 2011, and I planned to present it to Dad on Father's Day. But a conflict arose, so we drove up to Lincoln two weeks before Father's Day. After dinner Kim, Beth, Dad and I gathered in the living room.

While the video played on his TV, Dad and I discussed a few of the pictures. He made sure Beth saw what a strapping young man he used to be, back in the day. Dad's interest piqued when one of my brothers or I appeared and spoke about our most meaningful pictures. Toward the end of the video, our conversation died off, and I stopped glancing over at Dad. I wanted to give him his space.

When the video finished, Dad took off his glasses and cleaned them with his handkerchief. (He was never without a pocketknife or a handkerchief.) He put his glasses back on, took a deep breath, and spoke.

"My goodness, Mitchell. That was really something." He gathered himself again and continued. "I knew you were scanning the old slides, but I didn't know you could make a video like this. I can't thank you enough."

He reached out and shook my hand, a gesture usually reserved for when someone shot a deer or graduated from an institution of higher learning, accomplishments of comparable merit in his eyes. I had taken on this project for several reasons—preservation of family history, the joy I would experience looking through all these photos, and more—although pleasing this old man, my old man, was chief among my motivations.

"You're welcome. Happy Father's Day from Andy, Tom, and me. Those were only a few of the slides. I have over 1200 images on this disc," I said, holding up a DVD I had burned.

I downloaded the files to Dad's computer, which he used exclusively for emails and online cribbage, and trained him on how to access them. It wasn't easy. Teaching him something new never was, but he finally grasped it.

Before I left that day, Dad shared with me a rare moment of self-reflection. Throughout his life he had maintained that he would rather die young than experience the indignity of growing old. "Now that I'm eighty," he admitted, "I'm not ready to go. I want to stay around for a while longer."

"I'm glad to hear that," I said, "because we feel the same way."

Two days later, the trouble started.

* * *

Like many men of his generation, my father had a keen interest in war stories. Over his lifetime, he had read hundreds of war-themed books and watched as many movies and TV shows. Although he served in the Army during the Korean War, he never saw combat because he was stationed on another continent, protecting Europe from itself.

Dad also knew a thing or two about firearms, having been in the Army and having been a hunter for his entire life. He set an excellent example for us regarding gun safety. He handled every firearm he touched as if it were loaded and ready to fire. Because of his instruction, I've always done the same thing.

These facts, his love of war stories and his familiarity with firearms, came into play over his last few days. One Monday morning in

June of 2011, around 3 a.m., Andy received a phone call at his house in Bangor. He heard Dad say, "Andy, I need your help. I'm in trouble. I've done something wrong. The cops have surrounded my house, and I'm afraid they're going to shoot me."

Dad sounded frightened and confused. He rambled. Andy didn't know what to make of it because Dad had never exhibited any signs of dementia. Just then, Andy's cell phone rang, and he told Dad to stand by. It was Bill, one of Andy's childhood friends who had recently been named Chief of Police in Lincoln. Bill said to Andy, "We have a situation with your father."

There stood Andy, in the middle of the night, with a cell phone in one hand and a landline in the other. Forty miles north, there stood my father, with a phone in one hand, a loaded gun in the other, and a brain deprived of oxygen because he was suffering a heart attack.

Andy said to Bill, the Chief of Police, "I have my father on the other phone right now."

"That's good. Keep him on the line."

"He believes the police have surrounded his house."

"We have."

This confused Andy. From the way Dad sounded, Andy assumed he was delusional.

Bill continued. "My officers have peeked in the windows. Your father is in the kitchen and has all his guns laid out on the table. The neighborhood isn't safe, and we need to get him under control. Can you talk him through this?"

"Of course. What do you want me to say?"

"Tell him to put his guns down and walk out of the house with his arms up in the air."

Andy lowered the phone in his left hand and raised the one in his right. "Dad, listen to me carefully. You need to put the guns down and walk outside so the cops can see that you aren't going to harm anyone. Everything will be okay."

"I can't do that. I'm afraid they're going to shoot me."

"Dad, you called and asked me to help you. I'm in contact with those police officers, and I promise they will not harm you as long as you are unarmed, and your hands are up in the air."

After a few minutes, Dad agreed but added, "I'm not going to put the phone down. I need you to stay on the line."

When he stepped out of the garage, the police saw that he held something to his head, and in the darkness mistook the phone for a gun. Fearing he might harm himself, officers hidden just outside his door tackled him. Andy heard the brief scuffle, and the phone went dead. He sat alone, with the sound of his 80-year-old father crashing to the ground replaying in his mind over and over.

A few minutes later Bill got back on the phone with Andy and explained that they had called an ambulance because Dad was ill. Bill shared more information the police had collected from Beth, Dad's housemate. Earlier that evening Dad had begun to behave erratically. He envisioned himself a soldier and told Beth the enemy was coming.

He got his guns out, set them on the table, and said, "I'm going to shoot the first Jap that comes through that door."

If Vietnam was my childhood war, World War II was my father's. And if a hatchet was my weapon for attacking imaginary soldiers, Dad was employing real guns and ammo to play a more dangerous game.

After Dad's threat, Beth snuck out and ran to the neighbor's house to call the police. She warned them about Dad's condition, and that's why they surrounded the house instead of knocking on the door. They didn't want to be mistaken for Japs.

This situation could have ended so much worse. Beth did the right thing by getting out of the house and calling the police. The police showed restraint in surrounding the house but not pushing Dad into making a horrible mistake. Bill had the wherewithal to call Andy in the middle of the night. And without Andy's skilled handling of Dad's paranoia, who knows what may have transpired? If someone had been shot, the story would have been broadcast statewide, if not nationally. The headline "Everyone Did the Right Thing and Nothing Bad Happened" doesn't sell advertising.

Dad's condition stabilized at the Lincoln Hospital, and the doctor explained how lucky he had been to get there in time. Several small heart attacks over the preceding weeks had brought on the delusional behavior, but the doctor felt confident Dad would make a complete recovery. Andy looked in on him for the next few days and reported to me that Dad didn't recall any of the bizarre events of the night he was admitted to the hospital.

As the days passed, Dad's prognosis worsened. By mid-week, the doctor told Andy that, though he had stabilized, his heart had been damaged to the point where he could no longer live independently. Beth made it clear, after the excitement of Sunday night, she would be moving out. Only one option remained.

At several points throughout his life, Dad vowed he would never allow us to put him in a nursing home, as he had done to his own mother. He almost dared us to try. For a variety of reasons, neither my brothers nor I were in a position to take him into our homes. I called the local nursing home and scheduled a meeting with them on Friday in Lincoln to discuss intake for my father. Tom would accompany me. After the meeting, we planned to sit with Dad and give him the bad news. I never dreaded a conversation more.

On Thursday morning, Andy called and told me Dad had taken a turn for the worse. I jumped into my wheelchair van, picked Tom up on the way, and headed for Lincoln. The situation resembled the one we had experienced with my mother two and a half years earlier. Dad was suffering multiple organ failures, and the doctors could do nothing to save him. Once again, my brothers and I held a meeting and agreed to honor Dad's wishes by removing him from life support. Once again, his children and grandchildren gathered in the hospital room to say our goodbyes. Once again, our dying parent woke up long enough to interact with us in a positive way for a few minutes before falling asleep for good.

After Dad fell into an unconscious state, and the family dispersed, Kim and I left the hospital to grab a few hours of sleep at Dad's house, only a five-minute drive away. Powerful thunderstorms had rumbled through Lincoln that evening. When we arrived at his house on Edwards Street, we noticed a massive oak tree in the back-yard had succumbed to the wind and fallen over. If the birch tree I chopped down as a five-year-old symbolized Mom's paralysis, then the fallen oak tree marked Dad's imminent passing. Later I observed to Tom, "Two great oaks fell on this night."

The call came from Tom around 2:30 a.m. We all got up and made coffee, knowing there would be no more sleep for some time. A few minutes later, Tom arrived from the hospital, and we pondered the timing of Dad's death. Did he surmise he wouldn't be able to go home—that he would have to go into a nursing home—and did he will himself to die? I don't know if such a thing is even possible. However, if it is, my father possessed the motivation and determination to pull it off.

In another example of motivation and determination, I believe Dad died secure in the knowledge that he had protected the secret he always wanted to keep—the truth about what happened the night my mother got hurt. But that wasn't the case. He had leaked the real story out on a couple of occasions, and other people who were present the night my mother got hurt had leaked it out, too. He may have imagined a world where he could control the narrative, albeit for honorable purposes. However, like trying to hold an inflated balloon underwater, one slip-up and the truth would find its way to the surface.

If I had waited until Father's Day to show Dad the slides, as planned, instead of changing the date to two weeks earlier, he never would have seen them—a collection of photos mostly taken by him—an anthology of his life until middle age. What a shame that would have been. But I sometimes wonder if the emotions triggered when he watched the video and perused the slides led to his demise. More than once I have asked myself, *Did I hasten my father's death?*

When Kim and I started dating, Kim became amused by the sign Mom left taped on the door whenever Dad worked the night shift. Kim produced a beautiful, hardwood version which read "Welcome" on one side and "Don't Knock, Ted Is Sleeping" on the other. It hung on the door until my father retired from the mill, the appropriate message displayed depending on whether he was working the night shift or not. Kim and I recovered this sign from my parents' house after my father passed on. I considered making it a permanent feature at his gravesite, but several people told me that would be disrespectful.

I still haven't ruled it out.

CHAPTER 39

Karl Benz's Invention

In grade school I learned who invented the telephone, the airplane, bifocals, even the cotton gin, whatever that was. But I had to consult Wikipedia recently to find out that Karl Benz built the first automobile in 1886. This made me wonder, if Benz invented the automobile, who was Mercedes? It turns out, Mercedes was the name of a car made by a company that merged with Benz's company. There you have it.

Today, because of Karl Benz's invention, people live in the suburbs while enjoying access to work, shopping, entertainment, and so forth. But take away the automobile, or the ability to drive one, and the idyllic notion of suburbia crumbles. Life becomes a glorified house arrest. That's what I faced in 2011 with my advancing MS. Once I couldn't work or drive, I would have nothing to do except watch the grass grow. The time had come to move out of the suburbs.

We hired a realtor, put our house up for sale, and began a search for a new home. It had to be as accessible as the one we owned but in a more walkable neighborhood. Yes, I get the irony.

Urban areas have older homes. Older homes tend to be vertically oriented and not wheelchair accessible. After a couple of months, we became frustrated with the process and considered remaining in the suburbs. Then we stumbled upon an advertisement for a single-story home, built only ten years earlier and located in a downtown area.

As soon as we stepped inside, Kim and I looked at each other and knew we had found what we were looking for. The neighborhood suited us perfectly, and the house was even more accessible than the one we were in at the time—open concept, wide doorways, a large bedroom and attached bathroom. It also had features we didn't need but loved—vaulted ceilings and skylights, much-improved energy efficiency, and a view of the ocean. Yes, a freaking view of the ocean.

Unfortunately, we had seen little interest in the sale of our house, and we had no appetite for buying a new house before at least signing a contract on our existing one. So we waited and worried that we would lose this opportunity. After a couple of weeks, we received an offer from a man with MS and his wife. They wanted to move out of the city and into the suburbs so they could start a family, and our house was MS-ready. As soon as we signed a contract with them, we negotiated a purchase agreement on the in-town house. A little over a month later, we sold one house in the morning, became homeless for about an hour, and bought another house in the afternoon. Sometimes things just work out.

Our sixth, and I'm sure final house, is on a dead-end street in an urban area. We don't have as many trees nearby, low-flying jets interrupt our backyard conversations, and strange-looking characters walk by every day. However, we're right in the middle of things, and that's where we want to be.

Our city house is fully wheelchair accessible, but it's the neighborhood that's uniquely suited for me. In one short loop I can drop off a letter at the post office, register my car at City Hall, buy groceries at either of two supermarkets, pick up steaks for dinner at a butcher shop, get breakfast, lunch, or dinner at any of several restaurants, enjoy a glass of beer or wine at any of several bars, or sit and read in either of two city parks. If I have a little more time, I can visit a lighthouse or take the bridge over to Portland. If I'm particularly adventurous, the city bus transportation hub is only two blocks away.

For a short time after our move in the summer of 2011, I continued to drive. I compensated for my weakening left hand and arm in a couple ways. I overused the cruise control function, and I routinely placed the vehicle in park at red lights. People tooted their horns at me when I got off the starting line too slowly at green lights, but I learned to ignore them.

The end came in an unexpected way, though. I used my right arm, the good one, to operate the steering wheel by gripping something referred to as a suicide knob. By the fall of 2011, however, on certain 90-degree corners, I would let go of the gas and brake lever with my left hand to assist my right hand in turning the steering wheel. This caused a sudden deceleration—sometimes at busy intersections. It would only have been a matter of time before somebody rear-ended me.

I knew of more extraordinary driving accommodations I could have employed, such as a joystick-like device. If my disability had been stable—if I wasn't losing functionality—then incorporating these adaptations could have made sense. But I refused to throw a lot of money at solutions that might only serve my needs for a short time.

One day in November, on a 45-minute return trip from hunting, I drove worse than ever, especially on those 90-degree turns. After I arrived home safely, I entered the house, took my coat off, wheeled over to the desk, removed the scissors from the top right drawer, and cut my driver's license in half before I could change my mind.

The dreaded day had arrived, and I hadn't injured or killed anyone in the process. I didn't even have a fender-bender in the six and a half years I drove with my hands. I'm satisfied I gave up driving at just the right time.

The decision to stop driving incurred collateral damage. I still enjoyed hunting from my wheelchair and my van through the beginning of the 2011 season. I could take part in this activity without anybody's help, except in those rare instances when I shot a deer, like in 2010. A week after I stopped driving, I had my nephew Brad pick me up, take me to my hunting spot, and drive me home. I knew my friends and relatives would help out anytime I wanted, but it wasn't the same. Something else had changed, too. Dad was no longer there to answer the phone and hear my stories, having passed away that summer. I hadn't realized what an important role he played in motivating me to continue hunting. So, midway through deer season, without ceremony or regret, I placed my gun in the cabinet, for good I think. That was enough hunting.

Despite having mentally prepared myself for the end of driving, and despite all the benefits of our move downtown, losing the ability to drive frightened me. MS had threatened my independence many times, yet I had adjusted rather than succumbed. Even with public transportation and a walkable neighborhood, surrendering my driver's license meant giving up a degree of freedom and autonomy. Going forward, I would become more reliant on others. Each loss of this type—ability to walk, to work, to drive—chipped away at my quality of life. Every deficit pushed me from the mainstream to the fringe, to a place where, if I wasn't careful, I could be forgotten. A place where I could even lose myself. I feared that this loss of independence might lead me there.

But, as with my diagnosis, selling my snowmobiles, and other dreaded events, giving up on driving meant a weight had been lifted from my shoulders. "There, that's done," came into play again. Also, as with so many of my challenges, I had seen this happen before with my mother, and I witnessed her determination to thrive and live a rewarding life nevertheless.

It was these factors, and countless others, which allowed me to survive yet another loss. I marshaled on. If MS is ever to take away this coping ability, well, that may be the one loss I can't survive.

CHAPTER 40

Enchanted Island

As my MS continued to advance, the sensible course of action would have been to stay home, where everything had been set up to my liking. But I didn't want to live a cautious life. Once in a while I wanted to have a little fun.

We had never been on a cruise or gone to a resort in the Caribbean. Given my wife's frugality, I knew it would be a difficult sell.

"I've been thinking about something," I began.

"Oh, this should be good," Kim responded as she peered over the top of her Sudoku puzzle book.

"Please, let me lay out my case and finish my argument before you interrupt. We certainly have more important things to spend our money on, but I want us to go on a cruise . . . "

"I'm in. How about April?"

I stared blankly.

"Oh, forgive me for interrupting. You were about to show me a PowerPoint or an Excel spreadsheet with all the benefits, I assume."

That woman is full of surprises, most of them good.

We met our cruise ship at Port Canaveral, about an hour's drive due east of the Orlando airport. An employee directed us to a special section of the boarding area. As I looked around, I realized we had been herded together with all the other cripples. We watched as a wedding party walked on to the ship (the only people more privileged than we were), and then my group boarded. What a fine looking parade we were—wheelchairs, scooters, walkers, canes, too old, too fat, bearded lady, sword swallower, you name it. But I didn't feel conspicuous. These were my peeps now.

A few weeks earlier, I had spoken to Independence Technology, the manufacturer of the iBot, to purchase some new tires. While making small talk, I mentioned our upcoming cruise vacation. Five minutes after I hung up the phone, the representative from Independence Technology, Kristin, called me back.

"Because you told me you are going on a cruise, I must inform you that you cannot use the balance mode on board under any circumstances. The ship's swaying will cause a malfunction in the gyroscopes that control the iBot."

I responded, "Duly noted, Kristin. However, I must inform you that I've done a lot of things in the iBot I'm not supposed to do, and I *will* try out balance mode on the ship."

I used balance mode early and often on the cruise and encountered no problems. At one point, when the seas became rough, I appeared to move back and forth like a pendulum, about three feet to port and three feet to starboard. "Why are you moving around so much?" a bystander asked.

"I'm standing perfectly still. It's the ship and you people who keep moving back and forth." He realized I was right, and we had a good laugh about it.

Before we left for vacation, I had connected with a Jamaican taxi service on the Internet in preparation for our port of call in Ocho Rios. For $150, Duane agreed to drive us around the island in his wheelchair accessible van for about four hours.

On the morning we docked in Jamaica, Kim and I took a moment to stand on the top deck of our cruise ship and survey the island. We could see a city with traffic and shops and so on. Beyond the city lay densely forested mountains, dark and mysterious. "This island looks enchanted," I said to Kim.

We arrived at the taxi stand about half an hour before our agreed-upon meeting time with Duane. A no-nonsense lady took charge of matching up riders with taxis. She asked me if I wanted an accessible taxi. "Actually, I have a van reserved," I said.

"With who?" she snapped. I was wasting her time.

"Duane."

"I never heard of no Duane."

Not good. I began to wonder if he even existed.

The lady in charge motioned for a taxi driver nearby who had a wheelchair accessible van. He came over and asked if I needed a tour of the island. I repeated, "No thanks. I've already made arrangements with someone else. We're a little early." I'd seen a picture of Duane, and he was about 30 years younger than this guy.

"What's the name of the person you are waiting for?" the taxi driver asked.

"Duane," I replied, exposing my naïveté for all to see.

"Oh, I work for him. I spoke to him last night, and he told me to pick you up today. Didn't he mention it to you?"

"Oh, no," I said, becoming confused.

"And the deal was?" he asked.

"One hundred and fifty dollars for four hours," I responded automatically, as if telling the truth was the best or the only option in this transaction.

"Right," he said while accepting my greenbacks. "Follow me." We obeyed.

I was surprised to see another couple already seated in the large van—Diego and Erika—from the wedding party which had boarded ahead of us in Port Canaveral. They were lovely people, and we spent a lot of time with them the rest of the week, after braving Jamaica together.

The driver identified himself as Sebastián and assumed the classic Jamaican tour guide persona, which put us at ease (ya Mon). He pulled away from the curb, and we soon found ourselves at a low-budget strip mall. Sebastián said, "Don't buy anything from vendors other than the ones I tell you to, or you'll get ripped off."

Translation: "Don't buy anything from vendors other than the ones I tell you to, or I won't get a piece of the action."

Kim and I bought two T-shirts that disintegrated the first time we washed them at home.

As we boarded the van for our next destination, a younger man approached Sebastián. They had words, and Sebastián handed him some money. The younger man came up to me and said, "Hi, I'm Duane."

I recognized him from the photo he had sent me. "I'm glad to meet you. Was I supposed to go with Sebastián, or should I have waited for you?"

"Oh, it's cool, Mon. We all work together here to make sure you are happy." It was then I realized Sebastián had stolen our business from Duane, but Duane didn't want to admit as much to me. Apparently, they reached a financial settlement anyway.

As Sebastián pulled away from the strip mall the four of us informed him that we didn't want any more lame tourist traps like this one. We wanted to see the *real* Jamaica. Diego leaned over and whispered in Sebastián's ear. Kim turned to me and reported, "Diego asked Sebastián if he could buy some pot."

Kim scooched forward in her seat and said to Diego, "I can hear what you're talking about."

"Oh, I'm sorry. Is that a problem?" asked Diego.

Kim and I considered ourselves to be open-minded, almost hip, for our generation. "It's no problem at all," Kim said, letting him off the hook.

"Do whatever you want," I said. "It's cool."

"Thank you! I was so worried you would be freaked out," said Diego. We were a little freaked out, but we didn't want to show it.

During the next few hours, we met a variety of peculiar Jamaican characters, all of whom knew Sebastián by name. He showed us giant spider webs, mountainsides cultivated with pot plants, a mysterious, secluded beach, and a wooden carving of a man with an enormous, erect penis. They called him Ready Freddy. It felt like we had fallen through a rabbit hole into some alternate universe.

Before we saw these authentic Jamaican oddities, however, there was the matter of Sebastián filling the order for Diego. We pulled up beside a ramshackle house. Sebastián took some cash from Diego and left the four of us alone in the van. A couple of minutes later, he emerged with a small bag of the local harvest. He indicated that Diego couldn't smoke in the van. We needed to go to a special location to light up.

Sebastián parked in front of a private home on the side of a steep mountain, and had us follow him on to the back deck, which had been constructed from a mishmash of plywood and scrap lumber. A blue tarp served as the roof. Kim asked Sebastián, "Do you think this deck is safe for Mitch and his wheelchair? Together they weigh over 500 pounds."

"Yes, I'm sure it's all right," Sebastián replied. We accepted his judgment as if he were an expert on structural matters. This was his island, his universe after all, and maybe the laws of physics here were unique.

From the deck we were afforded a spectacular view of the harbor, allowing us to forget for a moment about any risk we might be taking: traveling the back roads with Sebastián, making drug deals, standing on a makeshift deck. Also, I found it somehow reassuring that I could see our cruise ship below. Two locals approached me with a selection of hand-carved pot pipes. "No thank you," I said. "That's your man, over there." I pointed to Diego.

Sebastián expertly rolled up a joint. He lit it and handed it to Diego, who took a long drag. Obviously, he had smoked a lot of pot in his day. Diego offered the lit joint to me. I thought about how regimented my life had become, how I had lost the ability to take risks to appease my adventurous side, how rare it had become for me to experience a unique thrill. I thought about how many people with MS raved about the positive effects of smoking the herb, and how I owed myself a non-blinded, non-placebo-controlled trial of this treatment option. I thought about all these things in about a half of a second and said, "Ya, fuck it." I took a hit, and another, and another.

Yes, I got stoned while sitting in my wheelchair on a ramshackle deck at some dude's house in Jamaica, with an American I had just met, and a mysterious taxi driving, spell casting, drug dealing, structural engineering, rabbit hole tour guide named Sebastián.

And it felt good.

CHAPTER 41

It's Always the Bathroom

Our parents leave us too early in life. Our spouses and children don't join us until later. It's only our siblings who might be with us for the whole ride, if we're so fortunate. In my case, Tom and Andy have always been there, and I hope they always will.

I can't remember who came up with the idea, but it made perfect sense. My brothers and I agreed to set aside a portion of our modest inheritance to commune on a tropical beach for a week. After much debate, we decided our wives could come along too, if they promised to behave themselves. They did promise, although two of them turned out to be liars.

We decided on the Sandals Royal Bahamian, near Nassau, Bahamas. The resort claimed to have a handicapped-accessible class of rooms, so we booked one for five nights, and my brothers reserved rooms nearby.

I've stayed in a lot of crappy, supposedly handicapped-accessible rooms in the past (mostly in greater New York City). Sometimes I didn't even have space to turn my chair around. When I opened the door to our room at Sandals, I felt a sense of relief. It was spacious and welcoming: flat screen TV, four-poster bed, stocked bar (complimentary). A large sliding glass door led to the ground level, private patio. Nice.

Then we looked in the bathroom. Damn. It's always the bathroom.

I couldn't pull under the sink in my wheelchair. The toilet sat too low with no grab bars nearby. The bathtub/shower was an oval-shaped garden style, tall on the outside and deep on the inside. The only grab bar in the shower was located at the far end. I couldn't even reach it. Per my request at the time of booking, Sandals did provide a shower seat.

We studied the situation, scratched our heads, and came up with a plan. I leaned my head over into the tub so Kim could shampoo my hair. Then I sat on the shower seat, outside the bathtub, and Kim hosed me down and provided what was essentially a sponge bath. I discovered that I loved sponge baths. They combine the best parts of a shower and a massage. I told Kim I would be cleaned in this manner henceforth, even when we returned from vacation.

I'm still waiting for that first sponge bath at home.

We complained about the room to the hospitality manager. She admitted the resort was woefully negligent in providing real handicapped-accessible rooms, apologized, and offered compensation. She gave Kim and me a voucher for a three-night complimentary stay on our next Sandals vacation. Not bad, but she wasn't done.

This all-inclusive resort didn't include everything. The most high-class restaurant sat at the end of a pier and charged $140 per couple to dine. As further compensation, the hospitality manager made reservations for the six of us there, on the house, a $420 value. Not bad at all.

When we opened the dinner menus, as expected, we saw no prices for the food items. However, the wine and champagne prices ranged from $50 to $200 per bottle. I asked the waiter, Shannon, "I thought the drinks were included in the $140 fee per couple?"

"Oh, our house wines and champagnes are included. This bottle list is for premium brands." The six of us laughed at the state of near panic we had talked ourselves into.

"Please bring a bottle of your house champagne and your house Pinot Noir to get things started," Andy said. We went through several bottles. This was the night Karen misbehaved, and that's all I'm allowed to say on the subject.

But I will go into some detail about the day Kim misbehaved. The DJ by the main pool announced a "Best Woman" competition. Before he even explained the events, Kim raised her hand. That's how she operates—dive in first, learn to swim later. I gave her several reasons why she should not participate, and I thought I had prevailed in the argument. I made the mistake, however, of leaving her alone for a few minutes while I went to the bathroom. Damn, it's always the bathroom.

When I returned to the pool area, I heard the DJ introducing the contestants, and there stood Kim as contestant number five. The first round of the competition consisted of an interview question. "Tell me why you are with your man." The DJ encouraged answers of the raunchy variety. The lady from Wisconsin said she was with her man because, like Wisconsin trees themselves, her husband had good wood. Another mentioned something about big hands and big feet.

For me to return to our table, I had to go right by the DJ and the contestants. The timing was perfect. I had elevated to balance mode in my iBot, and Kim pointed in my direction as she said, "I'm with my husband because I get to have sex in *that* whenever I want."

The DJ and the other guests loved her response. To keep the momentum going, the DJ walked over to me with the microphone and asked, "What do you have to say about that?"

"Once in a while she even lets me join in," I said, as smoothly as if we had rehearsed the interview.

The crowd roared, and the DJ declared Kim the winner of round one. Round two required the ladies to perform those adapted push-ups, the ones with knees on the ground. Each woman completed more push-ups than the woman before, and contestant number four churned out 55 of them. Then came Kim's turn. I couldn't watch, lest anyone accuse me of endorsing this fiasco. I heard the DJ count off her push-ups. She was so pumped up, she did them at twice the pace everyone else had. I thought, *she's going to crash and burn,* and I was right. At about 45 she started laboring but wouldn't give up. The DJ had to make her stop. Round two went to the lady from Wisconsin.

Round three required the women to pole dance, except they didn't have a pole, so they used an umbrella stand. The first competitor figured out the umbrella stand wasn't particularly stable. The doctors said she might one day walk without crutches but will never again pole dance. Once more, I couldn't watch. The crowd cheered and laughed throughout the first four seductive dances, and then Kim's turn came.

To this day, I don't know what she did. All I know is that it drove the crowd into a frenzy. By popular vote, Kim became "Best Woman."

Later that evening, more than one man approached Kim and asked if she could teach those pole dancing moves to their wives.

* * *

Despite the challenges of disabled travel, we decided to vacation in the Caribbean again the following year. After all, we couldn't allow that voucher for three free nights to go unused. This time, Andy and Karen couldn't make it, so it was only the four of us. We decided on the Sandals resort at White House, Jamaica. (No, I would not be calling Sebastián for taxi service.)

Having been to a Sandals resort just a year earlier, we knew what to expect. Upon arrival, they gave us moist, lemon-scented towels to wipe our faces and hands. Uber-friendly attendants carried our bags and helped us check-in. Champagne flowed. Worries melted.

Again, we booked a first-floor room with a private, walk-out patio. I had spoken with several people at Sandals, and they sent pictures, so I had confidence this room would be more accessible than the one in the Bahamas. However, upon inspection, it looked almost identical—no accessibility features at all. But it had a beautiful view and sat only a few feet from the beach.

We wondered what had happened to the accessible room in the pictures. We didn't wonder for long. The concierge called us to explain how happy he was to have been able to provide a complimentary room upgrade. That was fine, I explained, but they had upgraded us out of a handicapped room into a non-handicapped one. I asked if we could see one of the accessible rooms. We were underwhelmed. The handicapped features were legitimate, although the quality of the room came up short in every other way. We chose luxury over accessibility, and in doing so, I chose sponge baths over showers.

I always carried a portable urinal so I could empty my bladder while sitting in my wheelchair and then pour the contents into the toilet. Yes, the advantages we men enjoy in the bathroom, relative to women, extend even to the handicapped population. Most of the public bathrooms at the resort, however, afforded me no privacy for this task, because the stalls were too small for the iBot to pull into completely. Men don't expect privacy when urinating, but given my unusual technique, I would have appreciated it.

When it came to bowel control, I rocked. On this five-night visit, I only had to go twice. The toilet in my room had no accessibility features, so Kim and I scouted out some of the public bathrooms to find the one that worked best. Besides looking for a higher toilet, grab bars, and a spacious stall, we also wanted to find a less busy bathroom. This way, Kim could come in and assist me without being exposed to things she didn't want to see.

We found the best location we could, and the process went well. However, things didn't go as smoothly the second time, a couple of days later, at the other end of the resort. Instead of using the same toilet, I suggested we try a similar one much closer. With Kim's help, I transferred to the toilet. But when it came time for the more difficult upward transfer (the toilet sat lower than my wheelchair), this stall design differed enough from the other one that we couldn't figure out a way for Kim to help me transfer. We needed one more body.

I'm not self-conscious in these circumstances, so I asked Kim to walk out into the general area and find "the first Jamaican dude you see." The resort's male employees were plentiful, clearly identified by their clothing, and always willing to help. This girl, who had no problem pole dancing in public a year earlier, frowned at my suggestion. She considered it distasteful to approach a total stranger and ask him to accompany her into the men's room. I'll never figure her out.

When Kim didn't return in a couple of minutes, I surmised that she had set out to find my brother, not some Jamaican dude. Indeed, she hiked across the entire complex and found Tom lounging at the pool nearest our hotel rooms. Of course, he accepted the mission.

In my boredom, I contemplated alternative ways to gain leverage with my arms and transfer myself. It was a long shot.

After I had analyzed the problem—possibly solving simultaneous differential equations in my head, possibly not—I contorted my body into a precise configuration to optimize the applied forces. In doing so, I accomplished by myself what Kim and I could not accomplish together. I give credit to what remained of my once keen engineering mind. Or it may have just been shit luck. At the moment when Tom and Kim burst into the bathroom to rescue me from the swirling abyss, they found me sitting in my wheelchair and zipping up my shorts with a smug look on my face.

After five glorious days, we dragged ourselves back to the airport in Montego Bay, Jamaica, for our return to Portland, Maine via Charlotte. On major trips I bring two wheelchairs—in this case my iBot for obvious reasons and an inexpensive backup power wheelchair for use when the iBot was charging. Our flight from Charlotte landed in Portland late at night, and an attendant met me at the airplane exit with a manual wheelchair. He pushed me to the baggage claim area where we found all our bags. We looked around for my wheelchairs but didn't see them.

Kim found the USAir baggage agent and inquired about my chairs. The agent spoke to some people on the radio, made a phone call or two, and deduced that the wheelchairs were not in Portland. One remained in Charlotte, and the other one somehow made it to Philadelphia, of all places. I saw both chairs in Charlotte during our three-hour layover, so I had not expected trouble.

In a calm but firm manner, I expressed my disappointment to the baggage claim employee. She looked at our claim tickets and filled out a report for missing "luggage." She gave me a 1-800 phone number to check on the status of my chairs the next day.

"Obviously, I need to take this wheelchair that I'm sitting in now home with me. I'm unable to walk even a little," I said.

"I can't authorize you to do that. I'm a USAir employee, and this is an airport wheelchair."

If she had said something like, "Yes, clearly you can take the chair home with you. I'll let somebody who works for the airport know you borrowed it," things would have gone so much better for her.

Tom had stood by silently the entire time, but could withstand the indignity no longer. He explained the absurdity of her statement and the incompetence of her airline, employing colorful words and phrases. When he had exhausted himself, Kim suggested he fetch the wheelchair van from the parking garage and bring it to the curb outside baggage claim. He agreed. As soon as Tom went out of sight, I said to the USAir employee, "I'm sorry my brother yelled at you, but you need to know I WILL be taking this wheelchair home. If you like, you can tell your boss you did everything in your power to stop me."

Shell-shocked, she only nodded.

We couldn't retrieve the wheelchairs for another two days, and the airline had damaged the iBot, rendering it unusable. I called Independence Technology, and they couldn't come to my house and repair the chair until the following Monday. I didn't regain use of my iBot wheelchair for nine days. Not good.

After the technician repaired my iBot and sent the $1800 bill to USAir, I started negotiations with them for compensation over and above the repair costs. First, I requested a detailed explanation of how they had misplaced my wheelchairs. Their account made no sense, and the question went unanswered. I cannot imagine how baggage handlers could think misplacing power wheelchairs would not be disastrous for the wheelchair user—for me. Every USAir employee I met in person, I liked. But these nameless, faceless employees screwed me, not unlike the nameless, faceless administrators in the Rituxan trial.

I requested two first-class vouchers for round-trip flights anywhere in the world, one for Kim and one for me. They offered two $100 vouchers. After a couple of weeks of back-and-forth, we agreed on two $600 vouchers. Close enough.

Kim and I appreciate how fortunate we are to go on vacations like these. So many deserving people, healthy and disabled, don't have the vacation opportunities we do, for any number of reasons. We're not wealthy, but we have adjusted our spending decisions more toward living for the day than saving for a rainy day, given the progressive nature of my disease.

We didn't go on these trips confident the accommodations would be completely accessible, and our enjoyment of the vacations was not contingent upon that. Granted, the bathrooms were a huge disappointment. But, due to our creativity, a positive attitude by us and the local management, and a fair compensation package from the first resort, we didn't allow these issues to ruin our vacations. Were the trips worth it? Definitely.

It takes courage to travel with me; I am a prolific blogger. You never know how I'll portray you in my posts. For that matter, it takes courage to visit me at my house, have lunch with me, or even make eye contact with me on the street, for the same reason. What happens with Mitch doesn't stay with Mitch. It gets spread all over the Internet. So I thank my travel companions for the great material they provided for me.

It also takes patience to travel with me because I am a significantly disabled and thus generally inflexible person. I can't go to certain destinations, and I can only take certain flights. Although we won't spend all day, every day together at the resorts, you know if you want to hang out with me I can't do certain things. And of course, if you vacation with me, you know I'll bark out orders now and then so you can be more helpful.

"Do you think that piece of luggage is going to carry itself?"

"Get me another margarita."

"I said NO salt on the rim. Try again!"

"Get out of the way. You're blocking my view of the pool."

"Damn, I look good. Take a picture of me."

"Don't call it a night yet. If Kim has one more rum punch, you guys will have to put me to bed."

Everyone is tolerant of my orders, if largely insubordinate.

CHAPTER 42
Stabbed in the Back

My disease continued to progress, unabated. By early 2012 it had become difficult for me to transfer between wheelchair, toilet, and shower chair. I noticed problems at the dinner table—cutting steak for example. I hadn't tried any treatments since my second CCSVI procedure almost a year earlier, and I saw nothing on the horizon.

Then Marc (Wheelchair Kamikaze) introduced me to research conducted by his Manhattan neurologist, Dr. Sadiq. He had recently published the results of an open-label trial of over one hundred progressive MS subjects whom he treated with intrathecal methotrexate. Most of his PPMS patients either stabilized or improved after beginning this treatment.

Intrathecal means "injected directly into the cerebrospinal fluid, which surrounds the brain and spinal cord." Methotrexate is "an anti-cancer chemotherapy drug." That's right. I, the guy who once said he would never submit to another spinal tap, agreed to have a chemotherapy drug injected into my spinal fluid, via a lumbar puncture, every eight weeks.

I viewed Dr. Sadiq's trial results with a healthy skepticism. He had earned a reputation as a top-notch MS researcher and clinician, so why didn't I trust this study more?

In the medical field, countless encouraging, preliminary studies are later disproved by more substantial, blinded, placebo-controlled follow-up trials. Because no such trial, not even one, had ever been successful for PPMS, I had no reason to believe this treatment protocol would be different. But I was desperate. I didn't have the luxury of time to sit back and wait for everyone to figure this out to the nth degree. As I did with CCSVI treatment, I pushed my doctors, writing:

Good morning Dr. Muscat:

Attached is a retrospective, open-label analysis of over 100 patients that Dr. Sadiq has treated with intrathecal methotrexate. The results are promising:

Of 34 primary progressive patients, EDSS scores (a common measure of MS disability) were stable in 82%, with no significant progression in EDSS post-treatment compared to baseline.

Please review this paper and give me your thoughts. Regards,

Mitch Sturgeon

Dr. Muscat responded:

Mr. Sturgeon:

As always, I am open to trying most things. I certainly understand the risk of doing nothing (you are getting worse), and am willing to proceed with this treatment as long as you realize (which I know you do) the potential risks and uncertain benefit.

And I wrote back:

Thanks for your response. I am aware of the limitations of this study, but I've set the bar pretty low for what qualifies as *promising* when it comes to PPMS treatment.

Dr. Muscat introduced me to Dr. Aronson, a hematologist-oncologist who sometimes administered intrathecal methotrexate to his lymphoma and leukemia patients. I would be his first MS patient.

I never had a more thorough consultation. Dr. Aronson sat with Kim and me for 90 minutes and discussed the research papers I had provided, his experience with this treatment for cancer patients, and my medical history. We became comfortable with one another, and decided to proceed.

In early March of 2012, I had my first spinal infusion and found it moderately unpleasant. Dr. Aronson took a few tries before he found the spot in my back where he could slip the needle between the vertebrae and inject the medicine. But it went well enough that I returned eight weeks later for another round.

The second infusion took place on a Monday, and it felt a little better than the first one. However, I developed the dreaded post-lumbar puncture headache, like in 2001 when I had a spinal tap to confirm my MS diagnosis. I lay flat in bed or reclined in my wheelchair all week long. Sometimes these lumbar puncture headaches resolve themselves within a couple days. If they don't, then the standard treatment is called a blood patch, which I received on Friday afternoon.

The anesthesiologist took blood from an arm vein and injected it into the spinal cord at about the same location as the original puncture. So, I had the pleasure of enduring a second spinal tap that week to treat the side effects from the first spinal tap.

I was thrilled when the blood patch procedure delivered complete and immediate relief, as it almost always does. I once again sat upright in my wheelchair, read my emails, and completed other tasks I had difficulty with while lying flat on my back.

A little over 24 hours later I began to feel headaches again, and by Sunday morning they had resumed in full force. Two days later I went in for a second blood patch, nine days after my initial lumbar puncture. The second patch held.

I found the whole ordeal so unpleasant that I didn't know if I could continue with the treatments. The only thing less appealing, however, was the idea of giving up.

I researched post-lumbar puncture headaches and learned that some doctors used a 25-gauge needle, which is thinner than the standard 22-gauge one. The 25-gauge needles dramatically cut back on the incidence of post-lumbar puncture headaches. I suggested this to Dr. Aronson. He expressed hesitance; this thinner needle would be less rigid, and he worried that he might have trouble controlling its direction. But he agreed to try it, and he encountered no problems. We stuck with that needle the rest of the way.

Nobody enjoyed these infusions, but we all made the best of it. Dr. Aronson's nurse, Stephanie, went out of her way to make Kim and me comfortable and to schedule our visits around Kim's work. My lovely wife made every trip with me, helped me transfer from wheelchair to bed and back, assisted the doctor and Stephanie in contorting my body into the correct position for each infusion, and supported me in countless other ways.

Dr. Aronson didn't need this in his life either. He could have stayed in his comfort zone instead of taking on an MS patient he had never met and administering a procedure which couldn't have been fun for him. But he always said, "As long as you're willing to come in for these infusions, I'm willing to give them to you."

For a couple of reasons, Kim and I routinely go long periods of time without discussing how badly MS is kicking my ass. First, there's the concept of noise. For example, if you weigh yourself on an old-fashioned scale, the needle oscillates back and forth for a while. Of course, your real weight isn't changing, only the scale readout is. That oscillation represents measurement noise. But if you wait long enough, the noise dissipates, and your true weight becomes apparent. It's the same thing with determining disease progression. If we are impatient and try to assess changes in my condition over a short period, we might become confused by noise—day-to-day variation in how my body functions. When we assess progression over six months or a year, the noise cancels itself out, and the real answer becomes apparent.

The other reason we don't talk about disease progression more often is the psychological toll these discussions take on us. The news is rarely good, so conversations on this subject don't contribute to feelings of contentment and happiness. Living in denial is also unhealthy, so we don't forsake these conversations; we just spread them out.

By October of 2012, about eight months into the intrathecal methotrexate treatment, I initiated one of these talks.

"Kim, how do you think I've been doing since I went on the methotrexate?" I didn't give her my opinion first because I didn't want to bias her response.

"I don't know. What do you think?" We play this cat and mouse game at the beginning of every one of these discussions. I usually relent and go first.

"I haven't noticed any disease progression since I started on the stuff."

"I agree. I haven't had to help you any more than I used to. You don't seem to be worse at all this year."

"I hate to be premature," I said, "but I think it's fair to say that the intrathecal methotrexate is working."

Kim and I dance carefully around issues like this. Success is so fleeting, so fragile, that the very act of acknowledging it out loud feels reckless. But the world, my world anyway, wanted to know, and I enjoyed reporting that the treatment appeared to be having a positive effect. I posted as much on my blog and sent notes to Dr. Muscat and Dr. Aronson.

Throughout the next year I received six more infusions. In between, Kim and I went about our business. She worked. I blogged. We laughed. We cried. Well, she cried very little, and I, not at all. We nurtured some friendships, took others for granted, and maybe laid the groundwork for some new ones. We lived mostly in the present, regarded the past fondly, and thought little about the future. I can't say when I first noticed the progression returning. It's never a bang. It's more of a squeak that persists, a mosquito that buzzes and pesters and won't fly away. Toward the end of the second year of my treatments, Kim and I had another of our talks, and once again we reached agreement.

The MS onslaught had resumed, at full force. I struggled with this turn of events. Over the years I had accepted no longer walking, working, driving, and so many other aspects of my former life. Kim and I had developed strategies for my activities of daily living so I could shower, shave, dress, and so forth.

We had handled everything this damn disease had thrown at us. But the worsening disability, that insidious wasting away, threatened to shake my resolve. Whatever I did, it was never enough. MS could not be placated. It demanded so much of me, and then it demanded more.

I've heard it said, "It's not the heat, it's the humidity."

Instead, I say, "It's not the disability, it's the progression."

I shared my assessment with Dr. Muscat. He still had overall charge of my intrathecal methotrexate program, though Dr. Aronson administered the treatments. We agreed I would get only a few more infusions before giving up, unless it started working again.

Every oncologist, especially one with such a long and accomplished career, has witnessed untold human misery. When you sign up to be a cancer doctor, you know all your cases will be of the life and death variety. As a matter of personal survival, I assume oncologists must develop the means to temper their natural grief response. Of course, oncology isn't only about misery; it's also about guiding patients back to health, rescuing children for their parents or one spouse for another.

When Dr. Aronson greeted me for my infusion visit in early 2014, as usual, he asked, "How are you doing?" I had come to know Dr. Aronson reasonably well, and I had grown fond of him. I think he felt the same way toward me.

"Unfortunately, the relief I felt during the first year of this treatment has gone away, and my disease progression has resumed."

He said nothing, and he avoided eye contact with me.

I continued, "My legs are unresponsive, and my hands are headed in the same direction. Unless this changes in the next couple of months, we should stop the treatments." I delivered this assessment dispassionately, as if I were ordering replacement vacuum cleaner bags over the phone.

He finally looked at me and said, "I'm so sorry to hear that."

I noticed genuine pain in his eyes, and this surprised me, although it shouldn't have. I had assumed if I could speak with anyone so bluntly, it would be my oncologist. However, just like doctors sometimes fail to take into account a patient's emotional needs, I didn't give his feelings any consideration. By springing this information on him so directly, my behavior was no better than inconsiderate doctors I have complained about over the years.

We proceeded with infusion number thirteen and scheduled number fourteen.

I decided, with Dr. Muscat's agreement, not to go back for the fourteenth treatment. I informed Stephanie and Dr. Aronson via email, and that was that.

CHAPTER 43
Challenges

Mental Challenges

Our brains operate on two levels. I'm particularly grateful for my conscious self. Through it, I ponder complex issues and navigate unfamiliar spaces. I express myself, and I comprehend others. I experience life in an open-minded and thoughtful manner. My consciousness is the "be" in the question "To be or not to be?" It's my intellect, my individuality, my muse.

I'm not as intimate with the subconscious part of my brain. For most of my life, it has operated effectively in the background. One exception has been my struggle with claustrophobia. Even if the tight space I am in presents no risk, at any moment I might feel compelled to get out, and fast.

In 2012, a new problem developed. Deprived of drama by my ever-sensible conscious self, my subconscious invented and then over-reacted to problems that never existed. I began suffering brief anxiety attacks. They felt like the panicky sensation I had experienced with claustrophobia, except less intense. I categorized them as mini panic attacks. Over time they became more frequent.

Seemingly innocuous events triggered these attacks, and these events shared a common theme. Attacks occurred when I seemed to lose control of some basic physical function. No emergencies existed worthy of the spike of adrenaline, the increased heart rate, and the urge to flee that I experienced. For example, sometimes my feet would become tangled up in the blankets in the middle of the night, and I would have to ask Kim to help me free them. This was a harmless situation. In my subconscious mind, however, it rose to the status of an emergency, and a panic attack ensued. As a person who is, in fact, losing control of many core functions, perhaps I should forgive my subconscious for its overzealousness.

Given that these trigger situations would only become more common as my MS continued to progress, I thought it wise to act sooner rather than later. I visited a therapist for the first time in my life. She taught me that panic attacks are common and treatable. She introduced me to a set of techniques based on Cognitive Behavioral Therapy (CBT), which interrupt and mitigate the irrational spirals associated with panic attacks.

After six weeks of therapy, I noticed the intensity of my attacks had lessened, but they still existed at an unacceptable level. I talked this over with my therapist, and she encouraged me to visit my physician to discuss pharmaceutical options as a supplement to the CBT program.

Antidepressant drugs called SSRIs are effective not only for clinical depression (which I didn't have) but also for taking the edge off anxiety (which I did have). From the day I started using SSRIs, I have had zero panic attacks.

People with MS are particularly susceptible to depression and anxiety. It can be a direct result of nerve damage in our brains, or it can be a secondary consequence of the stress from dealing with a chronic disease. No matter the cause, the treatment is the same.

This episode dealt a blow to my ego. I thought my emotional stability and mental toughness set me apart from the crowd. In retrospect, this feeling of superiority was both misguided and self-defeating. I should no more be given credit for decades of panic-free existence than I should be blamed for the recent panic attacks. Notions of pride and shame are of no value in this discussion, and in fact, only muddy the waters.

Physical Challenges
Meanwhile, the physical challenges continued to mount. The transfer from toilet to wheelchair was my most complicated one—the long division of transfers, the Rubik's Cube of disabled maneuvers. I had become well practiced, however, and when properly executed, the

process went off without a hitch. At this house, with this toilet, I had enjoyed an unblemished record.

One day, while performing this transfer for the hundredth time, I felt myself lunge forward, and I knew I was screwed. My hand missed the wheelchair armrest, and I nosedived toward the hard bathroom floor. The sudden impact sent a jolt through my body, and I feared I had broken something. I solicited status reports from different parts of my body. My left knee and my right elbow felt they had been handled roughly. But I didn't sense any significant pain. I had survived the fall.

Zach, home on his college break, responded to my shouts for help. First, I asked him to pull up my pants to cover my bare ass. I'm not sure which of us felt more relieved when that was taken care of. Next, I had him roll me over on to my back and place a pillow behind my head. I reached in my shirt pocket, pulled out my cell phone, and called Kim at work. I knew it would take two people and some ingenuity to get me back into my wheelchair.

The three of us brainstormed for configurations that might raise me off the floor. Zach and Kim pulled and tugged on my arms and legs, but everything they did hurt me. My body had become stiff over the years, and I didn't respond well to pressure applied in unusual directions. Then I remembered that after my mother had passed away five years earlier, we took possession of her portable Hoyer lift, a device used to help transfer her from bed to wheelchair and back. Kim and Zach rummaged through the attic and found all the pieces.

Kim rolled me on my side and laid the canvas sling under my butt. Ever so slowly, Zach worked the lifting lever while Kim supported me. It wasn't pretty—we didn't know what we were doing—but eventually they raised me high enough that we could slide the wheelchair underneath me and release the lift. We uttered a collective sigh of relief. Kim went back to work. Zachary went back to his video games. I went back to my beloved computer.

Many folks would have been flustered, embarrassed, or disheartened by this experience. But I am blessed with that positive disposition—straight from my mother. For example, at several points in the Hoyer lifting process, much to Kim's annoyance, I called a time-out and had Zachary shoot a picture with my iPhone. Even in that stressful situation, I thought ahead to a blog post. I imagined I would appear composed and handsome throughout the whole episode. The photos instead revealed an old, balding, fat guy who looked and felt like a beached whale. I deleted them all. MS had taken so much from me, yet a smidgeon of vanity remained.

Communications Challenges

The importance of precise communications became apparent the next time I had an urgent need for Kim's help. While attempting to transfer from the shower seat into my wheelchair, I met with difficulty, and so called out Kim's name. I heard her talking to someone on the phone in the next room. After 30 seconds or so, I added some urgency and volume to my request. "Kim!"

"Oh," she said. "I heard you the first time, but I was talking on the phone and didn't realize the urgency."

We had to invent a better system—one that didn't rely on her interpretation of the level of panic in my voice. Here's what we came up with. If I needed Kim only at her earliest convenience, I would shout her name. If I needed her with some urgency, but it wasn't a critical situation, I would shout, "Kim, code yellow." When she heard this she would calmly, although without undue delay, stop what she was doing and walk over to assist me. In an emergency, I would need her to drop what she was doing and run to my aid with reckless abandon. In this case, I would shout, "Code red!"

It seemed a workable system. Then, as good luck would have it, no code yellow or code red situations arose until months later—on Kim's 49th birthday. It had been a while since I had tried to transfer from bed to wheelchair in the morning, without Kim's assistance. Because it was her birthday, and she was sleeping peacefully, I thought I'd give it a try.

I surprised myself by swinging my feet off the bed and sitting up with ease. The next step required me to lean forward as far as I could, almost kissing the wheelchair seat facing me. Then I marshaled the collective strength in my arms, my torso, and my legs, and in a coordinated, if not graceful movement, I raised myself upward. I stood, so to speak, with my knees against the front of the wheelchair. Each hand gripped a wheelchair armrest. I took a quick breather and prepared for the grand finale.

This culminating movement required me to pivot 180 degrees counterclockwise and gently fall back into the wheelchair. I'm not sure where the failure occurred. I may have missed the bed with my left hand or the armrest with my right. Perhaps my legs got twisted, or my knees buckled. No matter the cause, I found myself ever so slowly sinking into the gap between bed and wheelchair, as powerless as if I had stepped in quicksand on Gilligan's Island.

I yelled, "Code Red!"

Kim, still groggy, responded with, "What?"

Only half awake, she couldn't understand the unintelligible sounds I assaulted her with in the early morning darkness. Unwilling or unable to alter my communication strategy, I more urgently shouted, "Code Red, Code Red!"

If I had kept my wits about me and had not been in a state of semi-panic, I might have used my words to remind Kim of the meaning behind Code Red.

Finally, my pleas registered with Kim, and she sprang into action. With athletic prowess, she slid across the bed and wriggled one leg and one hand underneath me, preventing me from falling farther. She and I worked in unison to overcome gravity, a quarter inch at a time, until my butt sat on the wheelchair cushion. "Great save, Kim!" I said.

This is a common theme. Ever since I met Kim, she has been making one great save after another.

Intimacy Challenges

I remember my mother being physically affectionate with me before her accident—part of our silent promise. Hugs and kisses abounded. After her accident, the wheelchair got in the way. It didn't have to be like that. We could have made a conscious effort to be affectionate, but we didn't. For most of my life after her accident, I was disinclined toward affection with anybody, especially public displays thereof. Would I have been that sort of person anyway, or was it a reaction to having affection so abruptly removed from my life? I'll never know.

Kim has a normal, healthy desire for human touch. Back in my pre-MS days, when she became affectionate (in a non-sexual way), I didn't hate it, but I wasn't sad when it was over, and I rarely initiated. I would have been content with no physical intimacy at all outside of the bedroom.

It's difficult to achieve a quality embrace when you're sitting in a wheelchair. During a hug, shoulders touch, but that's about it. Because the standing person must lean over so far, the hug rarely lasts long. Now that physical intimacy has become more difficult for me to achieve, I've decided it's something I want. Isn't that always the way?

One opportunity for me to experience nonsexual physical intimacy is while lying in bed, liberated from my wheeled contraption. Our bed looks like a king-sized mattress, but it's actually two twin mattresses butted up against one another. We are always experimenting with hand railing systems on either side of my twin mattress to help me adjust my position a little bit in the middle of the night. Having a railing on the outside of my mattress doesn't interfere with intimacy. However, a railing between our two mattresses might as well be a brick wall. Recently, when we removed one of those center railings, Kim slid over and cuddled with me for a long while, and it felt nice.

We need to continue to eliminate barriers to physical intimacy because Kim's touch heals my damaged body and nourishes my aching soul.

Social Challenges

I only wish I could blame the following tale of social ineptitude on MS.

I am blessed with a strong and accurate gaydar. I can tell if a person is straight or gay almost immediately. I know, it shouldn't matter, and it doesn't. It's just the way my brain works. Incidentally, I'm a big supporter of gay rights, and I have lots of gay friends.

We used to own a Ford Explorer. The mileage got high, and the maintenance bills piled up, so we decided to sell it. I advertised on Craigslist and divulged the known problems. I received an email from Jessie, who wanted to look at the vehicle the next day.

A light, steady rain fell as I heard a knock on the door. I invited Jessie in. She stood at an average height, had a sturdy build, and sported a short haircut. She asked me detailed questions about the vehicle. This woman knew more about cars than I did. My gaydar started twitching, but I was far from certain.

Jessie seemed trustworthy, and I handed the keys to her so she could take the Explorer for a drive. I couldn't exactly accompany her. She drove around for about 10 minutes, returned, and crawled underneath the vehicle for a while. She didn't mind the rain. She was concerned about the brake fluid level, so she went to the local auto parts store, bought some fluid, topped off the reservoir, and went back under to see if the brake lines had any leaks.

Satisfied, she came in the house to start the negotiations. We went back and forth until we agreed on a price. The vehicle was registered in both my name and Kim's, so we needed Kim's signature, but she was at work.

Jessie said, "Well, my partner will be picking me up in a few minutes. I can take the paperwork to Kim at her school so she can sign it."

Ding, ding, ding. The word "partner" was all my gaydar needed to hear. *I am so good. I just see things other people don't.*

The general election was only a few weeks away, and there happened to be a gay rights referendum on the state ballot that year. I thought this would be an excellent opportunity to get a perspective on the issue from a member of the LGBT community.

"I'm curious to know, how excited are you about the gay rights referendum? If it passes, will it make a big difference in your life?"

"I don't know what you're implying. For your information, I've been married to my husband for twelve years, and we have two children."

"But, but," I stammered, "you said 'partner.'"

"My business partner. My business partner is coming to pick me up in ten minutes."

It served me right for stereotyping. I backtracked and apologized and tried to extract my foot from my mouth. Jessie forgave me, and we continued with the transaction. I called Kim to explain that the buyer would be arriving shortly with paperwork to sign.

I added, "Don't ask her if she's a lesbian. I already did, and she's not."

"You didn't."

"Oh yeah, I did."

CHAPTER 44

Lightning Strikes

Lynn (the girl from the Unfortunate Popcorn Incident) and I lost track of one another after that fateful night at the movie theater. Later in life, however, we discovered that we lived only a few miles apart in southern Maine. We met for lunch. When I recounted the story of our childhood breakup, Lynn was horrified. She had no memory of the circumstances, and after much questioning, I believed her. Kim, Lynn, and I have become close friends, confidants, and drinking buddies.

A couple of years after my father passed away, Lynn and her partner, Tim, rented a cabin in Lincoln for a week and invited us to spend a couple of days with them. By mid-afternoon we arrived at the rental cabin on Little Narrows Pond, the same pond where my mother had fallen and become a quadriplegic more than 40 years earlier. We hadn't been back to Lincoln since cleaning out my parents' house after Dad passed away.

The first order of business was to get me and my two wheelchairs up the five steps from the driveway on to the wraparound deck. Kim guided me and the iBot up without incident.

To help us get the Invacare chair into the house, we found some rusty metal ramps in a shed and laid them on the stairs. I was highly knowledgeable about the operation of this wheelchair, and I had managed several multimillion dollar engineering projects in my career, so I appointed myself foreman. I explained to the others that we needed one person manning the joystick and two people pushing on the chair from behind. I would coordinate from the top of the staircase.

There I stood in balance mode, lording over my subordinates. I barked out orders, but they openly defied me. Then I made suggestions, and they blatantly ignored me. As my $24,000 chair teetered on the edge, I pleaded with them, and they told me to get out of their way. I should have listened. The wheels suddenly caught a grip on the ramps, and the chair lurched forward and up on to the deck. My iBot wasn't capable of moving backward quickly in balance mode, yet somehow I averted a head-on collision with the out-of-control Invacare chair. We soon forgot the unpleasantness and basked in the glory of our achievement. Backs were slapped, hands shaken, songs written.

Next, we prepared the fresh lobsters Kim and I had brought with us from Portland. We added clams and mussels to the mix. A bucket of margaritas topped off the menu. The feast, like the company, was outstanding.

After the meal, we sat on the deck and took in the view of the lake. Several lightning strikes illuminated the twilight sky. For me, nothing matches the thrill of watching an evening thunderstorm unfold. Life in the city doesn't afford me a backdrop large or dark enough to experience the awesome beauty of a storm.

As the sunlight faded, the intensity of the lightning picked up. The activity occurred far enough away that we didn't feel a raindrop and scarcely heard a clap of thunder. The time between strikes grew shorter until multiple strikes illuminated different sections of the sky simultaneously. No fireworks grand finale could have matched this display. We sat in awe, aware that we were experiencing something rare and extraordinary.

Our seats for the show could not have been better. The stage extended for miles over a dark, placid lake, ringed by a carpet of dense green forests and rolling hills. On the opposite shore sat the camp where my mother had been injured. Above all this, set against the black sky, just enough puffy clouds drifted by to reflect and intensify the lightning flashes and create eerie, floating silhouettes.

As the storm inched closer, a chill air displaced the harsh, steamy stuff that had enveloped us all day. We breathed in its vigor and tasted its electricity. All at once, the trees nearest us bent and swayed, presenting the undersides of their leaves in a gesture of submission to the storm. The rain arrived as a roaring sheet, and we rushed into the house, satisfied we had squeezed every ounce out of the experience that we possibly could.

I enjoy being captivated like this, even more than I used to, because it diverts my mind. When my attention is focused on something beautiful, burdens wither away. Even though the experience may be short-lived, its effects on my emotional health can be profound and long-lasting.

The next day we attended the 66th annual Riverdrivers Supper. Along with hundreds of other vehicles, we turned off Route 2 in our wheelchair van and started down the short grass and dirt road that led to Ludden's Field. We knew that modified vans such as ours had little ground clearance, but the road appeared to be in decent shape. Then we saw the railroad track crossing.

Natural leader that I am, I once again took charge. After surveying the situation, I told Kim, "You need to stay to the right to get over these tracks." This time, she listened. Sure enough, we heard a dreadful scraping from the underside of our new van—fingernails on a chalkboard. There we sat, straddling active railroad tracks, with a dozen cars and their hungry passengers queued up behind us.

One of the event organizers relieved me of my leadership authority by barking out new orders. He had Kim back the van up. More fingernails on chalkboard. He instructed Kim to stay to the left instead of the right. She did, and we proceeded over the railroad tracks without further problems. A quick inspection of the vehicle revealed no visible damage. A quick inspection of my ego revealed moderate damage.

This feast, held in Ludden's Field along the banks of the Penobscot River, serves as the anchor event of Lincoln's Homecoming Week festivities. The cookies, coleslaw, and other sweets are prepared off site. Biscuits are cooked at the field using reflector ovens in front of a roaring fire, the way it was done during the height of the logging industry in northern Maine. For the main course, hundreds of pounds of beans are prepared and poured into huge cast iron bean pots. The pots are filled with water, molasses, salt pork, and other ingredients. On Wednesday evening, the pots are transported to Ludden's Field, where another crew has prepared the bean holes. When the hardwood fires in each hole have burned down to hot coals, the bean pots are lowered into place, and metal covers are laid over them. The holes are filled with sand to help retain the heat as the beans cook underground for approximately 20 hours. On Thursday, volunteers dole out bean-hole beans and all the fixings to between 800 and 1200 people.

As much as we looked forward to an old-fashioned meal, we were just as interested in chance encounters with people we hadn't spoken with for years. Some of them had never seen me in a wheelchair, so I was glad to be piloting my iBot. It made me look less unfortunate.

After gorging ourselves, we prepared to leave. Kim had an idea. Instead of loading me into the minivan, I would put the iBot in four-wheel-drive, head over the railroad tracks myself, and wait for Kim on the other side. No problem. Again, a steady stream of traffic inched along in both directions. Without the extra 500 plus pounds my iBot and I contributed, the ground clearance improved, and she cruised over the tracks without incident.

When it comes to these accessibility issues, there is no room in our lives for stubbornness, hurt feelings, or even right and wrong. Like everyone else, our days consist of occasional moments of joy, infrequent flashes of anger or sadness, and extended periods of routine endeavors. But with us, everything is overlaid with mobility challenges that require patience and a positive attitude.

CHAPTER 45

Boston Strong

We watched replay after replay of the two bombs exploding near the Boston Marathon finish line. Kim and I were appalled by the senseless violence, and our hearts went out, not only to the victims, but to the whole city. After a few minutes, Kim wondered out loud, "Should we still go to Boston tomorrow? Does that option even exist?"

In the spring of 2013, my dear friend and longtime Boston resident, Randi, purchased tickets to a traveling Broadway show, *Book of Mormon*, as a fiftieth birthday present for me. Our show would be on Tuesday, April 16, the day after the marathon.

Before responding to Kim I consulted Google Maps to see how close everything was to the action. "The hotel is near the finish line, so I can't imagine they will be open," I said. "But I'll call them and the theater and see what they say."

A few minutes later I reported to Kim, "The hotel will be open even though the businesses across the street from it are closed. The theater is quite a distance from the bombings, and tomorrow night's show will go on as scheduled."

"You still want to go?" Kim asked.

"I look at it this way. If the hotel will stay open despite all the chaos around them, and if the theater is keeping their schedule, I feel an obligation to give them our business. What better way to say 'fuck you' to the terrorists than to go on with our lives, uninterrupted?" I continued, "Plus, there's no safer city in the world than Boston right now, with all the security they have in place. And those terrorists—I'm sure they are long gone. But, I understand if you're not comfortable with it."

"I agree with you. Let's do it."

I was dead wrong about the terrorists being gone. That issue played out later in the week as the culprits were apprehended in a dramatic chase across several towns in the Boston area.

Randi and her significant other, Al, met us at our hotel, and we walked to the theater district. The atmosphere was surreal. Military-style vehicles roamed the streets. Heavily armed men walked through Copley Square and Boston Common like it was Fallujah or Kandahar. I felt at once sickened and awestruck, vulnerable and protected.

Such an assortment of uniforms. The city cops and the Massachusetts State Police stood out. But so many military and para-military individuals looked over us, I couldn't tell what organizations they represented. I approached one particularly impressive gentleman, both physically and in terms of his dress and his equipment. I asked, "What branch of the armed services are you affiliated with?"

"None. I belong to a private security company out of Worcester. We are made up mostly of retired Special Forces personnel. As soon as the bombs went off, the mayor's office hired us to come in and help."

Then, it was his turn. "Do you mind if I ask you a question?"

I knew what was coming. "Please, ask away."

"How do you balance on two wheels like that?"

Other than the throngs of military personnel and equipment, something else stood out on this walk from the hotel to the theater district—the number of news vans parked on every street corner, each with a satellite dish on top for sending their footage back to headquarters. A clear pecking order emerged. The network vans commanded the busiest street corners near the finish line. Local newscasters, often doubling as their own camera operators, were relegated to the side streets. I wondered how this came to be. If a small-time van happened to get prime real estate first, did the networks pay him off to get him to move? Was there bullying? Schmoozing? Who knows?

The show at the Boston Opera House that night was hilarious, as advertised. But more importantly, it served as a respite from the bizarre events taking place around us. When the actors came out for their curtain call, we may have extended our standing ovation longer than customary or justified, because we knew that as soon as the applause died down, we would have to march back through the turnstiles and return to the front lines like soldiers on a weekend furlough.

Six months later, in the fall of that year, we returned to Boston for the first time since April. It was Wednesday, October 30, 2013—game six of the World Series at Fenway Park. The Red Sox had taken the lead over the St. Louis Cardinals, three games to two. If they won on this night, they would become world champions, and Kim and I would witness it.

This was the biggest event in Boston since the marathon bombing back in the spring. I received an email from the Red Sox, and I read similar articles online, explaining that all the streets around Fenway Park would be closed to traffic and parking for security reasons. The notice encouraged everyone to use public transportation—essentially the subway system.

This scenario presented a couple of problems. First, no wheelchair accessible subways run to Fenway Park. As I explained earlier, the Green Line is advertised as accessible, but it's awful.

Second, we typically park at one of the handicapped spots on the streets around Fenway. Being in a power wheelchair, I could manage a long walk. But what about people who used crutches, canes, or walkers? I didn't like how the city handled this issue. I wrote to them but never heard back.

After locating a parking space for the van and walking through Boston for 25 minutes, we slipped into Fenway Park, a spot I sometimes refer to as my Happy Place. It's a prime candidate for the surreptitious spreading of my ashes, should I ever die.

We wondered what kind of day awaited us. Would the Red Sox lose, making this another in my list of *almosts*, or would our team persevere and treat Kim and me to a once-in-a-lifetime experience because the Red Sox had not won a World Series at home since 1918?

We sat in the right field bleachers, an area of the park where we hadn't been in several years. These are Fenway's cheapest seats. Nothing luxurious here—just loud, die-hard, obnoxious, and often drunken fans. The handicapped seats and spaces overlook the visitor's bullpen, so we enjoyed an unobstructed, if distant, view of the entire field.

The drunks treated me roughly. As they walked behind me, they couldn't help but bump into my wheelchair about every 30 seconds. I didn't mind. I knew what to expect when I bought tickets in this section.

I had never experienced so much camaraderie and solidarity among the fans at a sporting event. I believe all 38,000 of us in attendance that night honored a silent promise of sorts. Nobody mentioned the historic outcome we all yearned for. Each person had some reason for their silence on this point—superstition, psychology, history. But you could sense, by merely making eye contact, that each of us hoped beyond hope we would experience something special. We would be satisfied with nothing less.

The game started slowly. Through two and a half innings, nobody scored. Then, in the bottom of the third, with the bases loaded and the crowd aching for something positive to happen, Shane Victorino lined a shot off the green monster—Fenway Park's 37-foot-tall left-field fence—scoring three runs. Behind the outstanding pitching of John Lackey, and three more runs in the bottom of the fourth inning, the Red Sox cruised to a 6 – 0 lead.

Although these developments encouraged me, I couldn't forget the collapses my fellow Red Sox fans and I had endured in 1975, 1978, 1986, and 2003. Fool me once, shame on you. Fool me five times, shame on me. I braced for an incredible comeback by the Cardinals.

During games, I don't consume many fluids. Going to the bathroom takes so much time, and I hate to miss even a single pitch. Nevertheless, I usually have to go at least once. With the score still 6 to 0 in the top of the seventh inning, and the Cardinals batting, I told Kim we needed to make a run for the handicapped bathroom so we could watch the end of the game uninterrupted.

Kim reached the bathroom door first and looked back at me with a frown. A long line had formed, consisting entirely of youngish, healthy-looking people. Kim's face showed her anger, and rightfully so because these apparent cheaters would keep us away from the game for a long time. However, I rolled up to the front of the line in balance mode, acting as if I owned the bathroom, not even acknowledging the other people. When the door opened, and someone walked out, the person in the front of the line looked at me, stepped aside, and said, "It's all yours." I scanned the faces of the others in line, and nobody dissented. A little assertiveness and the spectacle of my iBot had done the trick.

When we returned to our seats, the Cardinals had rallied. But the Red Sox escaped further damage, and after seven and one-half innings the score was 6 – 1. My resolve weakened. Against my better judgment, I allowed myself to believe, if only a little, that this might happen, and right in front of our eyes.

Halfway through the eighth inning, the entire stadium sang along with Neil Diamond's "Sweet Caroline" like we always do at this point in a Red Sox game. On days when the Sox are losing, it provides consolation. When the Red Sox are winning, it can make you believe all is right with the world, and maybe, just for that moment, it is.

After "Sweet Caroline," the last vestiges of my cautionary safety net dissolved. I went all in. The Red Sox would win this World Series, or I would hibernate in an emotional cave for a week, again.

At the top of the ninth inning, we brought in our ace reliever, the Japanese pitcher Koji Uehara. As he jogged in from the bullpen, the entire stadium exploded in sustained applause. This would be the final, climactic act in a season-long drama. Everyone stood up, including me in my iBot, and didn't sit down again that evening. It took Uehara only 13 pitches to finish off the Cardinals.

These two sporting events, the Marathon and the World Series, one tragic and one triumphant, became the bookends for Boston's summer of 2013. As we stood in Fenway Park and hugged perfect strangers and watched the fireworks go off, something changed. Whether it was the cumulative frustrations of 95 years of never winning a World Series at home, or a lingering inability to feel comfortable, truly comfortable, in this city since the April 15 marathon bombings, we set all that aside, and the world changed for the better. We knew this euphoria couldn't last, but we hoped the redemption would. On that night, we poured out of the stadium and danced in the streets without guilt, inhibition, or fear. We were back, we were Boston Strong, and none of us would ever forget that feeling.

Amy, Zach, Mitch, Kim 2000, Sugarloaf Mountain.

Amy, Mitch, Kim, Zach 2001.

Vernice 2008, my last photo of her.

Kim, Mitch 2009, last kayak trip.

Mitch, Kim 2012, Bahamas.

Mitch, Kim 2013, Fenway Park World Series championship game.

Mom's card holder (now mine).

Andy, Tarr, Ted, Vernice, Mitch, Tom – Mother's Day 1972.

— PART THREE —

ↄ

CHAPTER 46

Our Mystical Connection

I inherited my mother's positivity, compassion, and resilience, which is not surprising. Kids take after their parents. But she also bestowed upon me her tragic legacy, as if misfortune could be passed from one generation to the next.

Because scientists have not yet identified a misfortune gene, what could possibly account for our shared hardship? Why would I develop a crippling disease, thirty years after the fact, in the exact location where my mother's spinal cord injury occurred? Why would my initial symptoms appear in the summer of my thirty-fifth year, the same age my mother was when she fell? Why is my body contorting into what hers had been? Could there be, mustn't there be, some deeper meaning here, perhaps of a mystical nature?

I doubt it. I don't think about life's great questions in terms of mysterious forces. I resist the urge to explain the unexplainable, to assign meaning where there isn't necessarily any. I don't subscribe to notions of karma or fate. You'll never hear me assert that "everything happens for a reason." I don't accept that supernatural beings like God, angels, or the Devil interfere with our lives, or exist at all, for that matter. To me, heaven and hell are but constructs of our vivid imaginations.

My mother raised me as a Congregationalist, but the church couldn't provide the type of answers I needed. By high school, I knew I would follow another path. As a young man, I hedged my bets while I transitioned through agnosticism by asserting, "If there is an all-knowing, all-powerful, benevolent deity, certainly he or she wouldn't punish me for using my God-given brain to probe and question and doubt."

I'm sharing my spiritual journey here not to change anyone's mind, but to give a glimpse into mine. It's important to note a couple of things. First, I didn't leave religion as a response to the bad things that happened in my life. Second, my heart doesn't have a hole in it where faith would otherwise reside. I find enough beauty and meaning in science, nature, and humanity. I don't want for more. I am a happy atheist.

Although my points of view on the ultimate questions may contrast with those of religious people, on the more objective, relevant issues, our philosophies converge. I espouse kindness and generosity, hard work and determination. I regard the world and the creatures who inhabit it as a gift. In my case, a gift from nature. I consider love an inherent human characteristic—not merely a social construct. I feel all these things and more, without animosity towards people who follow a different spiritual path.

I accept that this mysterious connection to my mother will confound me for the rest of my life, but I'm not driven to find truths unknowable. Acknowledging my ignorance and admitting I can't understand everything that happens in life isn't troubling for me. It's liberating.

In the world of coincidences, there are small ones, like when you bump into a friend at an out-of-town concert. Then, there are big coincidences, like the deaths of Thomas Jefferson and John Adams. These gentlemen were each prominent founding fathers, having signed the Declaration of Independence on July 4, 1776. They became bitter political rivals for a time and then reconciled late in life. Remarkably, on July 4, 1826, separated by hundreds of miles, both patriots passed away, 50 years to the day after signing the Declaration of Independence. This renders the coincidences between my mother's life and mine unremarkable by comparison.

Although our life stories are eerily similar, my mother and I had important differences, starting with the nature of our paralysis. Spinal cord injury is like getting hit hard, one time, with a hammer—a sickening thud and you're down. If you're lucky, and my mother was lucky in this sense, you remain somewhat stable after the acute event. PPMS, on the other hand, is like being beaten with a soft pillow—a thousand blows to the head and neck spread over the rest of your life. You don't feel pain from any single wallop, but gradually your central nervous system turns to mush.

My mother and I had some personality differences too. She relied on her strong Christian faith. I don't. She was subservient. I'm rarely outspoken or aggressive, but I advocate for myself more than she did. My mother radiated empathy. I'm also a caring person, though I have weak moments where I become indifferent to the plights of others. She never complained. I whine now and then. She was a private person. I splatter my every thought on to my blog for the world to see.

Another difference between us was that Mom didn't assume she, or other disabled people, had a right to public accessibility. She didn't want others going out of their way for her. She tried not to be a bother. I am less magnanimous, and I do advocate for disability rights even if my suggestions are unwelcome. I try to make my case in a positive way. I don't say, "I insist that we make this place accessible to disabled people," as much as I say, "How great would it be if we made this place accessible?"

Growing up, I viewed my mother through two different lenses. Being a good son of a good woman, I loved her deeply. I considered Mom an inspirational person, as I assume most people did. I never felt ashamed to be with her in public or to introduce my friends to her.

But I also viewed her in the same light that countless boys have viewed their mothers since the beginning of time. She was the woman who took care of me. The older I became, the more I took her for granted and backed away. I didn't treat her unkindly; I simply lost interest in my mother as I approached adulthood. I wonder if Mom found any consolation in this because my behavior demonstrated the normalcy of our relationship. I can only hope she did.

As an 18-year-old, I saw myself as strong, independent, ready to conquer the world. My mother wasn't like me at all. I considered her caring but meek, amiable but naïve, hardworking but subservient, lovable but tragic. I was an idiot in the way that all young men are idiots.

Throughout my adult life, I stayed true to my stoicism. It was all I knew. I treated my mother politely and respectfully. I visited often and brought along my wife and children. I saw her, or when I lived away from Lincoln, I called her, on Mother's Day, our birthdays, and Christmas. I loved my mother, and I loved to be around her. Yet I never called to see how she was doing, just to chat. To my credit, I never called anyone just to chat, other than Kim once in a while. When I visited my parents, I sat near my father to talk about sports, hunting, and the mill. I didn't avoid my mother, but I didn't seek her out either.

As I began writing this book and held my relationship with my mother up to the light for the first time, I experienced overwhelming regret for having wasted a lifetime of opportunities to develop greater intimacy with her. Worse yet, even when I knew my diagnosis, my likely future, and I saw my mother growing old, I didn't say the things I should have said or ask the questions I should have asked. Because of this, I could only imagine a final conversation with her in the hospital, as I related earlier in this book.

But, as I penned these closing chapters and forced myself to examine our relationship even more closely, I realized how the distance I had talked myself into ran counter to what my heart knew to be true.

All my life I have possessed a meager skill set for interpersonal relationships. I wasn't born with many, and I didn't augment the toolbox along the way. When I considered my relationship with my mother within these constraints, I accepted that connections between people occur at many levels. If Mom and I were not the type to talk things out, it didn't mean we were incapable of relating to one another. If we weren't comfortable discussing our common challenges, it doesn't mean we disavowed them.

There are countless avenues for knowledge to be shared and love to be expressed. I learned by observation of my mother: how she held her coffee cup (I do it the same way today), buttered a piece of toast, and baked what she called "wacky cake." I appreciated the pure joy she found in going for rides in the countryside and playing cards with her grandchildren. I noticed how she asked about other people, never complained about her life, and requested help only when she needed it. I admired how she never showed fear.

When I beat myself up for not fostering more intimacy, I had overlooked this part of our legacy. Growing up, Mom didn't approach me and give me a hug. Her physical limitations got in the way. Instead, she asked, "Do you want to help me make donuts?"

I didn't walk up to her and tell her how much I loved her. My emotional limitations got in the way. Instead, I said, "Yes, I'll help you make donuts. Where do we start?"

Spending time in my mother's house, eating the meals she prepared, watching her interact with Kim and our children, and enjoying the occasional conversation with her—it was medicine for the soul. Being around her meant being immersed in maternal love, which permeated her home like the fragrance of the mayflowers my father picked for her in the spring.

I've spent so much time these past three years with memories of my mother that I have grown closer to her, well after her death—a gift I couldn't see coming and had no idea was possible. I now understand the silent promise we had when I was five years old—that we would never leave one another—wasn't broken when she spent nine months in the hospital or when I went off to college. When she died, I was mistaken to think our promise died with her. She has been an important part of me all along: guiding, supporting, inspiring. I'm not facing my demons without her. I never was. I never will.

Mary Elizabeth Frye says it so eloquently in this poem that Mom requested we read at her funeral, and that I will have read on the occasion of my passing:

Do not stand at my grave and weep
I am not there. I do not sleep.
I am a thousand winds that blow.
I am the diamond glints on snow.
I am the sunlight on ripened grain.
I am the gentle autumn rain.
When you awaken in the morning's hush
I am the swift uplifting rush
Of quiet birds in circled flight.
I am the soft stars that shine at night.
Do not stand at my grave and cry;
I am not there. I did not die.

CHAPTER 47

My Parents' Truth

In the years after my mother's passing, Kim occasionally broached the subject of Mom's accident and what she had heard about it from my cousins. Each time I refused to engage with her.

I can't reconcile my feelings or my behavior on this matter; we're talking about repressed memories and deep psychological baggage here. Trying to work backward and figure out how I processed my mother's accident would be no less complicated than picking autumn leaves off the ground and reattaching them to their original places on the trees above.

Yet, I can't stop myself from trying. When Kim first raised the subject with me on the night of my mother's funeral, I responded with neither surprise nor skepticism, even though this refuted everything I had believed on the subject for 44 years. For me to have reacted this way, on some level I must have known something. Perhaps I had heard whispers in the past and had suppressed the memory of them. Maybe I appreciated how unlikely it was for my mother to fall and break her neck in the way my father had described. It's also possible that, even as a five-year-old, I picked up on my father's insincerity when he spoke to us that day in 1969. He wasn't an accomplished liar, after all.

Perhaps I subconsciously sympathized with my father's decision to put forth his version of events. What right did I or anyone else have to question my father's account? He and my mother owned the story—their personal collusion. My allegiance would be to my parents, not to the truth. The truth didn't give birth to me, raise me, clothe and feed me, love me. My parents did. The truth had no rights. It was irrelevant.

I'll never know for certain how I processed my mother's accident.

Today, I can only stare at the autumn leaves swirling around my feet and wonder where they fell from.

* * *

At the beginning of my memoir project, I knew I would have to conduct research with friends and relatives to learn more about my mother. I needed perspectives other than those of my brothers and me.

I had no idea how I would proceed if I confirmed there was more to my mother's accident than what my father had told us. Maybe the truth would guide me. Maybe the facts would come with instructions about what I should do with them once they came into my possession. I could only hope so.

I set out to interview my parents' surviving circle of friends and relatives, a shrinking group, most of them octogenarians. I had a wonderful time reconnecting with these individuals, people I had known so well in my childhood. Love flowed in both directions during these meetings.

I began with Debby, Mom's lifelong friend. After some pleasantries, I asked, "How did you and Mom meet?"

"We were classmates. In fact, if it weren't for Vernice, I would never have passed my bookkeeping courses and graduated from high school. She knew more than the teachers did. Vernice was smart. She was named salutatorian."

"What kind of activities did she enjoy?"

"In the high school play, Vernice portrayed the mother, and I was her daughter. She and I sang 'Now Is the Hour' in front of the whole school."

Debby went on to explain that when my parents were in their thirties, they maintained a circle of close friends who regularly enjoyed one another's company. In 1967, Kenneth, a man with a big heart and movie star good looks, was killed in a fiery, head-on car accident. The babysitter he had picked up and was bringing back to his home died as well. This was the first of three tragedies my parents' group of friends would endure over the next few years.

Before I could stop myself, I blurted out, "Do you know what happened the night Mom got hurt?"

"Oh yes. I was there."

This moment had been 45 years in the making. I paused, and then said the only thing I could. "Please, tell me everything you remember."

First, Debby listed off the names of the ten people who attended the party. I knew all of them, and four were still alive. Then she proceeded to give me the details. After I spoke with Debby, I interviewed the other three: Junior (her husband), Audrey, and Diane. Not all accounts of the evening were in complete agreement, but I think I've pieced together a narrative that captures the essential truth of Mom's accident. Through these interviews, I learned that the life of an innocent person was destroyed that night, and it wasn't my mother's.

* * *

Mom and Dad's friends, Roger and Diane, owned a camp on Little Narrows Pond in Lincoln. On Saturday, September 13, 1969, they held a party there during the day with many of my parents' core group in attendance. The families enjoyed swimming, barbecuing, and boating.

Late in the afternoon, the party shifted gears. Parents shuttled their kids back to town and handed them over to babysitters. Five couples gathered at the lake for the evening's festivities: Roger and Diane, Ted and Vernice, Debby and Junior, Jimmy and Audrey, and Albert and Lois.

They sat down for cards. The game might have been bridge, or dealer's choice poker, or some derivative like acey-deucy or scat. Although the adults likely sipped both mixed drinks and beer during the day, cocktails probably dominated the evening.

It must have been a while since my mother had enjoyed herself at a party because Debby heard her say to nobody in particular, "Tonight is my night to have fun," a reasonable expectation for a hardworking wife and mother of three.

The card playing ran its course, and the group wandered outside by the lake. It was shortly before or after sunset; the accounts vary. After having been holed up in the cabin, and after a long day of drinking, some people became rambunctious and playful. Roger, the owner of the camp, picked up my mother and threatened to throw her in the lake, clothes and all. Folks probably considered it nothing more than Roger being mischievous. Perhaps my father approved because of the party atmosphere and his close friendship with Roger. My mother surely didn't want to get wet, but I can picture her laughing and screaming, kicking her legs in gleeful protest.

Only Roger knew if he really intended to throw Mom in the lake. That became a moot point because this was the moment when things went wrong. Carrying my mother like an armload of firewood, he walked down to the dock. He stepped on the first rung of a wooden ladder on the side of the dock—no problem. But when he stepped on the second rung, located below the water's surface and covered with a layer of slime, Roger's foot slipped. He stumbled, and in doing so he dropped my mother. In one version, her neck struck the edge of the dock. In another, she landed neck-first on a rock jutting out of the water. Doesn't matter.

Mom lay still, and unconscious, with her face partially submerged. A group of people lifted her out of the water, and she came to almost immediately.

My mother said something like, "I'm really hurt. I need to go home." She didn't cry out in pain. Maybe she didn't feel any pain. My father carried her to their car and laid her down on the back seat. Lois jumped in beside Mom and stayed with her for the ride. Dad headed for home but switched course when Mom said something to the effect of, "We need to go to the hospital. I can't feel my legs."

Soon, they arrived at the Lincoln Hospital, nothing more than a sprawling house with bedrooms converted to patient rooms, where Mom had worked part-time until I was born. Somebody alerted Old Doc Gulesian, who wasn't so old at the time. He suspected a spinal cord injury and had Mom transported to Bangor.

Dr. Woodcock, Mom's attending physician at Eastern Maine Medical Center after her accident, absolved all parties of wrongdoing for having picked up and carried a spinal cord injury victim. Dr. Woodcock said Mom's cervical spine shattered the moment she hit the dock or rock, and subsequent handling of her did no further damage. He couldn't have been sure, and I expect he said this only to give peace of mind to the people who moved her. Many years later, not long before she died, one of Mom's doctors included in his notes a conversation where she said, "In those days, they didn't know about the need to stabilize your neck, so they just put me in the car and brought me to the hospital."

Introducing booze into a gathering like the one at the Little Narrows increases the likelihood of somebody getting hurt or killed. Few of us would argue that point. But we're still talking about rare chances. Misfortune is unprincipled, unfair, and capricious. It's not sprinkled about in small, equal doses. Virtues such as honesty, work ethic, or the number of good deeds done are irrelevant. These folks at the Little Narrows—they didn't deserve what happened to them. They were good people, just trying to blow off steam on a weekend.

Mom's accident was only the second of three great tragedies to befall this group of friends, after Kenneth's fatal car accident with the babysitter.

Although Dad knew Roger was at fault, he seemed to harbor no ill will. I'm sure the continued friendship from my parents and the support of his wife, Diane, helped Roger to some extent, but I doubt any of this made his life bearable. The foremost victim of this tragedy, one could argue, wasn't the woman who broke her neck but the man who dropped her.

Roger didn't carry his burden for long. In the winter of 1970, a few months after Mom's accident, he drove his snowmobile across a frozen Mattanawcook Pond, like he had done countless times before. In those days, it was not unusual to find automobiles on the ice as well. Because of dense fog, Roger couldn't see the station wagon until it was too late. Roger died instantly from multiple injuries, most notably a fractured cervical spine—a broken neck.

* * *

Roger probably wasn't the only one racked with guilt over my mother's accident. I can never know the degree to which Mom blamed herself, but I can make some guesses. Maybe she felt she could have been more insistent that Roger put her down. She could have taken a serious tone or lost her temper.

I can only guess how much onus Dad placed on himself. I don't even know if he saw it happen. If he did, he probably blamed himself for not stepping in before it turned tragic. Or maybe he experienced some version of survivor's guilt. On those issues, I'm only speculating, but I am confident he never felt vengeful toward Roger.

Maybe Diane or others at the party found a way to blame themselves. Perhaps someone egged Roger on or felt they should have intervened in some way. In these situations, guilt can work its way into the most innocent places.

When I heard the account of that evening from eyewitnesses, I assumed my father must have called a brief huddle before my parents left the camp and headed for town. In this huddle, my father would have said something like, "Nobody needs to know exactly what happened here. We will just say Vernice slipped on the step herself and hit the edge of the dock. Agreed?" Everyone would have nodded, and a conspiracy would have been born.

But no such meeting occurred. My parents gave their version of the story out to nearly everyone, and it became the predominant, although not exclusive, account of the evening. Those who knew better apparently understood my parents' desire to spin the events of that night the way they did and avoided contradicting them.

How different things are today. It would be impossible to keep something like this quiet in the age of social media, other than via an agreement among all the partygoers. The late 1960s were different, more private times.

As to the question of *why* my mother and father didn't want the real story to be made public, again, I can only guess. They must have felt embarrassed that a group of grown men and women behaved so irresponsibly and caused someone such harm. They may have also had a legal or financial reasons to hide the truth. I don't know. But I like to think, above all, my parents wanted to protect Roger, and minimize his pain—a noble yet unattainable goal.

Through the interviewing process, I discovered that this ship of secrets had many leaks. Versions of the truth surfaced here and there, though never in my presence. My father revealed the story to his friend Gardner Mitchell in Southwest Harbor. My brother, Tom, overheard a drunk Ted tell our Uncle Fuzzy the truth once, up at the hunting camp. Tom never revealed to Andy or me what he had heard until I interviewed him for this book. I know my father must have told other people, and they must have told more people, and so forth. And what about the other eight folks at the party? How often did they whisper the truth over the years? So many versions of the story were floating around.

Yet, I am amazed that certain individuals remained in the dark—Andy, me, most of the town gossips, and some of our closest family and friends.

Now that I know the truth, I've decided my father should have been the one to tell us. I would feel this way no matter how many other people knew the story, or some version of it, but especially because more than a few people did know, and some of them even heard it firsthand from my father. He gave us a sanitized version, suitable for children, but failed to circle back and provide the real story when we became adults.

My father's refusal to tell us what happened reminds me of the time he had me euthanize our family dog, Tarr, when I was 17 years old. In each instance, he didn't have the strength to do it, or he didn't want his sons to see him cry, or both. He should have helped me with the dog, and he should have told us about our mother.

Am I being too harsh? Perhaps. I don't know exactly what they went through. I don't know the whole story. Maybe I should rephrase it this way: I *wish* he had been able to help me with the dog, and I *so wish* he had been able to tell us about our mother.

Why do I refer to my father as the keeper of this secret? Why not my mother? As much as she deferred to his judgment before her accident—typical of marital relations in that era—she did so even more afterward. She probably felt he should decide. End of discussion.

Although the story of my mother's accident is heart-wrenching, it doesn't reveal character flaws in any of the people involved. It confirms their strength and integrity. The truth doesn't expose callousness, cruelty, or insensitivity by anyone. It shows their compassion. Yes, the story highlights poor decision-making, but no worse than the decisions human beings make every day. And yes, the true story acknowledges the suffering these people endured. I've had to rethink certain points of view. Above all, the burdens carried by my parents and their friends Roger and Diane were so much heavier than I thought they had been, and so their efforts to move forward were more extraordinary than I had known them to be.

After hearing eyewitness accounts of Mom's accident, I had two choices. I could honor a strategy that had not worked thus far—suppressing the truth—which had resulted in rumors of varying accuracy, woven among the people of Lincoln and our friends and relatives. If left alone, this mosaic of semi-truths would slowly fade with the generations until nobody cared about the story or remembered the folks involved. But if I shined the light of day on the narrative and rescued it from eventual oblivion, I could honor the lives of those most affected. I could also resolve whatever psychological stress the secret had created for me and others. And finally, I could set the record straight. The truth did come with instructions. It screamed, "I exist. I am relevant."

What have we learned? What are the lessons? First, we are reminded that bad things happen to good people, and this will never change. What matters is how the survivors process their grief and move on. The folks in this story are to be admired for their resilience.

The two widows, Betty, who lost her husband Kenneth in a car accident, and Diane, who lost her husband Roger in a snowmobile accident, each remarried and led long and at least outwardly happy lives. And my parents—well, you know their story. The tight-knit group of friends, the folks at the party and a few others, saw less of each other over the years, but not unlike any group of thirtysomethings who outgrow their youthful lifestyles. No matter how events and the passage of time had conspired to pull them apart, they were instead bound together by the sorrow of three tragedies and by the memories of better times.

We are also reminded that trying to keep a secret among a large group of people is a futile endeavor. I can understand why Dad devised and circulated the alternate story, but the narrative should have had a short lifespan. When it began to fall apart, when the people it was intended to protect no longer needed protection, and when multiple versions existed, I wish we had heard the truth firsthand.

And finally, my mother taught us this last piece of wisdom by her example:

No matter the misfortunes, the unfairness, the hardships, adjust to the new realities of your life and carry on. Whenever possible, do this with a smile.

CHAPTER 48
My Truths

Prominent neurologists and pharmaceutical reps have said, "MS is a highly treatable disease," or even worse, "It's a great time to have MS."

Bullshit.

Some patients climb mountains, run marathons, and start up companies. I'm happy for them, but for those of us who are significantly disabled from the disease, getting through each day is an accomplishment. Other than one PPMS treatment, with questionable efficacy, today there is nothing more to combat our disease progression than five, fifty, or a thousand years ago. Researchers, however, are currently focusing on primary and secondary progressive MS. Dozens of trials are underway, and more and better treatments may emerge in the not-too-distant future. But for now, it's still not a great time to have progressive MS.

Kim and I are in our fifties, the point in life when most couples rough out an exit strategy from the workforce and imagine what retirement might look like. Do we prefer Florida or Arizona? Golf or tennis community? Not us. I'm unable to picture how I'll get through each day twelve or even six months from now, but I'm confident we'll figure something out, at least for a while.

Eventually, I may no longer be able to sit up in a wheelchair or even live at home. We don't know what my life expectancy is. Things could plateau for a while, but probably won't. So we don't go there. We live in the moment, or a few months ahead of the moment. Our focus is where everyone's should be—on enjoying the now.

Besides not knowing what the future holds, another frustration is that nobody has discovered the root cause of MS. Even so, I have some guesses about what led to my MS. It might have been any one of the following, or some combination thereof.

I got drunk one night in college and felt the urge to stand on top of the bar at my fraternity house and flail my arms and legs about. I hesitate to call it dancing. Not surprisingly, I slipped and fell to the concrete floor behind the bar. I landed flat on my back, but I was Superman that night. I bounced up and continued to party.

The next morning, I awoke with a severely stiff neck. I was concerned enough that I visited a nearby walk-in clinic. When the doctor inquired about the circumstances of my injury, I had no intention of confessing the truth. Instead, I blurted out the first lie that popped into my head.

"Somebody had just mopped the stairway. I slipped on a wet step, fell backward, and banged my neck."

The doctor prescribed painkillers and rest, and after a few days the stiffness subsided. It flared up now and then for several years. Twice during that time, my entire left side went into spasm when I turned my neck in a particular direction. Eventually, the stiffness and the spasms became less frequent and then disappeared altogether. A theory, making its rounds in the MS world, suggests that trauma of the kind that I experienced could contribute to the development of MS, but the evidence is far from conclusive.

When I was 27 years old, 11 years before my MS diagnosis, I contracted viral meningitis, an infection of the spinal fluid, but not as deadly as its cousin, bacterial meningitis. The virus incapacitated me with a splitting headache for several days. Again, I know of no studies correlating this with multiple sclerosis. However, given that my MS lesions are bathed in spinal fluid, it makes me wonder.

At 31 years old, seven years before my MS diagnosis, I came down with mononucleosis, which is caused by the Epstein-Barr virus. Research indicates that a high percentage of people with MS have been exposed to this virus. There is some correlation, though we still know little about how or why Epstein-Barr and MS might be related.

People with MS probably have a genetic predisposition toward developing the disease. I am unaware of any ancestor of mine who had MS, and science has not identified a specific MS gene, but there appears to be some influence at the genetic level. We know this because the likelihood of the average person being diagnosed is about 1 in 800. The probability of a sibling or offspring of an individual with MS being diagnosed, however, is about 1 in 200. Are my kids worried about coming down with MS? I can't speak for them, but they have bigger concerns in life than worrying about a 1 in 200 chance of getting this disease. Yet, MS is paraded in front of them every time they see me, so yes, I'm sure they have concerns.

And finally, I worked as a chemical engineer in paper mills for 12 years. During that time, I became exposed to a lot of chemicals. I doubt that any chemical was wholly responsible for my MS, but any one of them could have been a trigger that set in motion one of the other potential root causes.

If my own reckless, drunken behavior, when I fell off the fraternity bar and injured my cervical spine, contributed to the development of my MS, this is yet another way my story is similar to my mother's, and I must live with that. At least my intoxicated behavior didn't cause direct harm to anybody else. That doesn't make me smarter or more responsible or in any way superior to Roger, the man who dropped my mother. It only makes me luckier.

* * *

I like to think about my situation, our situation, in different ways. For example, what if Kim had come down with MS instead of me? Answer: this would have been most unfortunate. First, Kim is so much better suited to be a caregiver than I am. She's a natural; it's in her DNA. I think I would have been an adequate caregiver, but I don't possess her rare combination of empathy and energy. Second, I am so much better suited to have MS than Kim is. Granted, she's a tough cookie and would have found a way to cope with MS had she contracted it. But Kim has no love for sedentary activities. I, on the other hand, enjoy relaxing endeavors, be they productive or not. So, if one of us had to suffer from MS, it's best for each of us, and for our marriage, that it worked out the way it did.

On rare occasions, my mind goes to dark places. I don't stop at the fear of being confined to a bed or even losing the use of all my limbs, which are legitimate concerns. Once in a while, I imagine being locked in a body that can't interact with the outside world at all. What if my brain remained alert and aware, but I couldn't see or speak or move? I envision people carrying on conversations around me as if I weren't there. It would be my own personal hell. I don't have any reason to worry about something like this, yet once in a great while, I do.

Those are daydreams, and I'm good at chasing them away. But what about my nocturnal dreams? More often than not, I walk in them. Sometimes my disability doesn't come into play at all. Other times, I'll remember my wheelchair in mid-dream. Thankfully, I don't have full-fledged nightmares about being locked in my body or about my disability worsening in any way.

I spend most of my time in the real world, however, and I continue to find contentment in a life interrupted by MS. My strength in the face of adversity is due more to my genetic makeup and the skills I learned from my mother than my own courage or intestinal fortitude. For this reason, I should be envied more than admired. Further, I don't consider myself in any way superior to those who are unable to find contentment. I enjoy so many advantages, not the least of which is that I don't suffer from clinical depression. My brain chemistry has remained intact thus far.

Throughout this book, I've portrayed myself as the picture of resilience. However, I can't promise I'll be able to handle anything thrown my way. At some point, I may succumb and lose my will. I hope that day never arrives, but if it does, it won't invalidate all I've done to remain resilient for so long.

I can't offer a single, unifying theory of how I've managed, and I won't attempt to provide a recipe for success. All I can do is share some common themes, some approaches that have worked for me.

My Keys to Leading a Contented Life as a Disabled Person (Works for healthy people, too!)

1. I appreciate my good fortune. For example, I live in a free country with outstanding medical care (although not an outstanding country with free medical care). I have favorable genetics, an amazing life partner, two children who never complain about my requests for assistance, supportive friends and relatives, and financial stability. I could go on. I realize how many things I have working in my favor, but I think everyone has something to be thankful for.

2. I don't ride emotional roller coasters, wringing my hands over situations that, in the end, fall into one of two categories: I can deal with them through accommodations, or they are out of my control. In neither case is handwringing helpful.

3. I never become so attached to any of my interests that losing the ability to enjoy a particular activity is devastating, and I've had to give up some passionate interests. In my healthy past, I identified myself as an outdoorsman, a snowmobiler, and a business professional. I am no longer any of those people, but in retrospect, I never was. These were only activities I occupied myself with. They didn't define me.

4. I have accepted that life doesn't owe me anything. Although I may experience a sense of loss, I don't feel cheated when things go poorly. Every one of my ancestors, for time immemorial, lived beyond adolescence and successfully reproduced before being eaten by sabertooth tigers, flattened by asteroids, or burned at the stake for believing in the wrong god. After being born, the rest is gravy. We are all living on bonus time.

5. I stay connected with other human beings, either remotely or face-to-face. I don't crawl into a hole of self-pity and turn away the people who have been close to me. Some folks have dealt with my changing situation well, and others haven't. I embrace the ones who have adjusted and don't worry about the ones who

cannot. It's as much their loss as mine, after all.

6. I remain inquisitive. I read, watch movies and quality television, and I scour the Internet for learning opportunities. I seek out interesting people with whom to converse. I write.

7. I take advantage of mobility aids to explore the world, where I view myself as an ambassador for the disabled community. I engage with people and try to make them comfortable around me. It does both of us a world of good.

8. I have hope, but don't rely upon it. I do everything in my power to improve my situation while preparing for the likelihood that I will endure further misfortune. The absence of hope is not necessarily despair. It can be acceptance and even peace.

9. I find the humor in life. I allow myself—even require myself—to laugh and smile because sometimes laughter is not only the result of happiness but the source of it.

10. I practice mindfulness and take the time to appreciate the simple things: a full moon rising over the ocean, my little dog wagging her tail when I come home, a pair of Cardinals zipping around our backyard.

11. I don't try to do it all. When I get tired, I rest. When I need help, I ask for it. When I want chocolate, I eat it. I take these liberties with humility and without apology.

I remain content despite this creeping paralysis. I still anticipate each day more for the wonders it might unveil than the suffering it could impart. In the future, when I've accumulated even more disability, I may scoff at myself for having been so naïve, but that's a risk I'm willing to take.

CHAPTER 49

The Weddings

The passion for life that Kim and I hold on to so tightly was epitomized by weddings in the summers of 2015 and 2016.

My childhood best friend Dave and I couldn't have followed more divergent paths. He became a musician in Las Vegas and remained a bachelor. I became an engineer in Maine, married young, and started a family. However, we remained close because of my visits to Vegas, his visits back East, and an occasional phone call. No matter how long the separation, we always picked up right where we'd left off. No awkwardness. No worrying where we stood with one another.

In the spring of 2015, Dave called to say he would be coming to Maine in late July. That's all the planning we did for his visit. That's all the planning we ever did for his visits. His one-time fiancée, Teena, who steered my scooter recklessly through the casinos, was no longer in the picture. This time, he would bring his girlfriend of several years, Stephanie. Kim and I had met her in Maine and Las Vegas, and we adored her even though we knew better than to get close to any of Dave's girlfriends. They had a habit of disappearing from our lives.

When they arrived in Maine, we hosted a get-together with about ten people in attendance. At this party, Stephanie revealed that Dave had recently expressed a willingness to get married, something she wanted very much. When Kim and our friend, Ann, heard this, they pounced. Before long, we found ourselves planning a Maine wedding, in our backyard, six days out.

Kim and Ann dropped everything and committed themselves to the wedding preparations, but lots of people pitched in. I contacted City Hall to work out the legalities. My brother Tom, a notary public, agreed to perform the service. Ann's husband, John, boiled 30 lobsters and helped pick them clean.

During the ceremony, I took advantage of the iBot's balance mode and stood up for Dave as his best man. The simple beauty of the wedding and the after-party suited this bride and groom perfectly. In front of 25 or so friends and family, another lifelong bachelor bit the dust.

After the ceremony, I made a long-winded toast and had some fun with it. I teased Dave about all the women he had known, and how I had tried my best to keep some of his relationships together. But it all turned out for the best because of Stephanie, whom I referred to in the toast as Serious Girlfriend Number Twenty. I ended it this way:

> From the moment I met her, I could tell Number Twenty was special. I tried to be standoffish and disinterested, but she countered with warmth and personality, topped off with a dose of authenticity. Damn.
>
> This connection was different; this girl was different. None of David's other relationships were as strong, as beautiful, as loving. I'm so happy these two found one another, and I'm thrilled I'll never have to say goodbye to Serious Girlfriend Number Twenty.

The toast was a success, the day a triumph. In our own backyard, on the patio Kim built using her bare hands, with our little corner of the ocean as a backdrop, two people made a lifelong commitment, not because they had to, or even because they should, but because they so, so wanted to.

Over the next year, we helped plan our daughter Amy's wedding. At first I was unsure about her chosen one, Nick. I had become a bit of a college snob over the years, and Nick wasn't planning on college. He was working toward becoming an electrician. Over the years, as I came to know him better, I appreciated how well he treated my daughter, and what a fine young man he was. Today, he's a successful electrician with a college degree and scant student loans. I'm no longer so judgmental.

Amy and Nick's wedding would be a more elaborate event than Dave and Stephanie's. We rented a farmhouse venue for the weekend.

Once again my brother Tom agreed to officiate. As with most weddings, the bride had been under considerable pressure in the weeks leading up to the big day—so many decisions to make. I could see the anxiety in her face, and I worried what the morning of the wedding day would be like for her.

As I sat at the kitchen table in the farmhouse a few hours before the wedding and tried to put the finishing touches on the script for the ceremony, I needed Amy's approval on certain, not insignificant, changes. And just as important, we had to decide on my role.

Amy and I both liked the idea of me walking her down the aisle in my iBot wheelchair. But the wedding was in the woods, and we weren't sure if it would be physically possible for us to march down the trail, side-by-side, without me running over her gown. We had planned to talk after the rehearsal the night before, but we didn't, and the issue remained unresolved as the ceremony approached.

Amy walked into the kitchen, and I ran the changes in the ceremony by her. As the pressures of a big wedding mounted, instead of nervousness and tension ruling the day, a peacefulness had come over her. She agreed with all the last-minute changes—said she loved them. I then pulled her aside.

"I would love to walk you down the aisle, but I completely understand if you'd rather I didn't."

"No, absolutely you should walk me down the aisle. If you run over my gown we'll just stop, have you get off the gown, and continue."

A couple of hours later, Zach escorted his mother to her seat. Kim's parents sat directly behind them. Most of our closest friends and relatives were in attendance. Five people came all the way from Cleveland for the wedding. We met so many wonderful folks from Nick's side of the family. What a gathering.

When the processional music started—a lovely instrumental version of Pure Prairie League's song "Amy"—my daughter grabbed my arm to steady herself. "Ready?" I asked.

"Yup," she answered, then she began taking long, deep, calming breaths. So did I.

With my iBot in four-wheel-drive mode, I elevated as high as I could, bringing the top of my head up to the level of Amy's chin. By the time we had covered 20 yards or so, we found our marching rhythm, and our breathing returned to normal.

The first obstacle was a wooden bridge with a gentle arch shape. When we reached the pinnacle of the arch, all the guests could see us. We both knew that *the stump*, this menacing tip of a terrestrial iceberg, stood ready to sink us if we steered too close to her. Like we had practiced at rehearsal, if only once, we descended from the bridge and made a wide turn around *the stump*. Nick couldn't stand back and watch any longer, and left his post in front of the trellis they would be married under. That worked for Amy and me, and the handoff, as it were, was successfully completed.

Kim later remarked that my tires and the hem of Amy's gown were in constant contact. There's no explaining how my wheelchair didn't grab Amy's dress and cause her to face-plant into the dirt on this, the most important day of her life.

Thirty years earlier Dave sang at our wedding reception—"Land-slide" by Stevie Nicks. After having flown all the way from Las Vegas, with Stephanie of course, Dave performed that same song at Amy's wedding. It was a moment. After the ceremony in the woods, we retired to the barn for festivities. At one point, amid the buzz of activity, Kim and I found one another in the center of the barn, the eye of the hurricane. While a storm of celebration and goodwill swirled around us, we were alone with each other for an instant.

In every direction friends, old and new, laughed, hugged, and toasted to bride and groom.

We joined in, toasting to a long and happy marriage.

"To the future," I said to no one in particular.

Kim and I, however, had grown to distrust the future. Too complicated. Too many unknowns. As my eyes met hers, I raised my glass in celebration of a simple, undeniable truth, "Here's to a magical day."

Kim smiled, touched her glass to mine, and echoed the sentiment. "Here's to the day."

Clair and Carole Sutherland, Kim and Mitch Sturgeon,
Vernice and Ted Sturgeon 1986.

Amy, Mitch, Nick 2016.

Acknowledgments

Teaching an engineer to write a book is no less daunting than teaching an English major to design a bridge, although the latter places the public at more risk (my opinion only). Here are some of the people who guided this engineer along his way.

First, I offer a huge thank you to the folks in Lincoln who told me stories about the old days: Colleen Scanlon, Sue Scanlon, Darlene Flood, Debby Bowers, Junior Bowers, Jack Weatherbee, Marilyn Weatherbee, Betty Goodwin, Diane Edes, Audrey Barton, and Martha Thomas.

Thanks to those brave souls who critiqued versions of this manuscript: Joanne Turnbull, Roger Pepper, Kevin Sheehan, Lindy Sheehan, Roger Pepper, Erica Bartlett, Stu Haddon, Juli Jerome, Cathryn Morrissette Bonica, Carla Mortensen, Robert Dana, Joe Souza, Jamie Michaud, Margaret Welch, Sandy Martin, Steve Pinette, Melinda Porter, Nanette Gutgsell, Dr. Paul Muscat, Dr. Salvador Sclafani, Dr. Peter Riskind, and Dr. Frederick Aronson.

Thanks also to Julie Zagorianakos for her steadfast research and Randi Cohen for coaching me on how to mine people's memories through interviews. Also, thanks to Lynn Easler for the cover photograph at Two Lights State Park and Jodi Jensen Miller for her marketing prowess.

I have two talented friends, Marc Stecker and Dave King, who came through for me. Thank you.

Thank you to my professional editors: Chuck Sambuchino, Mark Williams, and Louise Darvid. Thanks to my book shepherd, Grace Peirce. Thanks also to the Maine Writers and Publishers Alliance, and their workshop leaders including Elizabeth Peavey and Monica Wood. Thanks to the Portland Writers Workshop for introducing me to the craft of writing, one month at a time.

This memoir is a story of family, and I couldn't have done it without the encouragement and support of mine: Amy and Nick Doucette, Zach Sturgeon, Andy and Karen Sturgeon, Tom and Diane Sturgeon, and Carole and Clair Sutherland.

Most of all, thanks to my lovely wife, Kim, without whom this book, and this life, would not be possible.

About the Author

Mitch Sturgeon is a memoirist, blogger, and disability advocate. He was none of these things before being diagnosed with an aggressive form of MS in 2001. In the ensuing years he lost his ability to pursue outdoor passions like golf, snowmobiling, and hiking. In 2009, a year after he purchased his first wheelchair, he took medical retirement from his chemical engineering career and began writing.

Mitch authors an award-winning blog, enjoyingtheride.com, where he employs a mixture of humor, inspiration, and straight-talk to share his experiences as a disabled person. His essays can be found in periodicals such as *Down East Magazine* and in a variety of disability journals and websites. Mitch lives in South Portland, Maine, with his wife, Kim, where he can usually be found talking to his computer while gazing out over the ocean.

53839208R00165

Made in the USA
Columbia, SC
22 March 2019